ECHOES OF SCRIPTURE IN THE LETTERS OF PAUL

ECHOES OF

SCRIPTURE IN THE

LETTERS OF

PAUL

RICHARD B. HAYS

YALE UNIVERSITY PRESS
NEW HAVEN & LONDON

Excerpt from "Ash Wednesday" in *Collected Poems, 1909–1962* by T. S. Eliot, copyright
1936 by Harcourt Brace Jovanovich, Inc., copyright © 1963, 1964 by T. S. Eliot,
reprinted by permission of the publisher. Permission to reprint outside the U.S.
granted by Faber and Faber Limited, Publishers.

"The Nineteenth Century and After" reprinted with permission of Macmillan
Publishing Company from *The Poems of W. B. Yeats: A New Edition*, edited by Richard J.
Finneran. Copyright 1933 by Macmillan Publishing Company, renewed 1961 by Bertha
Georgie Yeats. Permission to reprint outside the U.S. granted by A. P. Watt Ltd. on
behalf of Michael B. Yeats and Macmillan London Ltd.

Designed by James J. Johnson
and set in Palatino Roman types by The Composing Room of Michigan, Inc.
Printed in the United States of America by Vail-Ballou Press, Binghamton, N.Y.

Library of Congress Cataloging-in-Publication Data

Hays, Richard B.
    Echoes of scripture in the letters of Paul / Richard B. Hays.
        p.   cm.
    Bibliography: p.
    Includes index.
    ISBN 0–300–04471–2 (cloth)
            0–300–05429–7 (pbk.)
    1.   Bible.   N.T.   Epistles of Paul—Relation to the Old Testament.
2. Bible.   O.T.—Quotations in the New Testament.   3. Bible.   N.T.
Epistles of Paul—Criticism, interpretation, etc.   I. Title.
BS2655.R32H39   1989
227'.066—dc19   89–30110
                                                                                        CIP

A catalogue record for this book is available from the British Library.

The paper in this book meets the guidelines for permanence and durability of
the Committee on Production Guidelines for Book Longevity of the Council
on Library Resources.

4 6 8 10 9 7 5

This book is dedicated to
George Hobson,
σοφὸς ἀρχιτέκτων,

and to the memory of
John Harold Gibbs
(1940–1982),
whose life was a true reading of the gospel.

Contents

Preface

Around the time I was finishing the manuscript of this book, I happened on George Steiner's review of *The Literary Guide to the Bible*, edited by Robert Alter and Frank Kermode.[1] In his learned and provocative essay,[2] Steiner castigates the contributors to the *Literary Guide* for avoiding what he calls the thorny and ugly theological issues raised by the relationship between the Hebrew Scriptures and the Christian interpretation of them:

> The all too precise prefiguration of Christ's role and agony in the Psalms, in Deutero-Isaiah, is only glancingly referred to. This, in turn, makes it hardly possible for the modern reader to apprehend the bitter, wholly consequent hatred of the Jew expressed in Romans—a hatred incomparably phrased, metaphorized by Paul, and one cannot but feel, bearing its death fruit in our century. It is just because the Psalms and the literature of prophecy in the Old Testament foretell Jesus so graphically that the rejection of Jesus by the Jews of his own day strikes Paul as a specifically suicidal blasphemy, as an act of self-negation which sets mankind on the treadmill of its imprisonment in history.

This passing reference to the apostle Paul cries out for response. If so erudite a literary critic as Steiner labors under such distressing misapprehensions about Paul and his argument in Romans, the need for the reading of Paul offered in the following pages is perhaps greater than I realized when I began to write.

"Hatred of the Jew"? As Paul would say, *mē genoito* (by no means)! In this book I seek to show, among other things, that Paul the Jew remained passionately driven, to the end of his life, by the desire to demonstrate that God had *not* abandoned Israel. Furthermore, the predictive christo-

logical interpretation of the Psalms and the prophets, which appears so
graphically obvious to Steiner, plays only a minor role in Paul's exposition of Israel's Scriptures. In short, although Steiner's remarks might be
applied, with some justice, to the evangelists Matthew and John, they
badly misrepresent Paul. If indeed we must reckon with "death fruit" of
the Christian tradition in our century, that fruit grows from soil made
fertile by Christian theology's perverse incomprehension of Paul's vision
for eschatological reconciliation, a vision that seeks—in Romans above
all—to embrace Jews and Gentiles alike within the scope of God's un-
fathomable mercy.

If we are to arrive at a properly nuanced estimate of Paul's theological
stance toward his own people and their sacred texts, we must engage him
on his own terms, by following his readings of the texts in which he heard
the word of God. My investigation is thus animated by the question, How
did Paul interpret Israel's Scriptures? In order to keep that question in
proper historical perspective, the reader should bear in mind a few
important facts.

First, Paul's letters are the earliest writings in the New Testament.
Although this fact is somewhat obscured by the conventional arrangement of the New Testament canon, these letters were all sent as pastoral
communications to particular churches long before the earliest of the
canonical Gospels had been composed. Consequently, the term *gospel* in
this book is normally used in the sense that Paul himself used it, as a
reference to the content of early Christian preaching, not as a reference to
specific narrative texts.

Following this first fact is a logically related second: because Paul
wrote in a time when there was no New Testament, no body of generally
acknowledged authoritative Christian writings, his Scripture was the
body of writings that constituted Israel's sacred text, which Christians
later came to call the Old Testament. Paul himself never referred to these
writings that way: the Scripture that he had known as a Pharisee remained Scripture for him after his call to proclaim the gospel of the
crucified Messiah, and he did not anticipate its supplementation by a
New Testament. Consequently, when I use the term Scripture in this
book, I normally use it in the sense that Paul himself used it, as a reference
to the Bible of the Jewish people (in Christian parlance, the Old Testament), not inclusive of any Christian writings.

It would be misleading, however, to refer to this Scripture as the
"Hebrew Bible," because the original Hebrew language of the biblical
writings was not a concern of Paul. His citations characteristically follow

the Septuagint (LXX), a Greek translation of the Hebrew Bible dating from the second or third century B.C.E., which was in common use in Hellenistic synagogues during Paul's lifetime. Rarely do Paul's quotations agree with the Masoretic Hebrew text (MT) against the LXX; even the few cases of apparent agreement with the Hebrew can be explained as evidence of variant LXX text forms that have been subjected to "hebraizing revisions," a tendency well attested elsewhere by the Greek versions of Aquila, Symmachus, and Theodotion. (A technical discussion of the biblical text employed by Paul can be found in the comprehensive study of Dietrich-Alex Koch, *Die Schrift als Zeuge des Evangeliums: Untersuchungen zur Verwendung und zum Verständnis der Schrift bei Paulus.*)[3] It appears that Paul, whose missionary activity concentrated on predominantly Gentile congregations in Asia Minor and Greece, normally read and cited Scripture in Greek, which was the common language of the eastern empire in his time.

Quotations from the LXX in this book follow the Greek text of Alfred Rahlfs, *Septuaginta.*[4] Translations of passages from the LXX are my own. Likewise, except where otherwise indicated, translations of the New Testament passages cited are my own, though I have generally not departed far from the Revised Standard Version (RSV) unless there was particular reason to do so. Italics in scriptural passages are mine unless otherwise indicated. Abbreviations in the footnotes follow the system set forth in the *Journal of Biblical Literature* 107 (1988): 588–96. Abbreviations for journals are italicized; abbreviations for titles of monograph series are set in roman type.

In this book I pursue questions that differ markedly from the normal range of issues posed by historical criticism of the Pauline letters. I approach the task of interpretation not by reconstructing the historical situation in the churches to which Paul wrote, not by framing hypothetical accounts of the opponents against whom Paul was arguing, but by reading the letters as literary texts shaped by complex intertextual relations with Scripture. Such an approach does not in principle preclude or invalidate other approaches that seek to describe the social world of the Pauline communities or the historical circumstances surrounding the production of the letters; indeed, a fully rounded understanding of these texts is impossible without such historical inquiry. To the trained eye, my debt to historical-critical scholarship is evident on every page. Nonetheless, I employ, for heuristic purposes, a set of analytical instruments different from those traditionally employed by Pauline scholars. I do this in part because I find the phenomena of intertextual echo intrinsically interesting and in part because I believe that the literary critic's "hearing aid" can disclose important elements of Paul's thought that have been left unexplored by other critical methods.

The results of my reading sometimes pose a challenge to current historical hypotheses. For example, if the structure and logic of Paul's elaborate contrast in 2 Corinthians 3 between Moses' ministry and his own can be explained through an understanding of the poetic function of dissimile, then it becomes unnecessary to postulate a pre-Pauline source for Paul's midrash on Exodus 34 in order to account for the internal tensions of the passage. My literary reading does not disprove the historical reconstructions of earlier commentators, but it does highlight the fact that these reconstructions are conjectural attempts to explain certain gaps or disjunctions within the text that might be patient of other explanations.

I would insist, nonetheless, that my treatment of Paul in these pages is not ahistorical. Attention to intertextuality, as I have defined it here, compels respect for diachronic concerns. The readings of Paul that I offer place him firmly within his historical context, as a first-century Jewish Christian seeking to come to terms hermeneutically with his Jewish heritage. This construal of Paul makes sense historically; indeed, I hope that it contributes to a more exact appreciation of Paul's place on the spectrum of emergent Jewish and Christian communities in the middle of the first century.

Furthermore, the intertextual approach to Paul may prove theologically fruitful. Questions about the relation between Judaism and Christianity, the authority of Scripture, the role of the church as an interpretive community, and the freedoms and constraints operative within that community are brought into sharp focus by the questions that I ask here of Paul's letters. If this book contributes to stimulating discussion of these problems, I will have achieved one of my purposes.

The aim of this study, then, is to undertake a reading of selected passages in Paul's letters, attending carefully to the scriptural echoes that sound there. This is neither a comprehensive study of Paul's use of Scripture nor an essay on literary theory as such; it is rather an attempt to probe the complex significations created by a representative sampling of Paul's intertextual reflections. Chapter 1 charts an approach to interpreting the echoes of Scripture in Paul and contrasts this approach to previous studies of Paul's use of the Old Testament.

Chapter 2 concentrates on the effects of intertextual echo in Romans, the letter in the Pauline corpus that bears the greatest concentration of Old Testament quotations. Romans centers on the problem of God's faithfulness to Israel: if uncircumcised Gentiles are now received into the people of God, does that mean that God has unjustly and arbitrarily abandoned his promised special covenant relation with Israel, that the word of God has fallen? Paul answers these questions with an intricately woven argument from Scripture, whose logic and effects are traced in this chapter.

One finding of chapter 2 is that Paul uses Scripture throughout Romans primarily to argue for a particular vision of the church. This perspective is expanded in chapter 3 through investigation of several other passages in which Paul finds the community of the church prefigured in Scripture. Because Paul sees the fulfillment of prophecy not primarily in events in the life of Jesus (as Matthew does) but in God's gathering of a church composed of Jews and Gentiles together, his hermeneutic is functionally ecclesiocentric rather than christocentric. The implications of this insight for interpreting key instances of intertextual reading as in 1 Corinthians and Galatians are explored.

Chapter 4 takes up the problem of whether Paul's revisionary readings are guided by an explicitly articulated hermeneutic. The question is addressed through an examination of 2 Cor. 3:1–4:6, a discussion of "letter and Spirit," where we find Paul not only using Scripture allusively but also reflecting on the illumination brought to Scripture for the new covenant people by the Holy Spirit. Here, more explicitly than in the texts discussed in the earlier chapters, Paul works out the claim that the true meaning of Scripture is made manifest in the transformed lives of the community of faith.

Finally, chapter 5 gathers and summarizes the findings of the interpretive probes of the previous chapters. Building on this summary, I offer some reflections about the hermeneutical implications of the reading of Paul that is developed in these pages. The poetic freedom with which Paul echoes Scripture poses intriguing problems and possibilities for communities in which Paul's own writings have come to be read as Scripture. If the word is so alive on the lips and in the hearts of the community of faith, how then must we read?

Parts of chapter 2 of this book were first published in various journals. A few paragraphs from my article "Have We Found Abraham to Be Our Forefather according to the Flesh?: A Reconsideration of Rom. 4:1," originally published in *Novum Testamentum* 27 (1985): 76–98, have been revised slightly for use here. I have expanded and adapted one paragraph from my article "Relations Natural and Unnatural: A Response to John Boswell's Exegesis of Romans 1," originally published in the *Journal of Religious Ethics* 14, no. 1 (1986): 184–215, for incorporation. I have also used brief excerpts from my article, "Psalm 143 and the Logic of

Romans 3," originally published in the *Journal of Biblical Literature* 99 (1980): 107–15. I am grateful to the editors of these journals for permission to reprint. I am also grateful to the University of California Press for permission to reprint the first two and last twelve lines of the poem "The Widener Burying-Ground" by John Hollander, originally published in *The Figure of Echo*.

Because I emphasize the hermeneutical role of community, it is essential that I acknowledge the important contributions of many colleagues, friends, and students in shaping the discourse that follows in these pages. My special gratitude is offered to Brevard Childs and Wayne Meeks for their discerning criticism, encouragement, and counsel in the formative stages of this project. Likewise, John Augustine, Gil Greggs, Steve Kraftchick, Regina Plunkett,and Barry Seltser read major portions of the manuscript in progress and posed perceptive questions that refined the argument in countless ways. The completed draft was read with great care by J. Louis Martyn and Eleanor Cook (readers for Yale University Press) and by Janna Jackson, all of whom made helpful editorial suggestions. The meticulous work of manuscript editor Carl Rosen has tightened and clarified the text at many points. The indexes were skillfully compiled by Regina Plunkett, with the aid of a grant from the Yale Divinity School Faculty Research Fund.

I would also like to thank the following people for their insightful comments: A. K. M. Adam, William Beardslee, Julie Calhoun-Bryant, Beverly Gaventa, Rowan Greer, Peter Hawkins, Judy Hays, John Hollander, Timothy Jackson, Luke Johnson, George Lindbeck, David Lull, Herbert Marks, Stephen Moore, Bernard Brandon Scott, Margaret Wimsatt, and Ben Witherington. The echoes of their good counsel whisper through the text of this book in ways that not even the author could adequately discern or credit. Looking over this roster of friends, I am grateful for many hours of joyful and edifying conversation. My students at Yale Divinity School, too numerous to name here, have also contributed valuable insights and questions and have kept me honest in the quest to understand Paul's interpretation of Scripture.

Finally, my wife, Judy, and my children, Chris and Sarah, have borne the weight of my authorial agonizing with the character quality that Paul calls *makrothymia:* "long-suffering steadfastness." Their sense of humor has kept me from self-importance, and their love has kept me from discouragement. Their presence has been a constant reminder to me of a simple truth articulated by my student Suzanne Carley in private correspondence: "After all, what good is a hermeneutic if you don't have a life?" In the end, that may be the best paraphrase of 2 Cor. 3:1–6.

CHAPTER ONE

The Puzzle of Pauline Hermeneutics

PAUL AS READER AND MISREADER OF SCRIPTURE

The apostle Paul introduces as spokesman for his gospel a character named The Righteousness from Faith,[1] who repeats lines penned long before in Israel's Scripture:

> Do not say in your heart, "Who will ascend into heaven?" . . . or "Who will descend into the abyss?" . . . The word is near you, in your mouth and in your heart. (Rom. 10:6–8)

The words echo Deut. 30:11–14, a passage in which Moses exhorts Israel to keep the commandments of the Law. Moses' point is that the *Law* is near: the commandments of God are neither esoteric nor impossible to obey, for they have been graciously given to Israel in "this book of the Law." In Romans 10, however, a puzzling shift occurs: as Paul interprets these words, they refer not to the Law but to "the word of faith which we preach" (Rom. 10:8b). Indeed, while claiming Moses' words from Deuteronomy, The Righteousness from Faith now appears to speak as Moses' adversary. Through a series of parenthetical interpretive comments, Paul takes possession of Moses' exhortation and transforms its sense so that Moses is made to bear witness to the gospel.

This tour de force is not an isolated instance. Paul repeatedly interprets Scripture in ways that must have startled his first audience. Consider the following examples: in Rom. 10:18, just a few sentences after his revisionary reading of Deuteronomy 30, Paul quotes Ps. 19:4 ("Their voice has gone out into all the earth"), a poetic description of the heavens' mute testimony to the glory of their creator, in order to prove that Jews are culpable for rejecting Christian preaching; in 1 Cor. 10:4 he

1

abruptly identifies the rock from which Israel drank in the wilderness as Christ; in Galatians 3–4 Paul appropriates the story of Abraham, the forefather of Israel who first received circumcision as a sign of covenant relation with God, in order to argue *against* circumcision. It is hardly any wonder that Paul encountered rejection and hostility from many Jews who shared his passion for the integrity of the Scriptures as the word of God.

In Paul we encounter a first-century Jewish thinker who, while undergoing a profound disjuncture with his own religious tradition,[2] grappled his way through to a vigorous and theologically generative reappropriation of Israel's Scriptures. However great the tensions between his heritage and his new Christian convictions, he insistently sought to show that his proclamation of the gospel was grounded in the witness of Israel's sacred texts. The trick lay in learning to read these texts aright. Christians accustomed to reading the "Old Testament" through the hermeneutical lens that Paul ground may find it difficult to appreciate how peculiar and scandalous many of his readings must have looked to his contemporaries. Consequently, defamiliarization is the first requirement of a critical examination of Paul's uses of Scripture.

The hermeneutical idiosyncrasy of Paul's reading can be highlighted by comparing Rom. 10:5–10 to a much-discussed talmudic passage that appeals to Deuteronomy 30 as a warrant for very different convictions. Although the Babylonian Talmud dates from a later period, it gives expression to certain sensibilities and conventions that Paul's interpretation violates. In *Baba Meşia* 59b appears the story of a dispute between Rabbi Eliezer and other sages; the issue at hand (whether a certain type of oven is to be deemed ritually clean or unclean) becomes the occasion for the articulation of fundamental rabbinic attitudes toward Scripture and its interpretation.

> On that day R. Eliezer brought forward every imaginable argument, but they did not accept them. Said he to them: "If the *halachah* [i.e., the legal teaching of Scripture] agrees with me, let this carob-tree prove it!" Thereupon the carob-tree was torn a hundred cubits out of its place—others affirm, four hundred cubits. "No proof can be brought from a carob-tree," they retorted. Again he said to them: "If the *halachah* agrees with me, let the stream of water prove it!" Whereupon the stream of water flowed backwards. "No proof can be brought from a stream of water," they rejoined. Again he urged: If the *halachah* agrees with me, let the walls of the schoolhouse prove it," whereupon the walls inclined to fall. But R. Joshua rebuked them, saying: "When

scholars are engaged in a *halachic* dispute, what have ye to interfere?"
Hence they did not fall, in honour of R. Joshua, nor did they resume
the upright, in honour of R. Eliezer; and they are still standing thus
inclined. Again he said to them, "If the *halachah* agrees with me, let it
be proved from Heaven!" Whereupon a Heavenly Voice cried out:
"Why do ye dispute with R. Eliezer, seeing that in all matters the
halachah agrees with him!" But R. Joshua arose and exclaimed: "It is
not in heaven." What did he mean by this? Said R. Jeremiah: "That the
Torah had already been given at Mount Sinai; we pay no attention to a
Heavenly Voice, because thou has long since written in the Torah at
Mount Sinai, 'After the majority one must incline.' " R. Nathan met
Elijah and asked him: "What did the Holy One, blessed be He, do in
that hour?"—"He laughed [with joy]," he replied, "saying, 'My sons
have defeated Me, my sons have defeated Me.' "[3]

While Paul appeals to Deut. 30:11–14 to demonstrate the nearness of
God's word—and therefore its living flexibility, its capacity for hermeneutical transformation to disclose God's grace in ways unfathomed
by prior generations of readers—R. Joshua seemingly adduces the same
text in order to foreclose hermeneutical deviation. For R. Joshua,[4] the text
proclaims its own already givenness, its stability as a bulwark against
human whim and delusion. Whereas Paul reads the passage as a promise
of ongoing revelation, R. Joshua reads it as a prohibition of appeals to
revelatory experience; as R. Jeremiah explains, "We pay no attention to a
Heavenly Voice." R. Joshua uses Moses' words to fix God's speaking in
the past, in a written text; Paul uses the same words to locate God's
speaking in the present, in his own kerygma.

The Talmud's construal of the text may appear to be closer than Paul's
to the original sense of the words in Deuteronomy, but both readings
execute major hermeneutical shifts. Despite R. Joshua's explanation,
Deut. 30:11, read in context, hardly prohibits God from continuing to
speak to his people; the point of the passage is that Israel cannot plead
ignorance of the Law as an excuse for disobedience. The rabbis extrapo-
late from Moses' declaration of the Law's accessibility a doctrine of its
closure. For R. Joshua, the exegesis of "it is not in heaven" (Deut. 30:11) is
governed by Deut. 30:10, which says that the commandments and statutes are "written in this book of the Law." For Paul, however, the exegesis of the passage is governed by Deut. 30:14: "But what does it say?
'The word is near you, on your lips and in your heart.' " In both cases, a
new global construal of the "Word of God" shapes the interpretation[5]: for
the rabbis the Word of God is the Mosaic Torah as mediated through

generations of oral explication; for Paul the Word of God is Jesus Christ as experienced in the Spirit-filled Christian community. Thus, *Baba Meṣia* 59b and Rom. 10:5–10 offer independent, rival readings of Deuteronomy, each of which assimilates it to a new symbolic world.

Despite the substantial theological differences between Paul and the rabbis, then, their actual interpretive practices are less divergent than their hermeneutical theories might suggest. Both sides of this artificially staged debate presuppose the legitimacy of innovative readings that disclose truth previously latent in Scripture; they differ primarily with regard to the warrant used to justify hermeneutical freedom. Paul gains leverage on the text by claiming immediate revelatory illumination; the rabbis gain leverage on the text by appealing to majority opinion within an interpretive community.

The rabbinic story, therefore, exposes the quest for hermeneutical closure as an illusion. Texts will always demand and generate new interpretation, as this halakhic dispute illustrates. Even a definitive divine Law written once for all cannot terminate interpretation; indeed, such a written revelation feeds the hermeneutical fire by compelling further interpretations.[6] Consequently, the story ironically undercuts the premise on which the rhetorical weight of the rabbis' appeal to the already written Torah rests. While Paul betrays no sign of ironic self-reflection in his audacious rereading of Deuteronomy 30, the Talmud winks at the reader, signaling recognition of the revisionary character of its own interpretation. How so? When the story portrays the Holy One, blessed be He, laughing and admitting defeat in matching exegetical wits with the sages, it implicitly concedes that R. Joshua and R. Jeremiah have succeeded in extracting from the text an interpretation that the Holy One, blessed be He, never intended at all. He is apparently so delighted by their hermeneutical ingenuity, that—like a father deliberately losing a game of checkers to his young son—he charitably forbears to point out that R. Jeremiah has egregiously misrepresented Exod. 23:2, which actually reads, "After the majority you must *not* incline to do evil, and you shall not bear witness in a suit to incline after the majority."[7]

This Torah text warns that, in a legal proceeding, majority sentiment must not be allowed to distort justice. R. Jeremiah's appeal to Exod. 23:2 in *Baba Meṣia* 59b, however, transforms its sense by converting what was originally a jurisprudential principle[8] into a general hermeneutical warrant. Furthermore, R. Jeremiah, through selectively quoting only the final three words of the Hebrew sentence, transmutes Moses' warning against group pressure into an admonition to let the majority rule.[9] One could hardly invent a more whimsical inversion. By allowing the sages to get away with this ruse, the Talmud tacitly concedes that its own pretense of propounding an interpretation ruled by the given Torah text is a benign fiction.[10]

My purpose in thus comparing Paul to the rabbis is neither to vindicate nor to castigate either party; the point of the comparison is to focus the distinctive character of Paul's hermeneutical perspective. Both *Baba Meşia* 59b and Rom. 10:5–10 represent readings—or misreadings, we might be inclined to say—of Scripture, extending its meaning in new directions.

Paul did not think of himself as a writer of Scripture; he was writing pastoral letters to fledgling churches, interpreting Scripture (by which he meant the texts that Christians later began to call the "Old Testament") to guide these struggling communities as they sought to understand the implications of the gospel. It requires a disciplined effort of historical imagination to keep reminding ourselves that when Paul wrote there was no New Testament; as Wayne Meeks has wryly observed, "That the Christian movement existed once without the canon which later become constitutive of it is a fact whose hermeneutical significance has not, even now, fully impressed itself on our theology."[11] This book explores the hermeneutical significance of reading Paul as a Christian interpreter whose Bible was Israel's Scripture. If we approach Paul's letters a priori as Scripture in their own right, we run the risk of distortion through a hieratic reading that loses sight of their historical contingency[12] and hermeneutical innovation. Paradoxically, we learn how rightly to read Paul's letters as Scripture only by first reading them as not-Scripture and attending to how he read the Scripture that he knew. The task of this book, then, is to retrace some of Paul's readings, seeking to grasp their novelty and to follow the intricate hermeneutical paths along which he led his readers.

CRITICAL APPROACHES TO PAULINE HERMENEUTICS

Paul's Interpretation of Scripture: State of the Discussion

Paul's appropriation of Scripture is a puzzle that has exercised the ingenuity of numerous scholars. Rather than tracing in detail the lengthy history of scholarship on the issue, I offer a summary characterization of the state of the discussion and propose a new approach to some traditional aporias.

Through much of the history of Christian theology and biblical interpretation, Paul's innovative readings of Scripture posed no problem because Christians heard the Old Testament through the translating headset of a Pauline hermeneutic: what Scripture really meant was whatever Paul (and other New Testament writers) said it meant. Historical criticism, however, has restored a proper sense of Scripture's identity as a separate voice (more properly, a chorus of separate voices, though Paul would not have so understood it) and thus afforded us the possibility of discerning how Paul plays the rebound of Scripture's voice off his own experience and confession. Such discernment, however, inevitably leads us to hear dissonances between the sacred texts and Paul's rendering of them.

At least since the beginnings of the critical study of the Bible in the Enlightenment, careful readers have noted the striking verbal divergence of many New Testament quotations from their putative Old Testament sources.[13] Early scholarly studies of these quotations often treated them as problems to be solved through textual criticism. Within the past century, however, scholars have generally conceded that Paul's use of Scripture cannot be explained simply through appeals to variant textual traditions and that the issues raised by his readings are fundamentally hermeneutical issues, because of the undeniable gap between the "original sense" of the Old Testament texts and Paul's interpretation, even in cases where the citations are in verbatim agreement with the LXX. This gap has generated a wide variety of critical responses, ranging along a spectrum from outraged dismissal to fervent apology.

Critics who represent what George Lindbeck has called the "experiential-expressive"[14] interpretation of religion, Schleiermacher's progeny, have found it easy to dismiss Paul's hermeneutical peculiarities, because they have seen his reading of Scripture as peripheral to the core of his religious experience. Percy Gardner, for example, writing in 1913, could casually declare:

When the great Apostle proceeds to throw the result of spiritual experience into intellectual form, all sorts of possibilities of error come in. The great source of these errors is his use of the Old Testament, which he interprets in the manner of the rabbis of his time, and therefore, it is needless to say, not in accordance with true critical methods. . . . [T]he close attention to the words of Scripture which came of the careful study of them in rabbinic schools, made him lay upon particular words and forms a stress quite foreign to the writers.[15]

If cultural conditioning caused Paul to misread the Bible quaintly, it mattered little, because the substance of his message was grounded in a preverbal experience of union with Christ. According to this view, Israel's Scripture was not a formative factor in his theology; he merely seized upon it to illustrate aspects of a (Christian) belief system that he already held on grounds extrinsic to his interpretation of Scripture. One of the most emphatic statements of this position was that of Adolf von Harnack, who contended that Paul did not intend to create a "book-religion" at all and that he wrote about the Old Testament in his letters only when he was forced to reply to issues raised by Judaizing opponents.[16]

A more theologically sophisticated development of this perspective can be found in the work of Rudolf Bultmann, whose exposition of Pauline theology in his *Theology of the New Testament* gives scant place to Scripture as a foundational element in Paul's thought. As Bultmann saw the matter, Paul was seeking to give expression to the kerygma through mythological language and symbols that were only provisionally adequate vehicles for it. Israel's Scripture occupies no privileged role in this scheme; in no sense is the Old Testament a material source for Paul's theology. Whatever vestiges of Old Testament mythology (such as apocalyptic eschatology) might remain in Paul's thought should be construed as evidence of his attempt to employ an outmoded religious idiom to express a new authentic mode of self-understanding.[17] Furthermore, interpreting Paul in light of the powerful traditional Lutheran antithesis between Law and Gospel, Bultmann saw the Old Testament as witness primarily to Law, which he understood phenomenologically as a representation of "the demanding will of God," the unfulfillable demand that is the necessary backdrop to the Gospel's word of grace. Consequently, though the Old Testament is "the presupposition for existence under grace," it serves only as a negative foil to grace.[18] Though Paul, through an accident of history, experienced the divine Law through the Old Testament, the consciousness of moral demand can arise equally well through "other historical embodiments of the divine Law."[19] The historical specificity of the Old Testament's narratives, commandments, and promises is of no importance for Christian faith, because "[i]t speaks to a particular people who stand in a particular ethnic history [*Volksgeschichte*] which is not ours."[20] The result of this analysis is a radical denial of the revelatory function of the Old Testament for Christian theology:

To the Christian faith the Old Testament is no longer revelation as it has been, and still is, for the Jews. For the person who stands within the Church the history of Israel is a closed chapter. . . . Israel's history is not our history, and in so far as God has shown his grace in that history, such grace is not meant for us. . . . The events which meant something for Israel, which were God's Word, mean nothing more to us. . . . To the Christian faith the Old Testament is not in the true sense God's Word.[21]

These breathtaking denials—which give expression to an attitude not uncommon in liberal Protestantism—are not uttered in ignorance; they represent the considered judgment of one of this century's outstanding New Testament scholars. It is extremely difficult, however, to see how such conclusions can be drawn from reading Paul's letters. It is hard to avoid the impression that Bultmann's a priori theological evaluation of the Old Testament—and of Judaism—prevented him from looking carefully at the evidence provided by Paul's actual uses of Scripture. (That is why Bultmann gave little attention to Paul's "misreadings" of the text.) I seek to explore the evidence more carefully and to present an account of the role of Scripture in Paul's thought that is diametrically opposed to Bultmann's. The pervasive influence of Bultmann within the discipline of New Testament (NT) studies in the twentieth century is surely one of the factors that has retarded investigation of Paul's interpretation of Scripture, not least because scholars reacting against Bultmann characteristically made the tactical error of asserting anachronistically that Paul read the Old Testament as "real history,"[22] thereby framing the debate in misleading categories.

At the other end of the spectrum from the tradition of Gardner and Harnack stand those interpreters who, even while acknowledging the hermeneutical gap between the original sense of Scripture and Paul's interpretations of it, seek to minimize the gap by emphasizing the importance of Scripture in Paul's theology and justifying his methods of interpretation.[23] Consider, for example, the stance of Richard Longenecker: "In the majority of his Old Testament citations, Paul adheres to the original sense of the passage. Or, if he extends it, it is possible to understand his rationale if we grant him the Jewish presuppositions of 'corporate solidarity' and 'historical correspondences' and the Christian presuppositions of 'eschatological fulfillment' and 'messianic presence.' "[24] Such a proposal asks us to grant a great deal indeed. Longenecker's analysis, which stresses the midrashic character of Paul's exegesis, illustrates the dilemma of most critics who seek to defend Paul's methods of interpretation. The more closely Paul's methods can be identified with recognized interpretive conventions of first-century Judaism, the less arbitrary and more historically understandable they appear; however, at the same time, such historical explanations of Paul's exegesis render it increasingly difficult to see how interpretations that employ such methods can bear any persuasive power or normative value for that mythical creature of whom Bultmann spoke with such conviction: modern man.

The great majority of critical studies of Paul's use of the Old Testament, however, have avoided frontal engagement with these hermeneutical perplexities, concentrating instead, more modestly, on essential technical tasks of scholarship. The Pauline quotations and allusions have been cataloged, their introductory formulas classified, their relation to various Old Testament text-traditions examined, their exegetical methods compared to the methods of other interpreters within ancient Christianity and Judaism.[25] The achievements of such inquiries are by no means to be disparaged: they have, as it were, unpacked and laid out the pieces of the puzzle. But how are the pieces to be assembled? Most of the "unpacking" of the Pauline citations was complete more than a generation ago, yet we still lack a satisfying account of Paul's letters as "hermeneutical events,"[26] discourse in which Paul is engaged in the act of reinterpreting Scripture to address the concerns of his communities.

The questions that scholars have traditionally asked about Paul's use of the Old Testament have been either answered in full or played out to a dead end. These questions may be grouped into five categories:

1. Questions of textual criticism: what form of the Old Testament text was known and used by Paul?
2. Questions of incidence of citation: which Old Testament books and passages does Paul quote?
3. Questions of sources and historical background: what sort of interpretive community tradition, if any, does Paul represent? Included here are the many recent efforts to demonstrate in detail that Paul's exegesis is midrashic, that it represents the exegetical methods and traditions of pharisaic (nascent rabbinic) Judaism. Also to be placed in this category are investigations of Paul's use of early Christian exegetical traditions and testimonies.
4. Questions of theological legitimacy: does Paul use the Old Testament with exegetical-theological integrity, or does he rifle it for prooftexts and twist its meaning? There is, of course, a long and inconclusive history of polemic and apology on this issue. At the

nerve center of this debate is the question of whether Paul's understanding of the role of Torah within the faith of Israel represents an
aberrant caricature of Judaism.[27]

5. Questions of biblical inspiration and authority: what doctrine of
the origin and normative claim of Scripture did Paul hold?

In practice, of course, these questions overlap one another; taken together, they provide a fair sketch of the scope of the discussion.

It is hard to escape the impression, however, that recent investigations, often burdened with an apologetic agenda, have tended to rehearse well-worn issues, making little headway on understanding Paul's
exegesis. The most creative interpreters of Paul have proceeded on other
fronts, using methods derived from the social sciences[28] or from the
study of ancient rhetoric.[29] Even those studies concerned with broadly
theological issues have little to say about Paul as interpreter of Scripture.[30]

This is a regrettable state of affairs, because the question of how Paul
read Scripture is of great importance for grasping the logic and purpose of
his arguments. Is there some method or hermeneutic that can account for
Paul's exegesis? Is he a completely idiosyncratic reader? How are we to
understand the literary and theological transformations that occur when
Paul cites and alludes to Scripture? As I contend below, many conventional assumptions about Paul's hermeneutics are in need of scrutiny and
revision.

Furthermore, if the letters are rightly described as "hermeneutical
events," then Paul's grappling with known texts provides a potentially
illuminating model for normative theological reflection on the task and
methods of biblical hermeneutics. Deliberation on such matters, however, must be deferred until the final chapter of this book, for fruitful
reflection on such issues cannot precede a fresh examination of Paul as
reader of Scripture.

Pauline Exegesis as Midrash?

In response to the recent proliferation of studies on rabbinic midrash,
the journals are full of essays arguing that this or that Pauline passage is
an instance of midrashic interpretation of Scripture.[31] In many cases,
however, it is not at all clear what such affirmations are supposed to
mean. If they mean simply that Paul writes as a Jew seeking to interpret
Scripture in such a way as to make it applicable to his own time and
circumstances, surely everyone would have to assent: the claim is true

but trivial. In that sense, all readings of Scripture by Jews and Christians always and everywhere are instances of midrash.[32]

Usually the categorization of Paul's exegesis as midrash seems to carry a stronger and more particular force: it is asserted that rabbinic midrash offers, in one way or another, the proper *historical* background against which Paul's thought is to be understood.[33] Sometimes the supposition is stated in the form of an antithesis: the sources of Paul's thought are Jewish rather than Greek or Gnostic or whatever. This antithetical approach has been explicitly promoted by the work of critics such as E. Earle Ellis and A. T. Hanson.[34] Apart from the fact that such Jewish-Greek dichotomies require careful qualification, there are complicated problems with the attempt to use rabbinic midrash as a historical background to Paul, not the least of which is simply the late date of the rabbinic sources. As Philip Alexander has written in a recent essay, anyone who does not reckon with the possibility of a profound discontinuity between Judaism before and Judaism after the catastrophes of 70 C.E. and 135 C.E. is likely to lapse into "massive and sustained anachronism. . . . The way in which NT scholars without more ado read back into pre-70 Judaism post-70 Rabbinic traditions is totally unjustified."[35] It is more valid methodologically to use Paul as a background source for the study of rabbinic traditions than vice versa.[36]

Rabbinic Judaism, no less than early Christianity, represents (along with the Qumran community and Philo's scholastic Alexandrian Judaism, inter alia), one of several different adaptations of the religious and cultural heritage represented by Israel's Scriptures. These different adaptations should be studied, at least initially, as parallel phenomena, related but distinct dispositions of that heritage. To argue that one of these phenomena represents a source or influence for another is likely to be misleading unless some documentable lines of historical dependence can be demonstrated. One thing that is clearly documentable is that all of them deliberately regard Scripture as source and authority for their own quite different theological developments. Thus, we are undertaking a valid and necessary (even if preliminary) task when we inquire independently into the way in which any one of them uses scriptural texts.

Reading Paul and the rabbis in conjunction with one another may illumine interpretive possibilities that would otherwise remain dark, but great caution is necessary in using one to explain the other. The methodological difficulties surrounding the appeal to midrash as an explanatory device for understanding Paul's exegesis may be illustrated by identifying three ways in which this appeal is often employed.

(1) *Midrash as form-critical "map."* There is a very strong tendency for

NT scholars to hope that midrash might give us the missing key to understand the formal structure of Paul's argumentation. If we could isolate form-critically a normative structural pattern of midrash, the pattern might be used to explain the structure of Paul's sometimes convoluted discourse. While this method can claim some positive results in passages such as Romans 4 and Romans 9,[37] the exegetical yield rarely seems to justify the investment of large sums of hope. Often the formal parallels between Paul's interpretations and the structural patterns of rabbinic midrash are to be found only at high levels of generality: both elucidate scriptural texts by referring to other scriptural texts, sometimes employing catchword associations.[38] The more specific one tries to become in tracing formal patterns, the less satisfactory the parallelisms appear to be.[39]

(2) *Midrash as hermeneutical method.* It is widely supposed that the rabbis addressed the task of interpreting Scripture through a series of clearly specified hermeneutical rules: the seven *middoth* of Hillel and the thirteen *middot* of Rabbi Ishmael are usually regarded as having special importance. If Paul interpreted the Old Testament by means of such rules, might it be possible to give a reasoned account of his hermeneutic on the basis of these rabbinic principles? Again, this hope is destined to lead to disappointment. Apart from the considerable difficulty of dating and interpreting the *middot*,[40] they do not in any case actually provide rules for the interpretation of Scripture. They are not rules or limiting guidelines, but an inventory of *tropes*[41]: the *middot* provide a descriptive account of a repertoire of possible imaginative operations that can be performed on the text in the act of interpretation. They do not tell the interpreter how to find out what a text means; instead, they suggest ways to make the text mean more than it says. The result of employing these tropes is aptly summarized by Jacob Neusner in his reflections on Leviticus Rabbah:[42]

> Scripture . . . does not allow us to predict what proposition a given set of verses will yield. On the contrary, because of the insistence that one verse be read in light of another, augmentative one, Leviticus Rabbah prohibits us from predicting at the outset, merely by reading a given verse of Scripture, the way in which a given theme will be worked out or the way in which a given proposition will impart a message through said theme. . . . So while the constant introduction of Scripture provides the wherewithal of speech, these verses serve only as do the colors of the painter. The painter cannot paint without the oils. But the colors do not make the painting. The painter does.

The interpreter holds the creative options, and the hermeneutic is no more dictated by the *middot* than the poet's vision is dictated by the availability of a range of poetic devices such as synecdoche and personification.

In any case, when we focus the discussion on the particular ways in which the *middoth* are actually thought to be employed by Paul, we discover that only two of them are of much importance: *gezerah shawah* (catchword linkage of two texts) and *qal waḥomer* (inference from the lesser to the greater). And, as David Daube has demonstrated, there is nothing peculiarly rabbinic about these rhetorical devices.[43] Furthermore, even when Paul does occasionally use such tropes in ways that bear a certain formal affinity to rabbinic practice, as, for example, in Romans 4, the material uses to which he puts Scripture differ fundamentally from those of the rabbis; his hermeneutic is materially informed by his Christian convictions much more than by some list of approved hermeneutical procedures. The message that Paul finds in the Old Testament is the gospel of Jesus Christ proleptically figured, a gospel proclaiming the inclusion of the Gentiles among the people of God; his exegesis of Scripture hammers relentlessly on this theme, a theme hardly central in rabbinic hermeneutics.[44]

(3) *Midrash as license.* Here the apologetic note sounds. The term *midrash* can serve as a convenient cover for a multitude of exegetical sins. One frequently finds Christian commentators explaining away their embarrassment over some piece of fanciful Pauline exegesis by noting solemnly that this is midrash, as though the wholesome Hebrew label could render Paul's arbitrariness kosher. Sometimes the commentator means that Paul is using an idea or motif already established in rabbinic tradition: the angels gave the Law at Sinai or the rock followed Israel in the wilderness. This is illuminating in the few cases where an antecedent tradition can be credibly established through other texts. (We should, however, be wary of interpretations that say in effect, "Don't blame Paul for this crazy idea: he didn't invent it." Paul adheres no less firmly to the traditions that he uses than to the ideas that he coins.)

More questionable are ascriptions of the midrash label to explain strange exegeses that have no antecedents or parallels in Jewish tradition: "the rock was Christ" (1 Cor. 10:4). When such a statement is explained as an instance of midrash, the term has come to mean loosely "free and playful interpretation." (This is precisely the sense in which midrash has caught the fancy of deconstructionists and other modern literary theorists who have found in rabbinic midrash a historical precedent and analogue for their own interpretive practices.)[45] The difficulty with this usage lies in its simultaneous imprecision and authoritative mysteriousness: the label *midrash* tends to bring the interpretive process to a halt, as though it had explained something, when in fact we should keep pressing for clarity: what poetic linkages of sound or imagery make this sort of imaginative leap possible, what effects are produced in the argument by it, and what sort of response does it invite from the sympathetic reader's imagination? Such questions need to be asked of rabbinic exegesis as well as of Pauline texts.

Intertextuality: A Proposed Approach

Rabbinic midrash and the letters of Paul are natural analogues because both are paradigmatic instances of intertextual discourse, both wrestling with the same great precursor. The phenomenon of intertextuality—the imbedding of fragments of an earlier text within a later one—has always played a major role in the cultural traditions that are heir to Israel's Scriptures: the voice of Scripture, regarded as authoritative in one way or another, continues to speak in and through later texts that both depend on and transform the earlier. Such intertextual processes do not begin only with the formal closure of the canon. Renée Bloch's seminal studies of midrash articulated an insight that has now been elegantly documented by Michael Fishbane in *Biblical Interpretation in Ancient Israel:* the revisionary hermeneutical operations that later came to be called midrash were already manifest in the work of the writers of the biblical texts, who collected, interpreted, and transmuted still earlier texts and traditions.[46]

> One may say that the entire corpus of Scripture remains open to these invasive procedures and strategic reworkings up to the close of the canon in the early rabbinic period, and so the received text is complexly compacted of teachings and their subversion, of rules and their extension, of topoi and their revision. Within ancient Israel, as long as the textual corpus remained open, Revelation and Tradition were thickly interwoven and interdependent, and the received Hebrew Bible is itself, therefore, the product of an interpretive tradition.[47]

To read Paul against this background of "inner-biblical exegesis" is to understand his place in the stream of tradition in a new way. He saw himself as a prophetic figure,[48] carrying forward the proclamation of God's word as Israel's prophets and sages had always done, in a way that reactivated past revelation under new conditions.

Of course, the phenomenon of intertextuality is by no means limited to texts that are understood as the Scripture of a religious community; this is one important lesson that biblical scholars can learn from literary critics,[49] who, no less than theologians, work with a canon, a body of traditions engaged in intertextual reflection. Beyond the Law and the Prophets, the Writings in their canon include Spenser, Shakespeare, Milton, Wordsworth, Stevens, and so forth. The boundaries of the canon will vary with the critic, but wherever there is a community of readers who hearken to earlier texts as powerful and evocative voices with a claim to be heard in the present, intertextual writing and reading will take place. The working hypothesis of this book, therefore, is that certain approaches to intertextuality that have developed within literary criticism prove illuminating when applied to Paul's letters.

The discussion, however, of intertextuality among literary critics has not been confined to the study of how writers cite and allude to specifically identifiable textual precursors. Julia Kristeva and Roland Barthes have been influential voices defining intertextuality as the study of the semiotic matrix within which a text's acts of signification occur.[50] All discourse, in this view, is necessarily intertextual in the sense that its conditions of intelligibility are given by and in relation to a previously given body of discourse. As Jonathan Culler observes, "Intertextuality thus becomes less a name for a work's relation to prior texts than a designation of its participation in the discursive space of a culture."[51] A criticism interested in intertextuality so understood seeks to explore the intertextual space by taking inventory of the cultural codes within which the text operates and of which it is a manifestation. This kind of criticism, which very quickly shades over into sociology or anthropology, actually converges with the traditional concerns of historical criticism of the Bible. The historical critic who seeks to find parallels and antecedents for a biblical text is also seeking to describe the intertextual space as a precondition for interpretation. The major difference in the approaches is that, where the historical critic traditionally seeks genetic or causal explanations for specific texts, critics such as Kristeva and Barthes are interested in describing the system of codes or conventions that the texts manifest.[52]

Without denying the value or intrinsic interest of such investigations, I propose instead to discuss the phenomenon of intertextuality in Paul's letters in a more limited sense, focusing on his actual citations of and allusions to specific texts. This approach to Paul is both possible and fruitful because Paul repeatedly situates his discourse within the symbolic field created by a single great textual precursor: Israel's Scripture. Thomas Greene's comment on long poems of the Renaissance is equally apt for Paul's compositions: they "tend to reach out to a single privileged predecessor and bind themselves to that authenticating model with par-ticularly intricate knots."[53] The vocabulary and cadences of Scripture—particularly of the LXX—are imprinted deeply on Paul's mind, and the great stories of Israel continue to serve for him as a fund of symbols and metaphors that condition his perception of the world, of God's promised deliverance of his people, and of his own identity and calling. His faith, in short, is one whose articulation is inevitably intertextual in character, and Israel's Scripture is the "determinate subtext that plays a constitutive role"[54] in shaping his literary production.

Such an approach to reading Paul in no way seeks to deny or exclude the presence of nonscriptural influences on his discourse. Paul's discur-sive space encompassed countless codes and elements "already read" from his Hellenistic culture; many other studies have investigated such presences in his letters.[55] The present investigation, however, giving the place of honor to the privileged predecessor that Paul himself explicitly acknowledged, is limited to an exploration of the intertextual echoes of Israel's Scripture in Paul.

The question of intertextuality (though not the term itself) has oc-cupied an important role in literary-critical discussion through much of the twentieth century, at least since T. S. Eliot's influential essay of 1919, "Tradition and the Individual Talent." Deploring the tendency of many readers and critics to prize novelty and individuality and to "dwell with satisfaction upon the poet's difference from his predecessors," Eliot for-mulated the provocative dictum that "not only the best, but the most individual parts of his work may be those in which the dead poets, his ancestors, assert their immortality most vigorously."[56] Of course, Eliot's own poetic practice illustrates the point: "The Waste Land" is a quintes-sential feat of "bricolage,"[57] a great mosaic of fragments self-consciously culled from Eliot's ancestors and shored up into a new poetic construction articulating the sensibilities of a disillusioned generation. The rather whimsical footnotes appended by Eliot to the poem offer explicit ac-knowledgment of debts no different in principle from the debts owed by every poet to his or her predecessors.

Since the publication of Harold Bloom's *Anxiety of Influence* in 1973, critical attention to problems of intertextual influence has intensified. Bloom's idiosyncratic approach, subsequently developed further in a se-ries of studies,[58] portrays the poet's struggle with tradition in the most vivid possible terms. "Every poem," asserts Bloom, "is a misinterpreta-tion of a parent poem."[59] Every poet is a latecomer who gains an identity only by misreading the works of formidable ancestors.

Poetic influence—when it involves two strong, authentic poets,—always proceeds by a misreading of the prior poet, an act of creative correction that is actually and necessarily a misinterpretation. The history of fruitful poetic influences, which is to say the main tradition of Western poetry since the Renaissance, is a history of anxiety and self-serving caricature, of distortion, of perverse, wilful revisionism without which modern poetry as such could not exist.[60]

In Milton's Satan, Bloom descries an allegorical figure of the poetic consciousness, trapped in a relation of inescapable dependence on a Father-Creator, yet openly rebelling by claiming and twisting the creation in accordance with his own will, seeking thereby to posit himself anew, to become his own creation rather than another's. Nietzsche and Freud, of course, loom in the background as the great theoretical influences on Bloom's program. The strong, authentic poet can be described as an *Überleser*, who asserts the will to power over tradition (here Nietzsche speaks through Bloom),[61] and the overcoming of the tradition enacts a symbolic Oedipal violence against the father (here, Freud).[62]

The result of Bloom's approach is to focus attention on the psyche of the poet as interpreter: to interpret a text is to render an account of it as the locus of the poet's *agōn* with tradition. At the same time, another result of this approach is to minimize the distinction between literature and interpretation: if every poem is hermeneutical, the inference lies readily at hand that every hermeneutic is poetic.[63]

This quick summary of Bloom's critical project hardly conveys either its complexity or its willful eccentricity. The whole undertaking, however outrageously formulated by Bloom, has the virtue of focusing our attention on essential aspects of poetic and religious creation. No one agrees with Bloom (the very spirit of his struggle discourages agreement: he wants to stand on a lonely critical-poetic peak); everyone acknowledges that he is onto something. Consequently, his work has stimulated a wide range of recent attempts to investigate the phenomenon of intertextuality.[64]

Literary criticism has long realized, to some extent at least, the importance of the use and reuse of traditions, and the best literary criticism has always recognized that a study of poetic influence must encompass far more than "the wearisome industry of source-hunting, of allusion-counting, an industry that will soon touch apocalypse anyway when it passes from scholars to computers."[65] To identify allusions is only the beginning of an interpretive process. Consider the way in which Reuben Brower, writing well before Bloom, described his purpose in studying allusion in the poetry of Alexander Pope:

> While there is some pleasure in recognizing the conventions Pope used and some pleasure in hearing echoes of earlier poets in his verse, it is more important to see how he used the poetry of the past for his own expressive purposes. . . . Through allusion, often in combination with subdued metaphors and exquisite images, Pope gets his purchase on larger meanings and evokes the finer resonances by which poetry (in Johnson's phrase) "penetrates the recesses of the mind."[66]

The critical task, then, would be to see what poetic effects and larger meanings are produced by the poet's device of echoing predecessors.

Such an undertaking could straightway drive the interpreter into a historical mode of research; to hear and understand the poet's allusions we need to know not only the tradition to which the allusion points but also the way in which that tradition was understood in the poet's time and the contemporary historical experience or situation with which the poet links the tradition. It is for this reason that some of the best recent investigations of intertextual phenomena have taken a strong historical turn (indeed, this approach might be described as the most important contemporary alternative to deconstructionist criticism). I have in mind here such elegant works as Barbara Lewalski's *Protestant Poetics and the Seventeenth-Century Religious Lyric*, George deForest Lord's *Classical Presences in Seventeenth-Century English Poetry*, and the studies of Milton by J. A. Wittreich (*Visionary Poetics: Milton's Tradition and His Legacy*) and Francis Blessington (*Paradise Lost and the Classical Epic*).[67] These investigations have in common a resolute intention to place their poetic subject matter within its proper cultural milieu and so to discern more sensitively the literary force and effect of the poet's allusive language. This means, in effect, that they are able to do precisely for Donne and Herbert and Milton what New Testament critics are able to do only imprecisely for Paul.

What then? Must New Testament critics merely stand apart and envy the wealth of sources accessible to scholars who have chosen to work in the seventeenth century rather than the first? Or is there another model for approaching intertextual allusions that will be more suitable to the character of the New Testament evidence, a method that will implicate us neither in Bloom's hermeneutical *hybris* nor in the dense texture of intellectual history offered by Lewalski and Wittreich? I think that such an alternative does exist, as illustrated by John Hollander's graceful study *The Figure of Echo: A Mode of Allusion in Milton and After*, which exemplifies a style of interpretation that focuses neither on the poet's psyche nor on the historical presuppositions of poetic allusions but on their rhetorical and semantic effects.

In contrast to Bloom's emphasis on the poet's struggle against predecessors, Hollander allows for an appreciative valuation of continuity within the tradition, as poets honor the voices of the dead even while forming echoes that transform their words in new acoustical environments. He gives us nothing so systematic as a methodology or even a theory of literary allusion[68]; rather, he gives us finely nuanced readings of particular instances in which Milton and other poets echo earlier voices, showing how such echoes work within the poems where they occur. Hollander's compact work seeks to "consider a way of alluding that is inherently poetic rather than expository, and that makes new metaphor rather than learned gestures." His concern is neither to investigate "problems of actual or putative audience" nor to speculate on the poet's "degree of self-awareness, of conscious design" in echoing an earlier text; instead, he concentrates on the poetic effects produced for those who have ears to hear. The important point, for Hollander, is that "the revisionary power of allusive echo generates new figuration."[69] This phenomenon occurs not only because old voices are overheard in new settings but also because "the rebounds of intertextual echo generally . . . distort the original voice in order to interpret it."[70] The twofold task of a criticism attuned to such echoes, then, is (a) to call attention to them so that others might be enabled to hear; and (b) to give an account of the distortions and new figuration that they generate.

Such concerns are, of course, not an idiosyncratic product of Hollander's fancy. Robert Alter, for example, argues that literary criticism as a distinctive discipline can be defined by its attention to matters of this sort.[71] He cites the instance of Yeats's quatrain, "The Nineteenth Century and After":

> Though the great song return no more
> There's keen delight in what we have:
> The rattle of pebbles on the shore
> Under the receding wave.

Taken by itself, this brief poem has a suggestive but cryptic quality. We understand only if we overhear in Yeats's verse the echo of Matthew Arnold's "Dover Beach," in which the poet, pondering "the grating roar / of pebbles which the waves draw back," hears in it "the eternal note of sadness" and laments the passing of older cultural structures:

> The Sea of Faith
> Was once, too, at the full, and round earth's shore
> Lay like the folds of a bright girdle furled.
> But now I only hear
> Its melancholy, long, withdrawing roar,
> Retreating . . .

Alter observes that Yeats, writing more than sixty years later, plays tacitly upon Arnold's imagery to make a sharply contrasting poetic statement.

> It is by no means pedantic to introduce "Dover Beach" into our consideration of Yeats because literature as a language is intrinsically and densely allusive, Yeats in this case defining his meanings by citing the Arnold poem and marking a certain distance from it, making a kind of affirmation instead of Arnold's plangent complaint and eschewing the declamatory aspects of Arnold's rhetoric for a haiku-like compactness and concreteness. . . . In any case, the larger meanings and cultural memories hinted in the sea imagery are activated by the recollection of Arnold's poem.[72]

"Recollection" is much the better description than "citing"; this is a pure case of echo rather than quotation or even overt allusion. Yet our reading of the Yeats poem will be impoverished if we fail to hear in Yeats' "rattle" of pebbles the echo of Arnold's "grating roar."

This example illustrates one further property of echo. Allusive echo can often function as a diachronic trope to which Hollander applies the name of *transumption*, or *metalepsis*.[73] When a literary echo links the text in which it occurs to an earlier text, the figurative effect of the echo can lie in the unstated or suppressed (transumed) points of resonance between the two texts. Yeats says nothing about the "Sea of Faith," but Arnold's explicit note lingers as an overtone in Yeats' lines. Hollander sums up in a compact formula the demand that this sort of effect places upon criticism: "the interpretation of a metalepsis entails the recovery of the transumed material."[74] Allusive echo functions to suggest to the reader that text B should be understood in light of a broad interplay with text A, encompassing aspects of A beyond those explicitly echoed. This sort of metaleptic figuration is the antithesis of the metaphysical conceit, in which the poet's imagination seizes a metaphor and explicitly wrings out of it all manner of unforeseeable significations. Metalepsis, by contrast, places the reader within a field of whispered or unstated correspondences. In the pages that follow, we will see that Paul's echoes of Scripture repeatedly bring the trope of metalepsis into play.

In proposing Hollander's criticism as a model for reading Paul's intertextual allusions, I do not mean that we should "apply" his method; it is
less a matter of method than of sensibility. I am urging that we should
learn from Hollander and other literary critics the discipline of tuning our
ears to the internal resonances of the biblical text. Is such a discipline
anachronistic?[75] The force of Fishbane's work is to suggest precisely the
reverse: within Israel as a reading community, "all significant speech is
Scriptural or Scripturally-oriented speech."[76] We will have great difficulty understanding Paul, the pious first-century Jew, unless we seek to
situate his discourse appropriately within what Hollander calls the "cave
of resonant signification"[77] that enveloped him: Scripture.

INTERTEXTUAL ECHO IN PHIL. 1:19

In order to hear how scriptural echoes lend resonant overtones to Paul's
prose, let us consider the case of Phil. 1:19. This text, rarely treated
in the critical literature on Paul's use of the Old Testament, allows us to
examine Paul's literary use of scriptural allusion in a place where there is
no labored history of theological polemic, a place where the ruts left by
our scholarly precursors are not too deep.

In Philippians, exegetical exposition of the Old Testament plays no
explicit role. Indeed, if we limit our consideration to quotations introduced with an explicit citation formula and exclude the instances of allusion and echo, this epistle of thanks and exhortation would appear to
contain no Old Testament references at all.[78] Certainly, in sharp contrast
to other letters such as Galatians and Romans, Paul's purposes in writing
to the Christians at Philippi do not center on controversial issues of scriptural interpretation: the generally cordial tone of this letter assumes a
theological and hermeneutical harmony between Paul and his readers.

In the course of framing an apologia for his own current imprisonment
(cf. 1:7, 12–14), Paul echoes a fragment of voice from Job. Despite his
chains, he assures the Philippians that "through your prayers and the
help of the Spirit of Jesus Christ this will turn out for my deliverance"
(1:19). The last part of this statement (*touto moi apobēsetai eis sotērian*),
though prefaced by no quotation formula, is a verbatim citation of words
lifted from Job 13:16 (LXX): "Even this will turn out for my deliverance,
for deceit shall not enter in before him." The echo is fleeting, and Paul's
sentence is entirely comprehensible to a reader who has never heard of
Job. A reader nurtured on the LXX might, without consciously marking
the allusion, sense a momentary ripple of elevated diction in the phrase,
producing a heightened dramatic emphasis. The reader whose ear is able,

however, not only to discern the echo but also to locate the source of the original voice will discover a number of intriguing resonances.[79]

The earlier passage is part of a lengthy speech in which Job, rejecting the facile insinuations of comforters who attribute his suffering to some secret iniquity in his character, proclaims his own integrity and his trust that he will in the end be vindicated before God. (Cf. 13:18: "Behold, I am near to my judgment; I know that I shall appear as righteous" [*Idou egō eggus eimi tou krimatos mou, oida egō hoti dikaios anaphanoumai*].) The imagery of the passage is thoroughly forensic, and indeed in 13:27 Job depicts himself as a prisoner: "You have placed my foot in the stocks." By echoing Job's words, Paul the prisoner tacitly assumes the role of righteous sufferer, as paradigmatically figured by Job. Awaiting trial, he speaks with Job's voice to affirm confidence in the favorable outcome of his afflictions; thereby, he implicitly transfers to himself some of the significations that traditionally cluster about the figure of Job.

There are important differences, of course, between the situations of the defendants in question. The greatest difference concerns their stances toward God: for Job, God appears to be the adversary in the litigation, the party inflicting injustice, at least temporarily. Paul, however, sees God as his own defender and vindicator, not as his adversary. This does not prevent him, however, from discovering in Job language that he can redeploy to portray his own situation. The lightness of the figurative assertion is a significant part of the literary effect here.[80] Paul makes no claim that Job was a type of which he is now the antitype, nor is there any direct citation formula solemnly claiming, in the manner of Matthew or Qumran, that Paul's own experience constitutes the fulfillment of a previously obscure prophetic passage of Scripture. His rather subtle echo of Job's plaintive self-defense establishes a figurative resonance between his plight (and ultimate fate) and that of Job, but stops far short of making any explicit claims or positing a typological scheme. Indeed, a full appreciation of the echo effect can lead the reader to reflect not only on the correspondences between Paul and Job but also on the contrasts: whereas Job, seeing through a glass darkly, endured his suffering with obdurate puzzlement, Paul, suffering as an apostle of Christ, interprets his suffering as a participation in the sufferings of the crucified Christ and thus finds himself able to rejoice in the midst of adversity. Job's tenacious assertion of his own rectitude becomes in Paul's mouth a triumphant affirmation of trust in the power and faithfulness of the God who raised Jesus from the dead. Those who have ears to hear will detect the contrapuntal effect and delight in it.

The effect that they discern, furthermore, will include certain figurative reflections on one other aspect of Paul's circumstances. Just as Job was afflicted by pious homilizers, Paul now finds himself beset by preachers who "preach Christ from envy and rivalry . . . not sincerely but thinking to afflict me in my imprisonment" (Phil. 1:15–17). Following the echo back to the source, we find Job in the earlier context hurling a challenge at his interlocutors: "Do you not speak before the Lord? But you utter deceit [*dolos*] before him" (Job 13:7). And again, immediately after the expression of hope that Paul quotes, we find Job contrasting his own vindication to the downfall of his accusers: "And this shall turn out for my salvation, for deceit [*dolos*] shall not enter in before him" (13:16). None of these phrases is picked up directly by Paul in Philippians. If, however, Paul tacitly likens himself to Job, the echo whispers a suggestion that the rival preachers have assumed the mantle of Job's hollow comforters; the falsehood of both will be exposed ultimately in the judgment of God.

This example illustrates Hollander's principle that "the interpretation of a metalepsis entails the recovery of the transumed material." At the explicit literal level of the discourse, Paul simply borrows a phrase from Job to express confidence amidst trying circumstances. But when the source of the phrase is read in counterpoint with the new setting into which it has been transposed, a range of resonant harmonics becomes audible. None of the correspondences between Paul and Job, or between Paul's rivals and Job's interlocutors, is actually asserted; instead, they are intimated through the trope of metalepsis. The trope invites the reader to participate in an imaginative act necessary to comprehend the portrayal of Paul's condition offered here.

The volume of intertextual echo varies in accordance with the semantic distance between the source and the reflecting surface. Quotation, allusion, and echo may be seen as points along a spectrum of intertextual reference, moving from the explicit to the subliminal. As we move farther away from overt citation, the source recedes into the discursive distance, the intertextual relations become less determinate, and the demand placed on the reader's listening powers grows greater. As we near the vanishing point of the echo, it inevitably becomes difficult to decide whether we are really hearing an echo at all, or whether we are only conjuring things out of the murmurings of our own imaginations.

In the case of Phil. 1:19, this "vanishing point" problem can be illustrated by attention to the phrase with which Paul introduces his allusion to Job 13:16: *oida gar hoti* (for I know that). The formal dramatic tone of this phrase contributes to the elevated diction of Paul's declaration, an effect that we have already noted. But suddenly another echo murmurs unbid-

den in the ear: "For I know that my Redeemer liveth."[81] We track down
the source of that voice: Job 19:25–26.

> For I know that my Redeemer lives,
> and at last he will stand upon the earth;
> and after my skin has been thus destroyed,
> then from my flesh I shall see God.[82]

If Paul is tacitly contrasting his own confidence in God to Job's defiance,
should we hear in his *oida gar hoti* yet another revisionary distortion of
Job's words? Or, in this case, does Handel's *Messiah* coincidentally hum
in our ear a harmony absent from Paul's score?

Consulting a concordance, we discover a teasing datum: the phrase
oida gar hoti occurs in the LXX only three times, all in the book of Job (9:28,
19:25, 30:23). Careful attention to these passages, however, casts doubt
on the supposition that Paul might be summoning up echoes of these
texts: "For I know that you will not leave me alone as innocent" (9:28);
"For I know that death will destroy me" (30:23). Even Job 19:25 (19:24 MT)
carries a sense far different from the serene confidence of Handel's sopra-
no air.[83] If the phrase *oida gar hoti* raises any ghostly reminiscence of these
texts, it beats dissonantly against the note of Paul's own affirmation. In
this case, in fact, the volume of the echo is so slight that it should probably
not be understood as carrying any allusive force at all. The echo, if echo it
is, is only a cadence in Paul's ear, perhaps subliminally recalled by his
evocation of Job but creating no semantic link between the earlier text and
the later. If we choose to hear a connection between Job 19:25 and 13:16,
we have performed a synthetic hermeneutical act, analogous to many of
Paul's readings but going beyond the scope of his own contribution in
Phil. 1:19.

I do not intend to spend hermeneutical energy pursuing such faint
echoes in this book. The following chapters concentrate on higher-vol-
ume echoes whose allusive character is more readily audible. We will be
attending primarily to intertextual references at least as explicit as the
reference in Phil. 1:19 to Job 13:16, including explicit quotations. Even
Paul's overt allusions and quotations can be explored by using some of
the same interpretive strategies ordinarily appropriate to subtler echoes,
because Paul's citations of Scripture often function not as proofs but as
tropes: they generate new meanings by linking the earlier text (Scripture)
to the later (Paul's discourse) in such a way as to produce unexpected
correspondences, correspondences that suggest more than they assert.

HERMENEUTICAL REFLECTIONS AND CONSTRAINTS

The Locus of Echo: Five Options

My reading of Phil. 1:19 adumbrates certain problems that riddle this book from first page to last: did Paul intend to echo Job 13:16? If so, how much of the interpretation that I give to the Paul-Job trope was in Paul's mind, how much would the Philippians have grasped, and how much is my own metaphorical fancy? Does the legitimacy of my reading depend on its correspondence to Paul's intention? Who has ears to hear the echoes and construe their significance? What criteria might help us to address such questions?

Although similar vexing issues haunt all efforts at textual interpretation, the problem is especially acute with regard to interpretations that hinge on allusions and echoes. John Hollander's poem, "The Widener Burying Ground,"[84] voices our predicament:

> In spite of all the learned have said,
> We hear the voices of the dead.
>
> . . . .
>
> Our marginalia all insist
> —Beating the page as with a fist
> Against a silent headstone—that
> the dead whom we are shouting at,
> Though silent to us now, have spoken
> Through us, their stony stillness broken
> By our outcry (*We are the dead*
> *Resounding voices in our stead*)
> Until they strike us, once more,
> Whispers of their receding shore,
> And reason's self must bend the ear
> To echoes and allusions here.

When we begin to speak of metaleptic effects that require the reader to uncover suppressed intertextual connections, "we must always wonder what our own contribution was—how much we are always being writers as well as readers of what we are seeing."[85] The text requires an act of interpretation to complete its sense, as both Paul and the rabbis, in their different ways, realized, but it is not always easy to account for the connection between the text and its reading. When I assert, for instance, that "Paul the prisoner tacitly assumes the role of the righteous sufferer, as paradigmatically figured by Job," I have proposed an interpretation of one intertextual link. But what sort of claim am I really making? Am I saying that Paul interpreted his own situation in these terms? That his original readers at Philippi would have perceived the intertextual trope? Or am I proposing an innovative reading grounded not on Paul's intent but on a self-validating retrospective critical intuition? In Bloom's terms, am I creating my own poem by misreading elements given by my precursor Paul?

If echo is a metaphorical way of talking about a hermeneutical event, an intertextual fusion that generates new meaning, in whose mind does that event occur, and how are claims about intertextual meaning effects to be tested? There are at least five distinguishable possibilities.

(1) The hermeneutical event occurs in Paul's mind. Claims about intertextual meaning effects are valid where it can credibly be demonstrated that Paul intended such effects.

(2) The hermeneutical event occurs in the original readers of the letter. Claims about intertextual meaning effects are valid where it can credibly be demonstrated that the Philippians would likely have perceived such effects.

(3) The intertextual fusion occurs in the text itself. (In this case, we cannot properly speak of a hermeneutical event.) We have no access to the author or to the original readers; we have only the text. Consequently, assertions about Paul's intention are intelligible only as statements about the implied author, and assertions about "the Philippians" are intelligible only as statements about the implied reader. Implied author and implied reader are epiphenomena of the text's rhetoric. Consequently, claims about intertextual meaning effects are valid where it can credibly be demonstrated that they are in some sense properties of the text's own rhetorical or literary structure.

(4) The hermeneutical event occurs in my act of reading. Claims about intertextual meaning effects are valid if I say so. In other words, the perception of intertextual effects has emerged from my own reading experience, and no further validation is necessary.

(5) The hermeneutical event occurs in a community of interpretation. Claims about intertextual meaning effects are valid where it can credibly be demonstrated that they conform to the hermeneutical conventions of a particular community of readers. (Such communities can, of course, be variously composed and disposed: the church, the guild of biblical scholars, the guild of literary critics, the readers of this book—and each of

these communities is, of course, fractured into various schismatic schools and subcommunities.)

When the options are laid out in this schematic fashion, we are bound to feel uneasy if we are forced to choose just one of them, because each in isolation has obvious deficiencies, yet each one describes an undeniably significant element of the hermeneutical process. Options 1 and 2 locate meaning in a historical act of communication between persons in the past, an act to which the extant text of Philippians bears witness. Options 4 and 5 locate meaning in the act of reading in the present, a direct encounter of present readers with a text not addressed originally to them. Option 3 is a heuristic fiction, an attempt to facilitate criticism by bracketing out the messy complications of the history behind the text and the experience of readers encountering the text.

I am neither prepared to embrace the doctrine of any of the hermeneutical schools represented by these five options (let the reader understand) nor inclined to jettison any of the elements of interpretation to which they draw attention. The working method of this book should be understood as an attempt to hold them all together in creative tension. That is a daunting task, of course, particularly when we are seeking to interpret ancient texts that interpret in turn still more ancient texts; as Greene remarks of his own efforts to read Renaissance imitations of classical models, "Reading imitations makes even larger claims on the historical imagination than most reading, and underscores even more cruelly our cultural solitude. It asks us not only to intuit an alien sensibility from a remote *mundus significans,* but also that sensibility's intuitions of a third. Nothing perhaps is more calculated to impress on us our temporal estrangement."[86] Yet, like Greene, we press ahead with the effort because "nothing perhaps immerses us so deeply in the flow of literary history,"[87] and because there is finally no escape from the task except into arbitrariness and desolation. What follows is a provisional account of my approach to this battery of hermeneutical problems.

Stated positively, my design is to produce late twentieth-century readings of Paul informed by intelligent historical understanding: to undertake a fresh imaginative encounter with the text, disciplined and stimulated by historical exegesis. The legitimacy of such a project rests on a single key hermeneutical axiom: that there is an authentic analogy—though not a simple identity—between what the text meant and what it means.[88] One might call this a proposal for "common sense" hermeneutics[89]: common sense not only because it is the way that sympathetic critics and faith communities have ordinarily read Scripture but also because it rests upon an assumption that readers ancient and modern can share a common sense of the text's meaning. If I, having learned something about Paul's historical circumstances and having read the same Scripture that Paul lived in so deeply, discern in his language echoes of that Scripture, it is not improbable that I am overhearing the same echoes that he and his earliest readers might have been able to hear, and there are specifiable criteria—which I will enumerate in a moment—for testing such intuitions. I offer this remark not as some breakthrough in hermeneutical theory, but as a modest account of what I suppose myself to be doing when I write a sentence such as "Paul the prisoner tacitly assumes the role of the righteous sufferer, as paradigmatically figured by Job." I am not coining a clever new intertextual trope; I am offering a reading of a trope that Paul wrote. It is possible—even likely— that I will understand the trope in ways that neither Paul nor the Philippians would have articulated, but I insist that my reading is an authentic explication of the intertextual fusion. My hermeneutical proposal can be summarized in the following way.

The hermeneutical event occurs in my reading of the text, but my reading always proceeds within a community of interpretation, whose hermeneutical conventions inform my reading. Prominent among these conventions are the convictions that a proposed interpretation must be justified with reference to evidence provided both by the text's rhetorical structure and by what can be known through critical investigation about the author and original readers. Any interpretation must respect these constraints in order to be persuasive within my reading community. Claims about intertextual meaning effects are strongest where it can credibly be demonstrated that they occur within the literary structure of the text and that they can plausibly be ascribed to the intention of the author and the competence of the original readers.[90]

Thus, my argument proceeds in the following way: I begin with my reading of the text—as I did in the case of Phil. 1:19—and try to persuade you, the reader of this book, that you should hear in it the same intertextual meaning effects that I have heard. In order to persuade you, I will argue both that the alleged echoes exist within the text and that Paul might have heard the same echoes; thus, the warrants brought into play in that process of persuasion are both literary and historical. The primary mode of reflection in this study is literary, but historical knowledge both informs and constrains my readings. Likewise, there are historical implications to the readings that I propose—especially for shaping our understanding of the relation between Jewish and Gentile Christians during Paul's lifetime, before the Jewish War of 66–70 C.E. We know Paul and his original readers primarily as characters in these literary texts, but what we learn about them as the implied author and implied readers can inform our reconstructions of the history behind the texts, though that is not the goal of this book.[91] (To note a single example, the implied readers of these letters appear to be primarily Gentile Christians with an extensive knowledge of the LXX and an urgent interest in its interpretation.)[92]

Because we know the readers of Paul's letters only through the letters themselves, it is in principle very difficult to distinguish between allusion and echo in these texts. The concept of allusion depends both on the notion of authorial intention and on the assumption that the reader will share with the author the requisite "portable library" to recognize the source of the allusion; the notion of echo, however, finesses such questions: "echo is a metaphor of, and for, alluding, and does not depend on conscious intention."[93] Since Paul's audience is known to us only hypothetically, it is hard to speak confidently about their capacity to recognize Paul's evocations of scriptural language. Is the evocation of Job in Phil. 1:19 an echo or an allusion? The difficulty of deciding how to classify such an instance illustrates my reasons for using the terminology flexibly: I make no systematic distinction between the terms. In general, throughout the following pages, *allusion* is used of obvious intertextual references, *echo* of subtler ones.

Hearing Echoes: Seven Tests

The foregoing discussion suggests that we must reckon with varying degrees of certainty in our efforts to identify and interpret intertextual echoes. Sometimes the echo will be so loud that only the dullest or most ignorant reader could miss it (e.g., Rom. 10:5–10); other times there will be room for serious differences of opinion about whether a particular phrase should be heard as an echo of a prior text and, if so, how it should be understood (e.g., Rom. 2:9). Precision in such judgment calls is unattainable, because exegesis is a modest imaginative craft, not an exact science; still, it is possible to specify certain rules of thumb that might help the craftsman decide whether to treat a particular phrase as an echo and whether to credit my proposed reading of it. I would propose the following criteria for testing claims about the presence and meaning of scriptural echoes in Paul. I do not use these criteria explicitly in my readings of the texts, but they implicitly undergird the exegetical judgments that I have made.

(1) *Availability.* Was the proposed source of the echo available to the author and/or original readers? In the case of Paul's use of Scripture, we

rarely have to worry about this problem. His practice of citation shows that he was acquainted with virtually the whole body of texts that were later acknowledged as canonical within Judaism,[94] and that he expected his readers to share his acknowledgment of these texts as Scripture. This criterion implies that echo is a diachronic trope: analyses of literary echo are possible only where the chronological ordering of different voices is known. That is why, for example, attempts to demonstrate allusions to the teaching of Jesus in Paul's letters have always proven inconclusive: the Gospels are written later than Paul's letters, and Paul shows relatively little direct evidence of having known the traditions that they contain. Consequently, particular claims that Paul may be echoing Jesus-tradition always bear a weighty burden of proof. Not so for echoes of Scripture.

(2) *Volume.* The volume of an echo is determined primarily by the degree of explicit repetition of words or syntactical patterns, but other factors may also be relevant: how distinctive or prominent is the precursor text within Scripture, and how much rhetorical stress does the echo receive in Paul's discourse? For example, 2 Cor. 4:6 should be understood as an allusion to Gen. 1:3–5, even though it echoes explicitly only the two words *light* and *darkness*. Here the source is the distinctive and memorable Genesis creation account, and Paul has placed the echo at the rhetorical climax of a unit in his letter.[95]

(3) *Recurrence.* How often does Paul elsewhere cite or allude to the same scriptural passage? This applies not only to specific words that are cited more than once, such as Hab. 2:4, but also to larger portions of Scripture to which Paul repeatedly refers, such as Deuteronomy 30–32 or Isaiah 50–54. Where such evidence exists that Paul considered a passage of particular importance, proposed echoes from the same context should be given additional credence.[96]

(4) *Thematic Coherence.* How well does the alleged echo fit into the line of argument that Paul is developing? Is its meaning effect consonant with other quotations in the same letter or elsewhere in the Pauline corpus? Do the images and ideas of the proposed precursor text illuminate Paul's argument? This test begins to move beyond simple identification of echoes to the problem of how to interpret them.

(5) *Historical Plausibility.* Could Paul have intended the alleged meaning effect? Could his readers have understood it? (We should always bear in mind, of course, that Paul might have written things that were not readily intelligible to his actual readers.) This test, historical in character, necessarily requires hypothetical constructs of what might have been intended and grasped by particular first-century figures. The value of the test is to make us wary of readings that turn Paul into (say) a Lutheran or a

deconstructionist. One implication of this criterion is to give serious preference to interpretive proposals that allow Paul to remain a Jew. However odd or controversial a reader of Scripture he may have been, he was a Jewish reader determined to show that his readings could hold a respectable place within the discourse of Israel's faith.

(6) *History of Interpretation.* Have other readers, both critical and precritical, heard the same echoes? The readings of our predecessors can both check and stimulate our perception of scriptural echoes in Paul. While this test is a possible restraint against arbitrariness, it is also one of the least reliable guides for interpretation, because Gentile Christian readers at a very early date lost Paul's sense of urgency about relating the gospel to God's dealings with Israel and, slightly later, began reading Paul's letters within the interpretive matrix of the New Testament canon. A radically divergent social and religious context engendered a major hermeneutical revision by locating Paul's letters within a different intertextual space: the space defined preeminently by the four canonical Gospels and the Acts of the Apostles. That is why I argue frequently in this book that the Christian tradition has distorted Paul's voice or missed its undertones. (As Frank Kermode observes, "the interpretive inadequacy of our predecessors is assumed by all of us, however we explain it."[97]) A historically sensitive exegesis can recover echoes previously dampened or drowned out. Hollander describes the critical discernment of echoes as a process of reclamation: "The reader of texts, in order to overhear echoes, must have some kind of access to an earlier voice, and to its cave of resonant signification, analogous to that of the author of the later text. When such access is lost in a community of reading, what may have been an allusion may fade in prominence; and yet a scholarly recovery of the context would restore the allusion, by revealing intent as well as by showing means."[98] An investigation of the history of interpretation can extend the range of possible readings of Paul's use of Scripture, but it also can lead us to a narrowing of the hermeneutical potential of Paul's intertextual collocations. Thus, this criterion should rarely be used as a negative test to exclude proposed echoes that commend themselves on other grounds.

(7) *Satisfaction.* With or without clear confirmation from the other criteria listed here, does the proposed reading make sense? Does it illuminate the surrounding discourse? Does it produce for the reader a satisfying account of the effect of the intertextual relation? This criterion is difficult to articulate precisely without falling into the affective fallacy, but it is finally the most important test: it is in fact another way of asking whether the proposed reading offers a good account of the experience of a

contemporary community of competent readers. We evaluate Hollander's study of echo—if we are willing to read him on his own terms—not by asking whether it provides an adequate theory of intertextuality in Milton but by asking whether his readings are good readings. We ask ourselves whether, when he beckons to us to listen, we do hear faint music reverberating around us. If so, he has taught us to read the text with a critical penetration that we could never have achieved apart from his example. Similarly, the final test of the present study of Paul will come only in the reading, and the case is necessarily cumulative.

There are always only shades of certainty when these criteria are applied to particular texts. The more of them that fall clearly into place, the more confident we can be in rendering an interpretation of the echo effect in a given passage. For example, in relation to Phil. 1:19, my reading is on very strong ground with relation to tests 1 and 4: Paul certainly knew the text of Job, and the reading does, in ways that I have described, fit nicely into the themes of Paul's discourse in Philippians 1. The volume of the echo (2), however, is only moderate: the words are repeated verbatim from Job, but the citation is short and not particularly prominent either in its original literary context or in Paul's letter. That is why it is usually overlooked. What about the test of recurrence (3)? The evidence here is not compelling. Paul does cite Job in several places, but nowhere else does he allude to this particular passage. With regard to historical plausibility (5), it is not at all improbable that Paul intended an allusion to Job, but it is perhaps rather improbable that his readers at Philippi would have picked up the allusion: it is rather too subtle. Modern critics have usually noted the citation (6), but I am unaware of any commentator, ancient or modern, who has seen in it the significance that I have proposed. In a case such as this, the evidence hangs uncertainly in the balance, and much depends on the reader's judgment, which I do not presume to prescribe, about criterion 7.

To run explicitly through this series of criteria for each of the texts that I treat would be wearisome. I trust the reader's competence to employ these criteria and to apply appropriate discounts to the interpretive proposals that I offer throughout. Against all this hermeneutical hedging, however, a final word must be spoken.

Beyond the Hedges

Although the foregoing tests are serviceable rules of thumb to guide our interpretive work, we must acknowledge that there will be exceptional occasions when the tests fail to account for the spontaneous power of particular intertextual conjunctions. Despite all the careful hedges that we plant around texts, meaning has a way of leaping over, like sparks. Texts are not inert; they burn and throw fragments of flame on their rising heat. Often we succeed in containing the energy, but sometimes the sparks escape and kindle new blazes, reprises of the original fire.

That is a way of saying that texts can generate readings that transcend both the conscious intention of the author and all the hermeneutical strictures that we promulgate. Poets and preachers know this secret; biblical critics have sought to suppress it for heuristic purposes. At times, the texts speak through us in ways that could not have been predicted, ways that can be comprehended only by others who hear the voice of the text through us—or, if by ourselves, only retrospectively.

Such phenomena occur repeatedly in all significant discourse: "The word is near you, on your lips and in your heart." The texts that envelop us speak through us; resonant speech discovers typologies that interpret present experience through the language of predecessors. But these typologies come to us unbidden, impose themselves upon us in ways that we understand through a glass darkly. Anyone who has ever acted in a play knows the experience of discovering that lines from the play come unexpectedly to mind in real-life situations different from the original dramatic context. The aptness of the quoted line does not depend on exact literal correspondence between the original meaning and the new application. Indeed, the wit and pleasure of such quotations lie partly in the turning of the words to a new sense. In such cases, the act of quotation becomes an act of figuration, establishing a metaphorical resonance between drama and life. Paul's uses of Scripture often have a similar character: Scripture is for him the text of the world-play in which he performs and from which familiar lines repeatedly spring to life in new situations.

To limit our interpretation of Paul's scriptural echoes to what he intended by them is to impose a severe and arbitrary hermeneutical restriction.[99] In the first place, what he intended is a matter of historical speculation; in the second place, his intertextual echoes are acts of figuration. Consequently, later readers will rightly grasp meanings of the figures that may have been veiled from Paul himself. Scripture generates through Paul new figurations; The Righteousness from Faith finds in Paul a new voice.

CHAPTER TWO

Intertextual Echo in Romans

RIGHTEOUSNESS AND WRATH PREFIGURED

The first sentence of Paul's letter to the Romans proclaims that "the gospel of God" was "promised beforehand through his prophets in holy texts" (*en graphais hagiais*). Even if, as many commentators have surmised, the uncharacteristic plural form *graphais* ("scriptures" rather than "Scripture") signals Paul's quotation of an already traditional Christian confessional formula,[1] his placement of this tradition at the opening of the letter discloses one of its urgent concerns: Paul is seeking to ground his exposition of the gospel in Israel's sacred texts.

Romans contains a heavy concentration of scriptural quotations and allusions. According to the tabulation provided by Dietrich-Alex Koch in *Die Schrift als Zeuge des Evangeliums*, there are eighty-nine Old Testament quotations in the Pauline letters, fifty-one of which occur in Romans.[2] Why such an agglomeration of "holy texts" in this particular letter? Do the quotations work together in some consistent way to support the letter's argument? Such questions are complex because the purpose and thematic center of Romans have themselves been disputed matters in recent scholarship.[3] If, however, we attend carefully to Paul's use of the quotations, we will discover them spiraling in around a common focus: the problem of God's saving righteousness in relation to Israel. The insistent echoing voice of Scripture in and behind Paul's letter presses home a single theme relentlessly: the gospel is the fulfillment, not the negation, of God's word to Israel.

In some instances (e.g., Romans 4, 9–11), Paul uses the texts explicitly as authoritative warrants in his argument; in other instances, his use of Scripture is allusive and indirect. As we shall see, the allusions, when examined carefully, converge with the overtly argumentative citations as indicators of the letter's theme and of the symbolic world within which that theme is articulated. Thus, the Old Testament texts that echo about within Romans provide important clues, both explicit and implicit, concerning the shape and texture of Paul's argument.

I propose to follow those clues, exploring Paul's use of Scripture in his letter to the Romans as a way of grasping the epistle's message. This approach, decidedly inductive in character, differs methodologically from the more usual historical-critical strategy of attempting to interpret the text through hypotheses about the historical circumstances surrounding the letter's composition or about the social composition of the community to which it is addressed. Without denying the importance of such historical questions, my reading of Romans embodies a hermeneutical assumption that is perhaps best made explicit at the outset: this text is most fruitfully understood when it is read as an intertextual conversation between Paul and the voice of Scripture, that powerful ancestral presence with which Paul grapples. Scripture broods over this letter, calls Paul to account, speaks through him; Paul, groping to give voice to his gospel, finds in Scripture the language to say what must be said, labors to win the blessing of Moses and the prophets.[4]

To be sure, Paul is writing to his contemporaries at Rome, and no doubt he has some practical purpose for doing so (cf. Rom. 15:14–33). Romans is, as J. Christiaan Beker has insisted, "a profoundly occasional letter," which seeks to bring the gospel into a contingent historical situation.[5] Unfortunately, however, Paul tells us little about that situation. Once the conversation begins, the addressees recede curiously into the background, and Paul finds himself engaged with an older and more compelling partner. The nuances of this conversation are complex; the partners know one another so well that much can pass unsaid, intimated through hints and gestures. No less crucial than Paul's explicit statements, therefore, are the intertextual echoes in the letter. We outsiders have to pay close attention to follow the conversation. But the effort pays dividends. To read Romans in light of conjectures about its historical purpose within Paul's ministry is, by contrast, a surprisingly unsatisfying speculative exercise.[6] Deeper comprehension will result if we treat the text as a hermeneutical event, listening carefully to the intertextual interplay within the discourse. Anyone still so disposed may ask at the end of such a reading what pastoral problems Paul is confronting as he writes; however, such questions are not the primary concern of our present inquiry.

In the case of this epistle, a thorough investigation of all the scriptural citations and allusions would be the virtual equivalent of a full-length commentary. We must therefore content ourselves with considering some representative instances of intertextual conversation in Romans. My reading works selectively but sequentially through the letter, with one exception: consideration of Rom. 10:5–10, the passage in which Paul seems to turn Moses against himself, is left for last, in the hope that this strange piece of interpretation can be better understood against the backdrop of the letter as a whole.

Let us then tune our ears to hear how Paul plays the scriptural texts into the letter's theme and what effects—semantic and aesthetic—are produced by their echoes, reverberating in air hushed by God's word.

The Apocalypse of God's Righteousness

The keynote of Paul's exposition sounds in Rom. 1:16–17: "I am not ashamed of the gospel, for it is the power of God for salvation [sotērian] to everyone who believes, to the Jew first and also to the Greek. For through the gospel the righteousness of God [dikaiosynē theou] is revealed [apokalyptetai], from faith for faith, just as it is written, 'The righteous one shall live from faith.'" All the crucial theological terms of this programmatic declaration echo the language of the LXX; indeed, in certain LXX passages these terms converge in ways that prefigure Paul's formulation strikingly. Consider, for example, Ps. 97:2 (98:2 MT): "The Lord has made known his salvation [sotērion]; in the presence of the nations [ethnōn] he has revealed [apekalypsen] his righteousness [dikaiosynēn]." This psalm verse tolls a Vorklang[7] of Paul's proclamation—a tone whose echo rebounds with greater force than the original sound. Paul means, of course, that God's righteousness is revealed through the death and resurrection of Jesus Christ, but his evocation of the psalmist's language hints at a conviction that he articulates explicitly elsewhere: God's grace in Jesus Christ simultaneously extends salvation to the Gentiles and confirms Israel's trust in God's saving righteousness (see Rom. 15:8–9a). Psalm 97:3 (LXX), the sentence immediately following the verse that Paul echoes, elaborates the theological frame of reference in which Rom. 1:16–17 must be understood:

> He has remembered his mercy to Jacob
> and his truthfulness [alētheias][8] to the house of Israel.
> All the ends of the earth have seen
> the salvation [sotērion] of our God.

The hope of the psalmist is that God's eschatological vindication of Israel will serve as a demonstration to the whole world of the power and faithfulness of Israel's God, a demonstration that will bring even Gentiles to acknowledge him. Paul shares the psalmist's eschatological vision; that is why he insists in Rom. 1:16 that the gospel is a word of salvation to the Jew first and then subsequently also to the Greek, although, as we shall see, he has subjected this scenario to certain dialectical revisions.[9]

Similarly, the promise of a future universal manifestation of God's salvation and righteousness sounds throughout the latter chapters of the prophetic book of Isaiah.

Hear me, hear, my people,
And kings, give ear to me.
For the Law will go forth from me,
And my judgment will go forth as a light to the Gentiles [ethnōn].
My righteousness [dikaiosynē] draws near quickly,
And my salvation [sotērion] will go forth as a light,
And in my arm [cf. dynamis in Rom. 1:16] will Gentiles [ethnē] hope.

(Isa. 51:4–5)

Or again:

And the Lord will reveal [apokalypsei] his holy arm before all the Gentiles [ethnōn],
And all the corners of the earth will see the salvation [sotērian] that is with God.

(Isa. 52:10)

In all these texts, Israel in exile is consoled by the promise of God's mighty act of deliverance. This act will be a manifestation of God's righteousness (dikaiosynē) because it will demonstrate, despite all appearances to the contrary, God's faithfulness to his covenant people; the promised salvation will constitute a vindication of God's name and of his people who have trusted in him through their suffering and exile.

Later in Romans, Paul will appeal directly to texts that articulate these themes (see especially 9:27–33, 11:26–27, 15:7–13, 15:21), employing them explicitly as warrants in his plea for reconciliation among Jews and Gentiles in the Roman church. In Rom. 1:16–17, however, there is not yet any direct quotation of these passages, no explicit reference made to the prophecies of Isaiah. Instead, Isaiah's vocabulary echoes subliminally in Paul's diction; the effect of the echo is to suggest—for hearers who share Paul's sensitivity to the cadences of the LXX—that the gospel must be

understood as the fulfillment of the ancient promise that God's righteousness would be revealed in an act of deliverance for the Jews first and
also for the Gentiles. This sort of figuration Hollander characterizes as
metalepsis: the reader, signaled by the echoes, is required to grasp together old text and new.

If we start tracing these echoes back to their sources, we find a cluster
of echoes emanating from the lament psalms and from exilic prophecy.
On reflection, this is hardly surprising: the nation's historical experience
of adversity calls into question the goodness and faithfulness of the God
who once made covenant with Israel. Consequently, the prophetic promise of God's righteousness comes precisely as the answer to this question,
that is, as an answer to the problem of theodicy. In Scripture the theodicy
problem is occasioned not by the general question of how a just God can
allow suffering in the world but rather by the particular problem of how
Yahweh can abandon Israel. As a careful reading of Romans will show,
Paul wrestles with an analogous problem. That is why he is able to play
the rebound of the Old Testament to good effect.

For example, if we take account of the frequency of echoes from the
lament psalms, we will understand more readily why Paul introduces his
proclamation with the otherwise puzzling affirmation that he is "not
ashamed" (*ou gar epaischynomai*) of the gospel. One still finds in major
commentaries (such as that of C. E. B. Cranfield) traces of a psychological
explanation of Paul's phrase: there is a natural temptation for Christians
to be embarrassed about a message as unimpressive as the gospel, but
Paul boldly declares that he has not succumbed to the temptation.[10] Only
slightly closer to the mark is Ernst Käsemann's description of the phrase
as "a fixed confessional formula" which is simply equivalent to
homologein, so that when Paul says "I am not ashamed," he means "I
confess."[11] Neither of these explanations takes adequate account of the
fact that *aischynein* and its near relatives *kataischynein* and *epaischynesthai*
appear repeatedly in the very prophecies and lament psalms from which
Paul's righteousness terminology is also drawn. The psalmist complains
that he (or the nation) has been put to shame before enemies (e.g., "You
have cast us off and put us to shame [*kateschynas*]" [Ps. 43:10 LXX]) or
implores the Lord not to allow him to be put to shame (Ps. 24:2 LXX) or the
prophet rejoices in the confidence that the one who trusts in the Lord will
not be put to shame (Isa. 28:16 LXX—a passage to which Paul appeals
directly in Rom. 9:33).

Oddly, although Bultmann observed that in passages such as 1 Cor.
1:27 and Rom. 5:5 Paul's usage of this "shame" language stands "wholly
on Old Testament ground,"[12] it has rarely been recognized that Paul's

epaischynomai in Rom. 1:16 also echoes off Old Testament rock. With Isaiah, Paul could say, "I know that I shall not be ashamed [*aischynthō*], because the one who justifies me [*ho dikaiōsas me*] is near" (Isa. 50:7–8). Paul is not ashamed in relation to the gospel precisely because the gospel is God's eschatological vindication of those who trust in him—and consequently of God's own faithfulness. Significantly, Paul transforms Isaiah's emphatic future negation[13] ("I shall not be ashamed") into a present negation ("I *am* not ashamed"). The present tense of Paul's denial corresponds to the present tense of his declaration that the righteousness and wrath of God *are being* revealed (1:17–18); thus, Isaiah's future hope rebounds through Paul's voice into a new temporal framework defined by God's already efficacious act of eschatological deliverance in Christ.

Paul's quotation of Hab. 2:4—the climax of his proclamatory keynote (Rom. 1:17)—must also be understood in the context of these same issues. Amidst the continuing controversy since the Reformation about how the expression *"ho de dikaios ek pisteōs zēsetai"* (the righteous one shall live by faith) should be interpreted, parties on all sides of the debate have been surprisingly content to assume that Paul employs the passage as a prooftext for his doctrine of justification by faith with complete disregard for its original setting in Habakkuk's prophecy.[14] However, in view of the theodicy theme evoked in these verses by Paul's apocalyptic announcement of God's justice and by his allusions to the lament psalms, the aptness of the Habakkuk citation immediately stands forth; in its original context, Hab. 2:4 speaks directly to the theological problem of God's faithfulness to Israel.

In Habakkuk, the passage that Paul quotes comes as the nub of God's answer to the prophet's complaint (Hab. 2:1) against the apparent injustice of God's ways, a complaint intoned throughout the first chapter of the book.

> How long, O Lord, shall I cry out,
> and you will not hear?
> Or cry to you when I am wronged,
> and you will not save?
>
> . . . .
>
> You whose eye is too pure to see evil,
> and who cannot look upon afflictions,
> why do you look upon despisers?
> Will you stand silent while the wicked man
> swallows up the righteous one?[15]

The affirmation, then, that "the righteous one shall live by my faithfulness [*ek pisteōs mou*]"[16] is God's response to the prophet's agonized outcry. Whatever else Hab. 2:4 might be construed to mean,[17] it is a response to the problem of theodicy, an implicit assertion of God's righteousness. The faithful community is enjoined to wait with patience for what they do not see: the appearing of God's justice. This hope God will not disappoint.

This interpretation of Habakkuk is no novelty of modern criticism. August Strobel has documented that Hab. 2:4 was widely deemed, both within Judaism—especially in its apocalyptic forms—and within early Christianity, a *locus classicus* for deliberation about the problem of the delay in the appearance of God's eschatological justice.[18]

Thus, when Paul quotes Hab. 2:4, we cannot help hearing the echoes—unless we are tone-deaf—of Habakkuk's theodicy question. By showcasing this text—virtually as an epigraph—at the beginning of the letter to the Romans, Paul links his gospel to the Old Testament prophetic affirmation of God's justice and righteousness. Like Habakkuk long before him and like Milton long after, Paul undertakes in his own way to "justify the ways of God to men" by proclaiming that the righteousness of God is now definitively manifest in the gospel.

Here as elsewhere, however, the echo is also a trope. Habakkuk's protest was occasioned by the military domination of the Chaldeans, "that bitter and hasty nation," over an impotent Israel (Hab. 1:5–11); Paul's problem arises instead from a different sort of historical phenomenon, not the occupation of Israel by a Gentile military power but the apparent usurpation of Israel's favored covenant status by congregations of uncircumcised Gentile Christians. The analogy between the situations is off-center and—precisely for that reason—metaphorical.[19]

Likewise, Paul's reading of the prophetic text filters the echo and thereby yields a complex semantic transformation. In the Hebrew text of Habakkuk, God's answer to the prophet is an exhortation to keep the faith: "The righteous one shall live by *his* faithfulness," that is, the person who remains faithful will be rewarded in the end by God. The LXX, however, has reinterpreted the dictum as a promise about the character of God: "The righteous one shall live by *my* faithfulness," that is, God's own integrity in preserving the covenant with Israel will ultimately be confirmed.[20] As Paul allows the quotation to reverberate into the text of Romans he elides the crucial personal pronoun, so that we hear only "the righteous one shall live by faithfulness." Whose faithfulness? We are not told. The ambiguity thus created allows the echoed oracle to serve simultaneously as a warrant for two different claims that Paul has made in his keynote formulation of the gospel: in the gospel *God's own righteousness* is revealed; and the gospel is the power of God for salvation *to everyone who believes*. Around these foci Paul plots the ellipse of his argument. That is why he writes that the gospel is revealed *ek pisteōs eis pistin* (out of faithfulness for faithfulness). Thus, Paul's citation of Hab. 2:4, rather than circumventing the text's original referential sense, draws on that sense—indeed, on at least two different traditional readings of it[21]—as a source of symbolic resonance for his affirmation of the justice of God's ways in the present time.

Thus, in Rom. 1:16–17, by mingling echoes from the Psalms, Isaiah, and Habakkuk, Paul locates his proclamation of the gospel within the sounding chamber of prophetic reflection on God's justice.

Judgment, Tribulation, and Distress

God's justice is shown forth not only in his faithfulness to the covenant with Israel but also in his activity of bringing judgment upon the wicked who refuse to acknowledge him. Paul introduces the theme of God's wrath immediately after the gospel keynote, in Rom. 1:18: "For the wrath of God is revealed from heaven upon all ungodliness and unrighteousness of human beings who suppress the truth in unrighteousness." Thus he sounds the first note in an indictment of fallen humanity, Jews and Gentiles alike, that runs all the way through Rom. 3:20. The indictment builds, like a fireworks display, toward a climactic explosion of scriptural condemnations in Rom. 3:10–18. While this thunderous cadence of quotations closes the first movement of Paul's argument, other biblical echoes sound more faintly through the early chapters of Romans, harmonically enriching the letter's central themes.

In Romans, chapter 2—strewn with exegetical stumbling-blocks for interpreters who presuppose that Paul must always and everywhere preach only justification by faith apart from works—Paul, while adopting the diatribe style of the popular Hellenistic moralists, delivers a message of judgment that weaves together themes and language reminiscent of Old Testament wisdom and prophecy as well as of several intertestamental Jewish writings. A glance at the copious marginal references in the twenty-sixth edition of Nestle-Aland's *Novum Testamentum Graece* suggests how densely allusive is the texture of Paul's language here. As an example, consider Rom. 2:5–11:

But by your hard and impenitent heart you are storing up wrath for yourself on the day when God's righteous judgment will be revealed.

For he will render to everyone according to his works: to those who by patience in well-doing seek for glory and honor and immortality, he will give eternal life; but for those who are factious and do not obey the truth but obey injustice, there will be wrath and fury. There will be tribulation and distress for every human being who does evil, the Jew first and also the Greek, but glory and honor and peace for every one who does good, the Jew first and also the Greek. For God shows no partiality.

In connection with this passage, the critical apparatus of Nestle-Aland[26] cites references or allusions to Wisdom of Solomon, Deuteronomy, Zephaniah, the Psalms, the Testament of Levi, the Psalms of Solomon, Proverbs, Isaiah, and 2 Chronicles.

For instance, Paul's affirmation that God "will render to every man according to his works" is a virtual quotation of Ps. 61:13 (LXX) and of Prov. 24:12, the future tense of the verb mirroring the psalm passage, its third person form and the relative clause construction (in the Greek of Rom. 2:6, not reproduced in the RSV's syntax) reflecting the Proverbs formulation.

Ps. 61:13b: You will render to each one according to his works.

Prov. 24:12: . . . who renders to each one according to his works.

Taken in isolation, the quotation might suggest a mechanistic conception of God's justice, but the wider context of the psalm, with its moving affirmation of God's mercy as source of hope and salvation, renders an account of God fully consonant with Paul's emphasis on God's kindness and forbearance (Rom. 2:4). However, the Proverbs text, especially in its LXX form, highlights the theme of God's omniscient judgment:

> If you say, "I did not know this,"
> know that the Lord knows the hearts of all,
> and he who formed breath in everyone,
> he himself knows all things,
> who renders to each one according to his works.

Thus, Paul's subsequent development of the idea that God knows and judges the secrets of human hearts (Rom. 2:15–16) is anticipated by the allusion to Prov. 24:12.

We need not suppose, in a case of this sort, that Paul intentionally selected a quotation that would allusively evoke from two discrete original contexts the dialectically paired notions of God's mercy and omniscience. No doubt he was aware of echoing Scripture when he wrote, "He will render to each one according to his works," but there is no reason to think that he went back and looked up the passages and then cleverly crafted his argument to weave their different themes together. Instead, the echo of Psalms and Proverbs recollects images of God that were in Paul's bones. We, belated rootless readers, can learn only through marginalia and concordances—like novice guitarists learning blues riffs from sheet music—what Paul knew by heart: to quote the confession that God will render to each one according to his works is to trigger overtones in which God's omniscience and mercy play in counterpoint and blend.

Some of the allusions here, however, are even more indirect. The phrase "tribulation and distress [*thlipsis kai stenochōria*] for every human being who does evil" carries an indistinct but suggestive echo of at least two different Old Testament passages. The stronger verbal echo comes from Isa. 8:22,[22] a part of a judgment oracle against the people of Israel for their failure to trust the word of promise. Rather than seeking the Lord, they consult "mediums and wizards who chirp and mutter" (8:19). Therefore, they will suffer a fate that Isaiah portrays in apocalyptic images: when the prophesied military destruction comes upon them, "they will look up into the heaven above, and they will look on the earth below, and behold, intense confusion and darkness, tribulation and distress [*thlipsis kai stenochōria*], and impenetrable darkness." Paul, in continuity with Jewish apocalyptic tradition, appropriates the imagery as an account of God's eschatological judgment, pointedly expanding the scope of the "tribulation and distress" to encompass Jews and Greeks alike, not just the elect nation (as in Isaiah) but all who do evil. Thus the prophetic announcement of judgment on Israel rebounds, in Paul's evocation of it, into a metaphor of universal judgment.[23]

The second Old Testament passage that echoes faintly here is Deuteronomy 28, in which Moses proclaims the blessings and curses attendant on the Lord's covenant with Israel. Those who fail to obey "all his commandments" (Deut. 28:15 ff.) will incur a gruesome catalogue of curses, including a thrice-intoned prophecy that they will eat the flesh of their own sons and daughters "in your distress and in your tribulation [*en tē stenochōria sou kai en tō thlipsei sou*], with which your enemy shall afflict you" (28:53, 55, 57). That this passage commanded Paul's attention we know from Gal. 3:10: there he declares that all who live on the basis of the Law are under a curse, and then proves the claim with a conflated citation of Deut. 27:26 and 28:58. (The conflation simply shows that Paul thinks of Deuteronomy 27 and 28 as a unit, setting forth the conditional blessings and curses of the Law.)[24] Consequently, when the combination of *thlipsis*

and *stenochōria* occurs in Rom. 2:9 as a characterization of the fate of
"every human being who does evil," a reader standing within the same
"cave of resonant signification" where Paul stood will perceive that he is
depicting the eschatological wrath of God with lingering overtones
drawn from the covenant curse of Deuteronomy. Greeks, however, as
well as Jews will encounter this wrath since "there is no partiality with
God" (Rom. 2:11). (This maxim is, of course, another echo: cf. 2 Chron.
19:7 and Sir. 35:12–13.)[25] This does not necessarily mean that Paul anachronistically interprets the Deuteronomic covenant to apply to Gentiles;
the echo makes no overt claims. Instead, his account of the revelation of
God's wrath draws metaphorical resonance from the allusive echo of the
covenant curse. The allusion is a trope, inviting the reader to picture the
eschatological wrath of God in terms of Deuteronomy's images. As we
shall see,[26] the trope is not casually chosen, for Paul sees in the Deuteronomic covenant a prefiguration of the gospel, and he sees the attendant blessings and curses as words addressed to his own time.

Blasphemed among the Gentiles

If the gospel is the power of God for salvation for Jew and Greek alike,
and if God's judgment falls impartially on Jews and Gentiles, is Paul
promulgating a teaching that effectually dissolves Israel's identity altogether? In Romans 2, he seems to entertain the possibility seriously. He
considers the hypothetical notion that Gentiles who "do not by nature
have the Law"[27] may in fact do "the things of the Law," thus showing
"the work of the Law written on their hearts" (2:15). At the same time, he
observes that circumcision is of no value for someone who breaks the Law
(2:25). This line of reasoning leads him to a potentially scandalous conclusion, as the RSV's paraphrastic translation indicates: "He is not a real Jew
who is one outwardly, nor is true circumcision something outward and
physical. He is a Jew who is one inwardly, and real circumcision is a
matter of the heart, spiritual and not literal" (Rom. 2:28–29).

Although such opinions would have been bitterly controversial
among Paul's Jewish contemporaries—including Jewish Christians—the
images that inform Paul's radical position allude to scriptural passages so
familiar that he need not cite them explicitly. The jarring metonymic
image of the "circumcised heart" appears both in Deuteronomy and in
Jeremiah as a way of calling Israel to radical, wholehearted obedience to
God (Deut. 10:16, 30:6; Jer. 4:4; cf. Jub. 1:23), and Jeremiah also employs
its negative counterpart when he accuses "the whole house of Israel" of

being "uncircumcised in heart" (Jer. 9:26). The vision of the Law being written on the hearts of God's people, classically expressed in Jer. 31:33 (38:33 LXX), also appears in Isa. 51:7, the same section of Isaiah from which Paul's proclamation of the revelation of God's righteousness emanates.

The innovative element here is not the images themselves but the use that Paul makes of them. When God, in Isaiah's prophecy, addresses "my people, in whose heart is my Law," he is speaking not of Gentiles but of Israel, urging them not to be discouraged by the contempt of the Gentiles. Paul's echo inverts the motif, turning it into something that the prophets had never envisioned: a warrant for speaking of uncircumcised Gentiles—Paul probably has Gentile Christians in mind[28]—as God's people.

A complementary semantic inversion occurs in the one text that Paul does cite explicitly in this section of the argument. The quotation is the rhetorical climax of a paragraph (Rom. 2:17–24) in which Paul interrogates an imaginary Jewish interlocutor, culminating in the decidedly hostile question, "You who boast in the Law, do you dishonor God through transgression of the Law?" Before the fictive debating partner can offer a denial, Paul produces a prophecy to prove that Israel's disobedience has been foreseen and deplored in advance: "For 'on account of you the name of God is blasphemed among the Gentiles,' just as it is written " (Rom. 2:24, quoting Isa. 52:5 LXX).[29] This is not only a low blow but also, from the standpoint of critical exegesis, a stunning misreading of the text. In Isaiah, the quoted passage is part of Yahweh's *reassurance* of Israel in exile: precisely because Israel's oppressed condition allows the nations to despise the power of Israel's God, the people can trust more surely that God will reveal himself and act to vindicate his own name. Thus, Paul transforms Isaiah's oracle of promise into a word of reproach. The marvel is that Paul's misreading has so often met with blithe acceptance by subsequent Christian commentators; this is testimony to the power of the new symbolic world that Paul's reading creates.

Yet, as Paul's convoluted dialectical argument unfolds, we begin to see that his provocative misreading of Isa. 52:5 is only provisional. He knows perfectly well that these chapters of Isaiah are portents of God's grace toward Israel; for instance, in Rom. 10:15 he paraphrases Isa. 52:7 as a foreshadowing of the proclamation of the gospel of Jesus Christ: "How beautiful are the feet of those who preach good news."[30] If he reads Isa. 52:5 as a reproach, it is a reproach only in the same way that the historical event to which it refers was a reproach: a heightening of the tension of grace, a painful reminder of the discrepancy between human unfaithfulness and the faithfulness of God who will never abandon his covenanted people.

The quotation of Isa. 52:5 works metaphorically in Paul's argument only if the reader castigated by the text imaginatively takes on the role of Israel in exile. Yet the reader who assumes that posture cannot then fail to hear also the promises of hope and deliverance that Isaiah speaks to Israel in exile. Paul will speak these words aloud later in the letter:

> I do not want you to be ignorant, brothers, of this mystery: . . . a hardening has come upon a part of Israel until the fullness of the Gentiles should come in, and so all Israel will be saved, as it is written,
>
> > The deliverer will come from Zion;
> > He will turn away impiety from Jacob.
> > And this will be my covenant with them,
> > When I take away their sins.
> > (Rom. 11:26–27, quoting Isa. 59:20 and 27:9)

Consequently, to read Paul's citation of Isa. 52:5 as unqualified condemnation of Israel is bad reading, or, more precisely, it is an interpretation possible only on a first reading of the letter. The letter's rhetorical structure lures the reader into expecting Israel's final condemnation, but the later chapters undercut such an expectation, requiring the reader in subsequent encounters with the text to understand the Isaiah quotation more deeply in relation to its original prophetic context. Paul depicts God scolding Israel, like a parent chiding a child who has brought dishonor to the family, only because Israel's covenant relation with God remains intact, as many other passages both in Isaiah and in Romans will insist. In Romans 2 the citation of Isaiah functions as a word of judgment; however, the judgment carries with it the same implicit promise that sustained Israel in captivity. Thus, even in the portion of Paul's argument that seems to threaten Jewish identity most radically, the scriptural quotation evokes, metaleptically, echoes of the promise that God, in vindicating his name, will also redeem Israel.

THE LAW AND THE PROPHETS AS WITNESSES OF GOD'S RIGHTEOUSNESS

In Rom. 1:18–3:20, even where Paul uses scriptural allusions to underscore the message of God's judgment, the texts themselves whisper the countertheme of God's mercy. Though it might seem odd to find the scriptural echoes drifting back against the flow of Paul's argument in these chapters, this countermovement makes sense when we consider two factors: the character of Scripture's original witness and the goal toward which Paul's own argument ultimately drives.

Paul, of course, is developing an account of his gospel that emphasizes God's unmerited grace toward the ungodly (cf. 4:4–5) and God's steadfast love toward Israel despite Israel's unfaithfulness. In the context of this discussion, the proclamation of God's judgment in 1:18–3:20 provides a dialectical foil to the word of grace; consequently, if the biblical texts cited in this section foreshadow the argument's subsequent resolution, they subliminally prepare the reader for the reversal wrought by grace.

Furthermore, the dialectical movement of judgment and grace that structures Paul's presentation of the gospel is in fact a recapitulation of the judgment/grace paradigm that undergirds the whole witness of Scripture, especially the prophetic writings of the exilic period. When Paul claims that the Law and the Prophets bear witness to "the righteousness of God," which reaches out to save the ungodly, he is calling attention to precisely this fundamental ground structure of Scripture. Because a text such as Isaiah 52 bears this dialectical stamp, it resists the ostensibly undialectical use to which Paul puts it in Rom. 2:24. Like a strong spring stretched to its limit, it exerts a powerful pull on the argument, causing both text and reader to recoil, returning to the original shape of Isaiah's prophecy.

"Let God be true though every man be false"

The recoil action begins in Rom. 3:1. Paul anticipates the question to which any critical reader will have been led by the insistent claim in Romans 2 that what matters in God's eyes is circumcision of the heart, not outward signs of membership in the covenant community: "What then is the advantage of the Jew, or what is the benefit of circumcision?" On the basis of Romans 2, we expect Paul to answer, "Nothing at all!" thus breaking cleanly with Judaism. Instead of giving this apparently logical answer, however, he reverses field, abruptly declaring that the advantage of the Jew is "much in every way."

What tethers Paul to this devout ethnocentrism? Scripture is the tether, because Scripture tells the story of God's election of Israel. If Paul's gospel nullifies this election, it means that God's past dealing with his people was false dealing, that he made promises on which he is now reneging. At issue is "the moral integrity of God."[31]

So, if Jews do have some special advantage in relationship to God, what is it? Scripture itself, affirms Paul, is the preeminent advantage: "First of all, they were entrusted [*episteuthēsan*] with the oracles of God. What if some were unfaithful [*ēpistēsan*]? Their unfaithfulness [*apistia*] doesn't nullify the faithfulness [*pistin*] of God, does it? No, never!" (Rom. 3:2b–4a). No failing of the Jewish people can change the facts that "the oracles of God"[32] are addressed to them and that the very story of their faithlessness becomes, as Isaiah proclaimed, the occasion for God's invincible faithfulness to shine forth. With or without her consent, Israel has been made the bearer of God's promise. This is advantage indeed.

In support of the assertion of God's faithfulness,[33] Paul adduces a prooftext, Ps. 51:4 (50:6 LXX), "Just as it is written, 'So that you might be justified [*dikaiothēs*] in your words and triumph when you are judged.'" The psalmist's emphasis on the justification of God, however awkward for theologians who insist on interpreting *dikaiosynē theou* (the right-eousness of God) as a status conferred by God on believers,[34] suits Paul's purposes precisely, because Psalm 51, like Paul's argument in Rom. 3:1–20, pivots on the contrast between God's blamelessness and human guilt. Indeed, the psalm's powerful implicit reinforcement of Paul's case has frequently impressed commentators.[35] Psalm 51 is a penitential psalm, confessing sin and calling on God's mercy.

> Have mercy on me, God, according to your great mercy,
> and according to the multitude of your compassions blot out my
>   transgression.
> Wash me thoroughly from my iniquity
> and cleanse me from my sin.
> For I know my iniquity,
> and my sin is constantly before me.
> Against you only have I sinned,
> and I have done evil before you,
> in order that you might be justified in your words
> and triumph when you are judged.
>
>   (Ps. 50:3–6 LXX)

The psalm's superscription places it into a traditional haggadic setting: "A Psalm of David, when Nathan the prophet came to him, when he had gone into Bathsheba." The familiar story to which the superscription alludes is found in 2 Samuel 11 and 12. The prophet Nathan, sent as God's special prosecutor, spins a parable of a rich man who takes a poor man's lamb. David's pious indictment of the fictional scoundrel ("As the Lord lives, the man who has done this deserves to die") is—as Nathan and reader both recognize—an ironically fitting pronouncement of self-condemnation. Nathan shatters David's self-deception ("You are the man"), and David—living as he did before the invention of executive "deniability"—dramatically repents, confessing openly, "I have sinned before the Lord." Surprisingly, Nathan's response mediates God's forgiveness to David: "The Lord has also put away your sin; you shall not die."

Paul neither mentions this narrative framework nor cites from Psalm 51 any portion of David's confession of sin; the omission is intriguing. He quotes the one verse in the psalm that points to the vindication of God as one who justly bears wrath toward sinful humanity—even toward David, whispers the echo, even toward the man after God's own heart who is the mythic precursor of the Messiah—but muffles the psalm's confessions of guilt and pleas for forgiveness. In this case, no reader familiar with the psalter could possibly fail to hear the resonance of the psalm's unquoted verses with the theme of Romans 3. Rather than spelling out all the connections, Paul opts for metaphorical understatement, allowing this well-known psalm's echoes to sound subliminally beneath the overt argument.

The interplay of texts here is complex. Psalm 51, which Paul cites, is represented by its own superscription as a prayer that ought to be interpreted in relation to an earlier narrative. Thus, there are already two textual layers beneath the surface of Rom. 3:4. Paul offers a homiletical commentary on a psalm that in turn offers a devotional expansion of a narrative. This sort of multilayered intertextual interpretation of traditions is an ongoing and pervasive phenomenon in Israel's Scriptures, as well as in the hermeneutical traditions to which these Scriptures gave rise.[36]

In this particular lineal linkage of texts, the rhetorical structure of Romans 1–3 recapitulates the narrative structure of its textual grandparent, the story of Nathan's confrontation with David. The reader of Romans stands in David's role, drawn by the invective of Rom. 1:18–32 to pronounce judgment on pagan immorality, then unmasked and slapped by Paul's Nathan-like pronouncement: "Therefore you have no excuse, O man, whoever you are, when you judge another; for in passing judgment upon him you condemn yourself, because you, the judge, are doing the very same things" (Rom. 2:1).[37] Romans 3, then, like the denouement of the David story, sets forth a pattern of human guilt, met by divine judgment and mercy; for the reader of Romans, as for David, there is no escape from the righteousness of God. There is little evidence in Romans to suggest that these structural parallels are deliberately crafted by Paul. It is more likely that the subconscious structural parallels between Paul's message and the Nathan/David encounter led Paul to hit on Psalm 51 as an appropriate text to cite.

The point made explicitly by Paul's citation of Ps. 51:4 is that Scripture proclaims the justice of God's judgment. The point made implicitly is that Psalm 51 (and its narrative precursor in 2 Samuel 11–12) models the appropriate human posture before this righteous God: not challenging his just sentence of condemnation but repenting and acknowledging desperate need. The allusion to the David tradition foreshadows Rom. 4:6–8, in which David (Ps. 32:1–2) is called as witness of the blessedness of those whose sins are not "reckoned" by God (cf. 2 Sam. 12:13). In Rom. 3:4, however, all these connections remain in the cave of echo. A reader unfamiliar with 2 Samuel and Psalm 51 would read right past, recognizing that a prooftext had been quoted but missing the more complex resonances between Davidic psalm and Pauline kerygma.

Impossible to miss, however, is the jackhammer indictment of human sinfulness in the scriptural catena of Rom. 3:10–18. Assembled from parts of at least five different psalms as well as from Ecclesiastes, Proverbs, and Isaiah, this anthology of condemnation relentlessly pounds home the charge enunciated by its opening line: "There is no righteous person, no not one" (cf. Ps. 14:1–3 and Eccl. 7:20). Why this unremitting attack on the moral integrity of human beings? In the context of Paul's argument, the catena of quotations[38] provides a powerful rhetorical warrant for his assertions that all humanity, Jews and Greeks alike, is "under sin" (3:9), and that the whole world is therefore accountable (*hypodikos*) to God (3:19). The indictment is framed in the words of Scripture; this is crucial for Paul's purposes, because it demonstrates that "those in the Law" (Jews) are addressed by the Law (Scripture)[39] in such a way that their own culpability before God should be inescapable: in an echo of Ps. 62:12 (LXX), Paul observes that Scripture speaks this way "in order that every mouth might be stopped." Those who are entrusted with the oracles of God are thus given the paradoxical privilege of learning from those oracles the truth of their own depravity, a truth that remains hidden from the rest of humanity.

Thus, the underlying purpose of Rom. 3:9–20 is to establish beyond all possible doubt the affirmation that God is just in his judgment of the world. The passage rebuts the rhetorical suggestion of Rom. 3:5–7 that God might be considered unfair (*adikos*). The righteousness of God, proclaimed by Psalm 51, is highlighted by Scripture's contrasting account of human unrighteousness, which simultaneously cuts away any ground for human protest against God's justice.

Paul sums up this train of thought in Rom. 3:20 with one last scriptural allusion, this time to Psalm 143: "Therefore, by works of the Law no flesh shall be justified before him." Paul has tinkered with the wording of Ps. 143:2 in several ways. The phrase "by works of the Law" is his own explanatory exegetical comment, and he has changed the LXX's *pas zōn* (every living being) to *pasa sarx* (all flesh); furthermore, he has transmuted the psalmist's direct address to God ("No living being will be justified before you") into a declarative generalization by changing the personal pronoun from second to third person singular. The effect of these modifications is to render the intertextual relation indirect rather than direct. The psalm is not adduced as a proof for Paul's assertion, but his assertion echoes the psalm, activating Israel's canonical memory. A reader formed spiritually by the psalter, with or without recognizing the specific allusion, will know already that before God no one can claim to be justified; thus, hearing Paul's proclamation, the reader will be disposed to assent.

Attested by the Law and the Prophets

The echoes of Psalm 143 do not end, however, with the word of universal condemnation in Rom. 3:20. In order to overhear the full range of echoes, we must listen to the psalm as a whole, not just the phrase allusively cited in verse 20. The psalm itself is an urgent prayer for deliverance; consequently, the statement that "no living being will be justified before you" is not a speculative exercise in theological anthropology but a confession integral to the psalmist's petition for help. The psalm's opening and closing verses disclose the spiritual context in which Paul learned the words that he echoes in Rom. 3:20.

Lord, hear my prayer,
Give ear to my petition in your truth [*en tē alētheia sou*]
Hear me in your righteousness [*en tē dikaiosynē sou*];
And do not enter into judgment with your servant,
Because no living being will be justified before you.
. . . .
For the sake of your name, Lord, you will give me life;
By your righteousness [*en tē dikaiosynē sou*] you will lead me out of the oppression of my life.
And in your mercy you will obliterate my enemies,
And you will destroy all those who oppress my life,
Because I am your servant.

(Ps. 142:1–2, 10–11 LXX)

The psalmist's appeal to God's truthfulness (*alētheia*; cf. Rom. 3:4, 7) and righteousness (*dikaiosynē*; cf. Rom. 3:5, 21–22) as ground of hope and instrument of deliverance provides the background against which all of Romans 3 must be read. The psalm provides Paul not only with the language for a blanket indictment of humankind but also with the expectant language of prayer that looks to God's righteousness as the source of salvation. Thus, when Paul writes in Rom. 3:21 that "now, apart from Law, the righteousness of God has been manifested, *witnessed by the Law and the Prophets,*" he is making a claim that anyone who had ever prayed Psalm 143 from the heart would instantly recognize: God's saving righteousness, for which the psalmist had hoped, has at last appeared. The witness of the Law and the Prophets to the righteousness of God is not merely, as Christians have sometimes strangely supposed, a witness concerning a severe retributive justice; rather, it is a witness concerning God's gracious saving power, as Psalm 143 demonstrates.[40]

The effect of this intertextual echo in Rom. 3:20–21 is to bridge paragraphs that are often read in disjunction from one another. Paul cites Ps. 143:2 in verse 20 to anchor his argument that no one is righteous (*dikaios*) before God. Rippling outward from this anchor, however, are echoes recollecting God's righteousness; these echoes in turn are amplified explicitly as the theme of proclamation in Paul's next sentence, Rom. 3:21. Thus, the allusion to Psalm 143, which contains both an affirmation of the unconditional inadequacy of human beings to stand before God and an appeal to God to exercise his own righteousness in order to rescue the psalmist, anticipates the next turn in the argument.

The implications of this analysis are theological as well as aesthetic. The psalm language provides Paul with more than a clever segue. If Psalm 143 implicitly spans verses 20 and 21 of Romans 3, then the righteousness of God proclaimed by Paul is the same righteousness invoked by David's prayer, and Israel's Scripture becomes a positive witness to God's righteousness rather than a negative foil to it. If the righteousness of God proclaimed in Rom. 3:21–22 is the same as the righteousness of God expected in Psalm 143 and acknowledged in Psalm 51 (cf. Rom. 3:4–5), then the righteousness in question must be God's own righteousness, that is, God's own moral integrity.

This means that Rom. 3:21 is not the introduction of a new theme in the argument, explaining how individuals can find acceptance with God, as so many commentators since Luther have thought,[41] but the climax of a continuous discussion that goes back at least to the beginning of the chapter, or indeed all the way back to Rom. 1:16–17. Rom. 3:21–26 provides Paul's definitive response to the issues raised in 3:1–8. Is God unjust? No, God has put forward Jesus Christ as an "indication of his righteousness [*endeixin tēs dikaiosynēs autou*]"—a phrase repeated twice in verses 25–26—"in order that he [God] might himself be righteous even in justifying the person who lives through the faithfulness of Jesus."[42] These remarks about Jesus Christ as the demonstration and vindication of God's righteousness make sense only when they are understood as Paul's answer to the challenges raised earlier in the chapter about God's justice. The question of theodicy continues to govern the discussion throughout Romans 3, and the scriptural echoes provide the proper context for the interpretation of Paul's references to *dikaiosynē theou*.

The problem of the proper interpretation of *dikaiosynē theou* in Romans has been one of the hotly debated issues in New Testament studies over the past generation,[43] but rare is the critic who even considers the possibility of interpreting Paul's "righteousness of God" language against the background of the LXX. Learned scholars have argued bitterly whether *dikaiosynē theou* was a technical term in Jewish apocalyptic thought, as attested especially in the Qumran texts, or whether it was a new creation of Paul's theological genius, without ever observing that the very Old Testament texts quoted by Paul in Romans 3 already introduce the idea of God's righteousness.[44] This remarkable oversight illustrates the power of hermeneutical conventions in shaping a community's reading of its canonical texts. The Reformation theme of justification by faith has so obsessed generations of readers (Protestant readers, at least) that they have set Law and gospel in simplistic antithesis, ignoring the internal signs of coherence in Rom. 3:1–26; consequently, they have failed to see that Paul's argument is primarily an argument about theodicy, not about soteriology. The driving question in Romans is not "How can I find a gracious God?" but "How can we trust in this allegedly gracious God if he abandons his promises to Israel?" Christian caricatures of the Old Testament have made it difficult for belated generations of Gentile readers to grasp Paul's passion for asserting the continuity of his gospel with the message of the Law and the Prophets. By following the echoes of Psalm 143, however, we can rediscover the scriptural idea of God's saving justice at the foundation of Paul's argument in Romans.

That is why Paul insists (Rom. 3:31) that his gospel does not annihilate the Law but establishes it. How so? First of all, Paul's proclamation presents the righteousness of God not as some unheard-of soteriological novelty but as the manifestation of a truth attested by Scripture from the first. When he says that his message confirms the Law, he refers not to the specific commandments of the Pentateuch but to the witness of Scripture, read as a *narrative* about God's gracious election of a people.[45] That is why the Abraham story becomes for Paul the crucial test case. If he can show, as he sets out to do in Romans 4, that the story of Abraham supports his reading of God's Gentile-embracing grace, then he will have demonstrated, to his own satisfaction at least, the unity of gospel and Law.

Abraham as Father of Jews and Gentiles

In Romans 4, the process of intertextual reflection is made fully explicit. Here no echoes entice the reader back to shadowy origins; instead, Paul argues explicitly about the interpretation of texts that he places in full view. Even here, however, Paul's handling of the scriptural text is so idiosyncratic that misunderstanding is easily possible. We must reckon with the way in which Paul's interpretation of the Abraham story fits into his broader argument, attending first of all to the meaning of the enigmatic sentence that introduces the patriarch into the discussion.

The RSV translates Rom. 4:1 as follows: "What then shall we say about Abraham our forefather according to the flesh?" Such a rendering, however, runs recklessly over the Greek text. For a formidable series of reasons having to do with the manuscript evidence, with Greek syntax, and with Pauline style, the verse must instead be translated, "What then shall we say? Have we found Abraham to be our forefather according to the flesh?"[46] The answer demanded by this rhetorical question, as by other similar rhetorical questions in Romans (3:5, 6:1, 7:7, 9:14) is an emphatic negative.

Why is finding or not finding Abraham to be our fleshly progenitor an issue that Paul must address? The logic of his argument can be clarified by a paraphrase, picking up the thread of the discussion in Rom. 3:29.

> Is God the God of Jews only and not also of Gentiles? Of course not! He is surely the God of Gentiles also. But that means that if God, who justifies Jews on the basis of faith, is consistent in his integrity, he must justify Gentiles also through faith. Then through this faith are we invalidating the Law? No! Instead we are confirming the Law. Look, do you think that we Jews have considered Abraham our forefather only according to the flesh?

Paul wants to argue that Judaism itself, rightly understood, claims its relation to Abraham not by virtue of physical descent from him (*kata sarka*) but by virtue of sharing his trust in the God who made the promises. In that sense, the gospel, which invites all people, including Gentiles, into right relation with God through faith, confirms the Law; it is consistent with the real substance of the Law's teaching. This is the proposition that Paul sets out to demonstrate through his exposition of Genesis.

This reading of the text will appear odd only if we are committed to the presupposition that Paul is expounding a message that stands in an antithetical relation to Judaism. If we do not hold such a view a priori, it will be clear that Paul means precisely what he says: the gospel confirms the Torah. Only a narrowly ethnocentric form of Judaism, Paul insists, would claim that God is the God of the Jews only[47] or that Abraham is the progenitor of God's people "according to the flesh," that is, by virtue of natural physical descent. For the purposes of his argument, Paul associates these (evidently false) notions with the (disputed) claim that Gentile Christians must come under the Law. Paul, speaking from *within* the Jewish tradition,[48] contends that the Torah itself provides the warrant for a more inclusive theology that affirms that the one God is God of Gentiles as well as Jews and that Abraham is the forefather of more than those who happen to be his physical descendants.

In order to make the case, he weaves together Gen. 15:6 ("Abraham believed God, and it was reckoned to him for righteousness") with Ps. 32:1–2:

> Blessed are those whose iniquities are forgiven
> and those whose sins are covered.
> Blessed is the man whose sin the Lord will not reckon.

David, in the psalm, pronounces a blessing on the man whose sin the Lord does not "reckon." (This pronouncement is fraught with poignancy for the reader who has already heard the echoes of Psalm 51 in Rom. 3:4: David, who confessed his own guilt and God's justice, now speaks blessings in acknowledgment of God's forgiveness.) Paul uses the catchword *reckon* to connect David's blessing with Gen. 15:6 and Abraham. It has long been recognized that this is a very rabbinic-sounding piece of exegesis, employing the device of *gezerah shawah* (catchword linkage). Paul works this intertextual web into a temporal tangle by assuming that David's blessing applies in the first instance retrospectively to Abraham and then, in a derived fashion, to others symbolized by Abraham; thus, David, speaking in a prophetic mode, utters a blessing that looks backward to Abraham and forward to the world of Paul's readers. While the blurring of narrative temporal boundaries is ingredient in *gezerah shawah* as a hermeneutical device, this passage illustrates clearly Paul's tendency to treat the word of Scripture as a word spoken to the present time.

In Rom. 4:9, Paul asks, in relation to the Psalm quotation, "Is this blessing pronounced upon the circumcision [Jews] or upon the uncircumcision [Gentiles]?" In order to answer this crucial question, Paul reverts to the narrative context of Gen. 15:6. He is no longer concerned with the problem of *how* Abraham was "reckoned righteous" but instead with the question of *when*. Was it before or after he received circumcision? This question arises not because Paul wants to refute the view that Abraham was justified by a "work" (circumcision) but because Paul regards Abraham as a representative figure whose destiny contains the destiny of others. The blessing pronounced on him applies not only to him but also to his "seed" as well. Therefore, the fact that Abraham was reckoned righteous while he was still uncircumcised has symbolic—or typological—significance: he can thereby be the father of Gentiles as well as Jews. Paul spells this out explicitly in verses 11–12: "And he received a sign of circumcision, a seal of the righteousness of the faith which is in the uncircumcision *in order that* he might be: (a) the father of all who believe while uncircumcised in order that righteousness might be reckoned to them; (b) the father of circumcision to those who are not only circumcised but also walk in the footsteps of the faith which our father Abraham had while he was uncircumcised."

The story of Abraham is told as it is told (or, as Paul would say, these things happened to Abraham in the order in which they happened) in order that Abraham might fitly serve as the archetype for Gentile believers as well as Jewish believers. He is said to be the father of both groups not because they are descended from him *kata sarka* but because their faith mirrors his and because their destiny is prefigured in him: they are included vicariously in the blessing pronounced upon him by God, a blessing which is specifically said to apply to "all the nations [*panta ta ethnē*]."

Paul reiterates the same theme in verses 13–18, supported by quotations from Gen. 17:5 ("I have appointed you as father of many nations / Gentiles") and 15:5 ("Thus shall be your seed"). The quotations continue to emphasize Abraham's paternity of an elect progeny that transcends the boundaries of Jewish ethnic descent and Torah observance. Philo of Alexandria, a Jewish contemporary of Paul, sought to universalize Abraham's significance through a double-level interpretation that portrayed Abraham both as the exemplary wise man and as an allegorical figure for the soul's true quest for God. The moral of the tale for Philo is that "the mind did not remain forever deceived nor stand rooted in the realm of sense, nor suppose that the visible world was the Almighty and Primal God, but using its reason sped upwards and turned its gaze upon the intelligible order which is superior to the visible and upon Him who is maker and ruler of both alike."[49] Paul, however, follows a strategy very different from Philo's: he treats the Abraham story not as a philosophical allegory but as a narrative of divine promise which declares God's purpose to work in human affairs so as to create a unified new people of Jewish and Gentile believers.

Paul contends that his gospel, which offers God's salvation to Gentiles apart from the Law, is in fact a consummation and confirmation of the Torah's promises; his reading of Scripture—juxtaposed to an ethno-centric misreading—is in fact the right reading of what Israel's Scriptures have always proclaimed. Jews (at least those with circumcised hearts) have found Abraham to be their father not according to the flesh but according to promise. Paul has developed this reading of the story directly through exegesis of Scripture, without any appeal to the language of Christian confession. This reading intends to be and is a Jewish theological interpretation of the significance of Abraham. Insofar as Paul has mounted a persuasive argument within the acknowledged rules of the Jewish exegetical game, he has sustained his claim (3:31) that his gospel of justification for Gentiles outside the Law is consistent with the Law.

Thus, Rom. 3:21–4:25 asserts openly what the biblical echoes earlier in the letter only suggested: Scripture (the Law and the Prophets) bears witness to the gospel in such a way that the continuity of God's grace is upheld. Despite the subsequent protests of Marcion and his seed, the God whose righteousness is shown forth in Jesus Christ is Israel's God, the God of Abraham, who paradoxically affirms his unwavering faithfulness to his covenant with Israel precisely by electing to embrace Gentiles among his people.

SHEEP TO BE SLAUGHTERED

The early chapters of Romans testify that Paul regards the present as a time out of joint, an age riddled with anomalies: despite the revelation of the righteousness of God, human beings live in a state of rebellion and sin, and Israel stands skeptical of its appointed Messiah. Under such circumstances, God's justice is mysteriously hidden and the people of God are exposed to ridicule and suffering, as Israel learned during the period of the exile. Paul's pastoral task thus entails not only formulating theological answers to doubts about God's righteousness but also interpreting the suffering that the faithful community encounters during this anomalous interlude.

In Rom. 8:18–38, Paul reflects on the suffering that Christians experience in the present age. Toward the end of this theologically pregnant deliberation, he quotes Ps. 44:22 (43:22 LXX): "For your sake we are being killed all the day long; we are regarded as sheep to be slaughtered" (Rom. 8:36). Many commentators note that Paul has appropriated a lament of exilic Israel and placed it in the mouth of the early church. "The main effect of the quotation," says Cranfield, "is to show that the tribulations which face Christians are nothing new or unexpected, but have all along been characteristic of the life of God's people."[50] It would be more accurate to say, however, that Paul reads the Psalm as a prophetic prefiguration of the experience of the Christian church, so that the text finds its true primary meaning in Paul's own present time. The point is not that "righteous people have always suffered like this"; rather, Paul's point in Rom. 8:35–36 is that Scripture prophesies suffering as the lot of those (i.e., himself and his readers) who live in the eschatological interval between Christ's resurrection and the ultimate redemption of the world. Thus, in this instance as in many others that we will examine subsequently, Paul discerns in Scripture a foreshadowing of the church.[51]

Other echoes, however, cluster about the quotation, echoes sympathetic with the central themes of Romans. Consider the source of the quotation: Psalm 44 is a complaint psalm, raising agonized doubts about God's justice and faithfulness to his covenant with Israel. The passage that Paul quotes appears as part of the psalmist's protest against Yahweh's somnolent disregard for his people's suffering.

> All this has come upon us,
> but we have not forgotten you,
> or been false to your covenant.
> And our heart has not turned back,
> but you have turned aside our paths from your way,
> for you have laid us low in a place of affliction,
> and the shadow of death has covered us.
>
> If we had forgotten the name of our God,
> and if we had spread forth our hands to a strange God,
> would not God discover this?
> For he knows the secrets of the heart.
> For your sake we are slain all the day long,
> and accounted as sheep for slaughter.
>
> Wake up! Why do you sleep, O Lord?
> Arise, and do not cast us off for ever!
> Why do you turn your face away?
> Why do you forget our poverty and affliction?[52]

This psalm raises plaintively the issue that we have already seen to be the central theological problem of Romans: the question of God's integrity in upholding his promises to Israel. Paul is struggling to vindicate God from the suspicion of capriciousness in choosing to "justify" Gentiles who do not observe the Torah. Is God a fickle god who has cast off Israel (cf. 3:1–8, 3:21–26, 3:31, 9:14, and all of chapters 9–11)?

If we recognize the centrality of these concerns in Romans, we will be able to discern the echoes that Psalm 44, once quoted, sends ricocheting throughout the text. The psalmist raises a question precisely analogous to the one that Paul is seeking to answer: does the community's experience of suffering indicate that God has abandoned them? The psalm first despairingly indicates that God has indeed abandoned Israel (*Nyni de apōsō kai katēschynas hēmas"* [but now you have cast us off and put us to shame]; cf. Rom. 1:16), but it ends with a plea to the Lord: *anastēthi, kai mē apōsē eis telos* (arise, and do not cast us off forever). The answering echo is found in Rom. 11:1: *legō oun, mē apōsato ho theos ton laon autou; mē genoito* (I say then, has God cast off his people? By no means; cf. Ps. 93:14 LXX). And this, of course, is the same point made in the rhetorical questions and answers of 8:31–39, where Paul insists that no adversity can separate us from the love of Christ. The psalm quotation (Rom. 8:36), far from having the reassuring effect that Cranfield suggests, serves to intensify the depiction of suffering and to sharpen the question of God's faithfulness. It serves as a foil for the answer that Paul gives in 8:37–39.

Does this mean that Paul is playing Christianity off against Judaism or the gospel against the Old Testament? By no means! It means that Paul has found within the Old Testament words that give utterance to the inarticulate cry of the heart of all those—including Christian believers—who ache and groan along with the whole unredeemed creation (8:23, cf. Ps. 43:26 LXX). Moreover, his affirmation of God's ultimate faithfulness is, as we have seen in our examination of Romans 3, deeply rooted in the canonical witness of Israel's Scriptures. If there were any remaining doubt of that point, it should be dispelled by Paul's depiction of God as vindicator in Rom. 8:31–34: "What then shall we say to this? If God is for us, who is against us? . . . Who shall bring any charge against God's elect? God is the one who justifies [*ho dikaiōn*]; who is the one who condemns [*ho katakrinōn*]?" Paul's diction rings with echoes of Isa. 50:7–8 (LXX):

I know that I shall by no means be put to shame [*aischynthō*],
Because the One who justified me [*ho dikaiōsas me*] draws near.

Who enters into judgment with me [*tis ho krinomenos moi*]?
Let him confront me.
Indeed, who enters into judgment with me?
Let him draw near to me.
Behold, the Lord helps me.
Who will do me harm?

In vocabulary, in sentence-rhythm, and in substance Paul's declaration of trust in God resonates deeply with Isaiah's. Without recourse to quotation or prooftexting, Paul has formulated his confession in language that wells up out of Israel's hope.

But there is still one more significant overtone to be heard in Paul's quotation of Psalm 44. The psalmist's main point in verses 17–22 is that the suffering of Israel cannot be construed as a punishment for unfaithfulness or idolatry; on the contrary, God's people suffer precisely because of their faithfulness to him. Heavy emphasis falls on the *heneka sou* in verse 22: "for *your* sake" we are being put to death. This fact provides the basis of the psalmist's concluding appeal for God to vindicate his own name by coming to the rescue (v. 26).

Paul, for his part, is laboring to refute the charge—whether rhetorical or historical—that *he*, as a promulgator of a startling new teaching incorporating uncircumcised Gentiles into the people of God, has abandoned the ways of the God of Israel.[53] His anxiety on this score is betrayed by his uncertainty whether his offering (and his message?) will be acceptable to the Jewish Christians in Jerusalem (Rom. 15:31) and by numerous emphatic disclaimers throughout the text asserting the continuity of his proclamation with the Law. With such issues in the air, the citation of Ps. 44:22 whispers another disclaimer, this time sotto voce: by identifying himself and his Christian readers with the suffering Israel of the psalm, Paul evokes (metaleptically) the psalmist's denial of any charge of idolatrous defection. Fundamental to Paul's whole theological project is the claim that his gospel represents the authentic fulfillment of God's revelation to Israel. This claim receives symbolic reinforcement in his deft subliminal linkage of himself and his churches with the psalmist's stout insistence that "we have not forgotten you, or been false to your covenant." This linkage is an act of figuration that occurs almost entirely in the realm of echo: the apologetic motif does not appear overtly in the text at this point. Precisely for that reason, this passage clearly limns the effects created by the trope of metalepsis.

At the same time, Paul's suggestive fragmentary quotation of Psalm 44 raises a cloud of issues that loom over the letter as a whole and that finally precipitate, in Romans 9–11, an extended discussion of the fate of Israel. Paul's extraordinary interpretation of the "stumbling" of his Jewish contemporaries as divinely ordained becomes less dissonant when read against the choral background of Psalm 44. If exilic Israel's suffering is interpreted by the psalmist not as punishment but as suffering for the sake of God's name, then perhaps even the temporary unbelief of Israel can be understood as part of God's design to encompass Jews and Gentiles alike with his mercy. And indeed, so Paul argues in Rom 11:11–32. "So I ask, have they stumbled so as to fall? By no means! But through their trespass salvation has come to the Gentiles, so as to make Israel jealous. Now if their trespass means riches for the Gentiles, how much more will their full inclusion mean! (Rom. 11:11–12)."

In warning his Gentile readers against being "wise in [their] own conceits," Paul employs the metaphor of natural olive branches being broken off so that a wild olive shoot (i.e., the Gentiles) could be grafted on, but he suggests strongly that the broken branches will also be regrafted, "For God has the power to graft them in again" (Rom. 11:23). In this metaphor as in the preceding discourse it is clear that the breaking of the branches is God's act, aimed at salvation of the Gentiles.

Of particular interest here is the way that Paul describes this breaking: "If God did not spare [ouk epheisato] the natural branches, neither will he spare you" (Rom. 11:21). This language of "not sparing" should trigger a chain of reminiscences for Paul's readers. In Rom. 8:32, Paul had already written, "He who did not spare [ouk epheisato] his own son but gave him up for us all, will he not also give us all things with him?" By describing the fate of unbelieving Israel in the same language that he had used to describe Jesus' death, Paul hints at a daring trope whose full implications subsequent Christian theology has usually declined to pursue. What Paul has done, in a word, is to interpret the fate of Israel christologically. If Paul can write in Galatians that Jesus "became a curse for us . . . in order that in Christ Jesus the blessing of Abraham might come upon the Gentiles" (Gal. 3:13), he can say in Romans 11 something very similar about Israel's role in the drama of salvation. Israel undergoes rejection for the sake of the world, bearing suffering vicariously.

This intertextual play between Rom. 8:32 and 11:21, bold as it might seem, presupposes an older and deeper resonance with the Genesis narrative of Abraham's near-sacrifice of Isaac, in which God stays Abraham's hand, saying, "Do not lay your hand upon the child or do anything to him, for now I know that you fear God and you did not spare [ouk epheisō] your beloved son on account of me" (Gen. 22:12). Commentators have sometimes proposed, with varying degrees of confidence, that early interpretations of Jesus' death might have grown out of this Akedah tradition.[54] If Paul presupposes such a tradition, he does not say so explicitly, but his comments about Israel in Romans 11 suggest that the pattern runs deep in his imagination. The parallels between these three beloved ones "not spared" are too rich to be fortuitous. Abraham did not spare his son Isaac but bound him to the altar, only to receive him back through God's intervention. God did not spare his son Jesus but offered him up to death for the world, then vindicated him through the resurrection. God did not spare his people Israel but broke them off like branches for the sake of the Gentiles; surely that is not the end of the story, "for if their rejection means the reconciliation of the world, what will their acceptance mean but life from the dead?" (Rom. 11:15). In each case, the rejection/acceptance pattern plays itself out to the vicarious benefit of others.

Paul's grasp of the logic of this "pattern of exchange"[55] is so firm that he can write, "I could pray[56] to be myself accursed and cut off from Christ for the sake of my brethren, my kinsmen by race" (Rom. 9:3). The prayer sounds peculiar or even heretical by subsequent Christian standards, but it embodies Paul's fundamental conviction that the people of God do and should manifest in their own lives a conformity to the sacrificial example of Jesus Christ, a pattern which is rooted in the story of Abraham and Isaac and—paradoxically—reenacted in Paul's own time by the "breaking off" of Israel.[57]

Thus, when Paul in Romans 8 quotes the words of Psalm 44,

> For your sake we are being killed all the day long;
> We are reckoned as sheep to be slaughtered

he is sounding a theme that reverberates in complex patterns with and against his letter's other images of election, faithfulness, and sacrifice. This quotation prepares the way for his direct exhortation in Rom. 12:1: "I beseech you then, brothers, through the mercies of God to present your bodies as a living sacrifice."[58] That is what is required of the eschatological people of God; God's elect must suffer and groan along with—and even on behalf of—the unredeemed creation (cf. Rom. 8:18–25).

One intertextual echo that Paul puzzlingly suppresses has remained suppressed in this discussion so far. When Paul uses the psalmist's language to describe the people of God as "sheep to be slaughtered" (*probata sphagēs*), he can hardly fail to hear, sounding in sympathetic harmony, Isaiah's moving account of the fate of the servant of the Lord:

> He was oppressed, and he was afflicted,
> yet he opened not his mouth;

like a lamb that is led to the slaughter, [*probaton epi sphagēn ēchthē*]
and like a sheep that before its shearers is dumb,
so he opened not his mouth.

(Isa. 53:7)

The letter to the Romans is salted with numerous quotations of and allusions to Isaiah 40–55, including several passages that seem to echo the Suffering Servant motif of Isaiah 53 (e.g., Rom. 4:24–25, 5:15–19, 10:16, 15:21). Why, then, does Paul not draw this prophecy into the open and use the servant figure as an explicit basis for his interpretation of Israel, or of the church, or of Jesus? Paul's motive for this evasion or reticence, whichever it is, remains forever lost to us, but the effect of his rhetorical strategy can be readily described. He hints and whispers all around Isaiah 53 but never mentions the prophetic typology that would supremely integrate his interpretation of Christ and Israel. The result is a compelling example of metalepsis: Paul's transumptive silence cries out for the reader to complete the trope. Those who have ears to hear will hear and understand that the people of God, reckoned as sheep to be slaughtered, are suffering with Christ (Rom. 8:17: *sympaschomen*) and thus living out the vocation prophesied for them according the Scriptures. Upon them is the chastisement that makes others whole, and with their stripes is creation healed.[59]

HAS THE WORD OF GOD FALLEN?

The reader who has attended carefully to the echoes of Scripture in the first eight chapters of Romans will hardly be taken by surprise when Paul at last in Romans 9–11 undertakes an explicit discussion of the fate of Israel. This is not some excursus or appendix peripheral to the letter's theme; it is the heart of the matter, around which scriptural echoes have rumbled since Rom. 1:16–17. The psalmist's complaint that the people of God are "sheep to be slaughtered" modulates immediately into Paul's lament over the Jewish people ("my brothers, my kinsmen according to the flesh") in Rom. 9:1–5: "my grief is great and unceasing is the anguish in my heart." If suffering is the vocation of the church as well as the destiny of Israel in exile, the distinction between Israel and church is not sharply drawn for Paul. What was predicated of Israel can now be predicated of the church. There is one crucial distinction, however: Israel has refused to believe the gospel of Jesus Christ. If indeed nothing can separate "us" from the love of God in Christ Jesus our Lord (Rom. 8:39), what is to be said of Israel? Are they included or excluded by Paul's "us"? Has Israel been separated from the love of God? Does their refusal to accept

Jesus Christ as Lord exclude them from the sphere of God's mercy? This is the explosive question that Paul confronts in Romans 9–11.

Despite the difficulty of interpreting many of its individual statements, Romans 9–11 has a clearly recognizable overall structure,[60] broadly analogous to the structure of a lament psalm:

> 9:1–5: Lament over Israel.
> 9:6–29: Has God's word failed? Defense of God's elective purpose.
> 9:30–10:21: Paradox: Israel failed to grasp the word of faith attested by God in Scripture.
> 11:1–32: Has God abandoned his people? No, all Israel will be saved.
> 11:33–36: Doxological conclusion.

The density of scriptural citation and allusion increases dramatically in these chapters, as Paul seeks to show that Israel's unbelief, though paradoxical, is neither unexpected nor final. As Paul reads Scripture, he finds not only manifold prefigurations of God's mercy to the Gentiles but also promises of Israel's ultimate restoration. The purpose of Romans 9–11—as of the letter in its entirety—is to show that God's dealing with Israel and the nations in the present age is fully consistent with God's modus operandi in the past and with his declared purposes. Both the narrative of God's past action and his prophetic promises for the future are found in Scripture. Thus, Romans 9–11 is an extended demonstration of the congruity between God's word in Scripture and God's word in Paul's gospel.

If there is no such congruity, then the word of God has "fallen" (Rom. 9:6), and the God with whom we have to do is either untrustworthy or impotent. The fact that Paul stares this horrifying prospect in the face and wrestles with it at such length is a significant measure both of the discontinuity between Scripture and gospel—why else such hermeneutical exertion?—and of Paul's tenacious integrity in holding to the proposition that unless the Law and the Prophets really do bear witness to the gospel there is no gospel at all.

The intertextual linkages in Romans 9–11, then, are structural girders, not filigrees. If Paul's reading of Scripture in these chapters is flimsy, then there is little hope for his proclamation to stand.

"In Isaac Shall Be Called for You a Seed"

To prove that the word of God has not fallen, Paul first seeks to establish that Scripture has always told stories that illustrate the selective character of God's grace. God's will is disclosed through these stories as *hē kat' eklogēn prothesis tou theou* (God's purpose that operates according to election) (Rom. 9:11). Paul begins the argument by appealing once again to the Genesis narrative about Abraham, this time quoting Gen. 21:12, "In Isaac shall be called for you a seed" (Rom. 9:7b). The quotation, adduced in support of the claim that "not all the children of Abraham are 'seed' "[61] (Rom. 9:7a), is followed by a pesher-style commentary (i.e., a commentary that cites a text line by line and glosses each line with a brief explanation): "That is, not the children of the flesh are children of God, but the children of the promise are reckoned as 'seed' " (Rom. 9:8). Why is Isaac identified with promise rather than flesh? The answer is given by the tidy prooftext of Rom. 9:9, quoting loosely from Gen. 18:10, 14 to show that Isaac's birth was specifically *promised* to Abraham: "According to this time I will come, and there will be for Sarah a son." This quotation reinforces the link between *Isaac* and *promise,* a link supporting the more general claim that God singled out Isaac from among Abraham's children as the special bearer of election.

Thus, Gen. 18:10, 14 becomes the first of many passages tied by Paul in Romans 9 into an intricate intertextual web[62] suspended from Gen. 21:12. The key terms of this programmatic quotation ("In Isaac shall be *called* for you a *seed*") are recapitulated in quotations from Hosea and Isaiah (in Rom. 9:25–29) that create an *inclusio* encompassing verses 6–29. Within this unit, Paul brings forward a series of scriptural illustrations of God's selectivity: Abraham, Sarah, and Isaac (vv. 7–9); Jacob and Esau (vv. 10–13); Moses and Pharaoh (vv. 15–18); the potter and the clay (vv. 20–23). While the first two texts appeal to the patriarchal narratives to show God's elective will in action, the latter two illustrations serve to defend God's right to do as he pleases with his own creation, thus answering once again the recurrent rhetorical question about God's justice (Rom. 9:14: "What then shall we say? Is there injustice with God?").[63]

The metaphor of the potter and the clay—evoking complex echoes from numerous scriptural antecedents[64]—alludes powerfully to a parable of Paul's precursor Jeremiah:

> So I went down to the potter's house, and there he was working at his wheel. And the vessel he was making of clay was spoiled [LXX: "fell"; cf. Rom. 11:11, 22] in the potter's hand, and he reworked it into another vessel, as it seemed good to the potter to do. Then the word of the Lord came to me: "O house of Israel, can I not do with you as this potter has done? says the Lord. Behold, like the clay in the potter's hand, so are you in my hand, O house of Israel." (Jer. 18:3–6)

The potter/clay image must not be read simply as a rebuke to silence impertinent questions, nor is the effect of the allusion—unmarked by Paul—limited to the obvious immediate purpose of establishing God's absolute power to do whatever he chooses (like the five hundred pound gorilla); it also resonates deeply with Paul's wider argument about God's dealings with Israel. The parable suggests that the potter's power is not destructive but creative: the vessel may fall, but the potter reshapes it. The parable, spoken in prophetic judgment upon Israel, is simultaneously a summons to repentance and a reassurance of the benevolent sovereignty of God, persistently enacted in his love for his people Israel even in and through the pronouncement of judgment. Thus, the allusion to Jeremiah 18 in Rom. 9:20–21, like other allusions and echoes earlier in the text, anticipates the resolution of Paul's argument in Romans 11.[65] The reader who recognizes the allusion will not slip into the error of reading Rom. 9:14–29 as an excursus on the doctrine of the predestination of individuals to salvation or damnation, because the prophetic subtexts keep the concern with which the chapter began—the fate of Israel— sharply in focus.

Paul's development of the potter metaphor concludes with a reference to God's preparation of "vessels of mercy." Then, abandoning the metaphor in midsentence and speaking directly of Christian believers, Paul describes these vessels as *"called . . . not only from the Jews but also from the Gentiles"* (Rom. 9:24). With the word *called*, he picks up the motif of vocation sounded in the Genesis quotation with which the unit began (Rom. 9:7), and this motif becomes the hook on which the quotations from Hosea are hung: "as indeed he says in Hosea, 'Him who was "not my people" I will *call* [*kalesō*] "my people," and her who was "not beloved" I will call "beloved." ' . . . 'And in the place where it was said to them, "You are not my people," there sons of the living God shall be *called* [*klēthēsontai*]' " (Rom. 9:25–26, paraphrasing Hos. 2:25 and quoting Hos. 2:1 LXX).

The extraordinary feature of Paul's appeal to this text is not the freedom with which he paraphrases the wording[66] of Hos. 2:25 (2:23 in most English translations)—including his introduction of the link-word *call* into the passage—but the revisionary interpretation that he places on the prophecy. In its original setting, Hosea's prophecy promises the restoration of a sinful and wayward Israel (i.e., the northern kingdom) to covenant relationship with God. Though God provisionally disowns Israel through a dramatic reversal of the covenant promise ("for you are not my people and I am not your God" [Hos. 1:9b, cf. Exod. 6:7]), he ultimately will supersede Israel's covenant violation through his own steadfast love, symbolized by Hosea's faithfulness to the harlot Gomer: "And I will betroth you to me for ever; I will betroth you to me in righteousness [*dikaiosynē*] and in justice, in steadfast love, and in mercy. I will betroth you to me in faithfulness [*pistei*]; and you shall know the Lord" (Hos. 2:21–22 LXX). Where Hosea clings to the poignant hope of Israel's privileged place despite her "harlotry," Paul deconstructs the oracle and dismantles Israel's privilege; with casual audacity he rereads the text as a prophecy of God's intention to embrace the Gentiles as his own people.

This hermeneutical coup is so smoothly executed that Gentile Christian readers might miss its innovative boldness—and therefore its potential scandal to Jewish readers. Paul is *not* arguing by analogy that just as God extended mercy to Israel even when Israel was unworthy so also he will extend grace to the Gentiles. Instead, Paul is arguing that God was speaking through the prophet Hosea to declare his intention to call Gentiles to be his own people. It is as though the light of the gospel shining through the text has illuminated a latent sense so brilliant that the opaque original sense has vanished altogether.

Or has it? If the quotation is a warrant for the claim made in Rom. 9:24 that God has "called us *not only from the Jews* but also from the Gentiles," then a real ambiguity exists in Paul's use of it. On the one hand, the Gentiles are historically the ones who have no claim on being called God's people, in direct contrast to the Jews (cf. Rom. 9:1–5); thus, in the first instance, Paul is reading the prophecy as a promise of Gentile inclusion among God's people (cf. Eph. 2:11–13 and 1 Pet. 2:9–10 for analogous formulations from a Christian point of view). However, the whole argument of Romans 9–11 presupposes that, *para doxan*, the Jews have in fact stumbled or been broken off so that it is now they who are "not my people," despite their birthright. In the scandalous inversions implied by the analogies of Romans 9, it is the Jewish people who stand in the role of Ishmael, the role of Esau, and even the role of Pharaoh. It is they who have experienced hardening and rejection, so that their contemporary situation is exactly analogous to the situation of the unfaithful Israel addressed by Hosea. But if that is so, then may they not also be included in the number of the nonpeople whom God calls and loves? This is exactly the conclusion toward which Paul works in chapter 11 with his discussion of the regrafting of the broken branches and his declaration of the mystery that after the full number of the Gentiles comes in, "all Israel shall be saved" (Rom. 11:25–26). Thus, if in Romans 9 and 10 Paul deconstructs Scripture's witness to Israel's favored status, Romans 11 dialectically deconstructs the deconstructive reading, subverting any Gentile Christian pretension to a position of hermeneutical privilege.

For that reason, some ambiguity hovers about the citation from Isaiah that Paul juxtaposes (Rom. 9:27–28) to his revisionary reading of Hosea. Turning from a prophecy that he construes as an oracle concerning Gentiles, Paul now cites a prophecy about Israel. The introductory formula is a peculiar one, however: "But Isaiah cries out *hyper* Israel" (Rom. 9:27a). Though the preposition *hyper* can sometimes mean "concerning" (equivalent to *peri*; cf. 2 Cor. 1:8), in the idiom of the Greek New Testament it more typically means "on behalf of, for the sake of." If the latter sense were followed, Isaiah's cry might be heard not as a threat, but as a voice of hope: "But Isaiah cries out for the sake of Israel, 'If [*ean*] the number of the sons of Israel[67] be as the sand of the sea, a remnant *will* be saved.' " (The rendering "*only* a remnant will be saved," found in many English versions,[68] is an interpretive paraphrase with no textual basis in any Greek manuscript.) Indeed, if we remember that Paul is adducing prooftexts in support of his claim that God has called vessels of mercy from among Jews and Gentiles alike (Rom. 9:24), it makes much better sense to read the Isaiah prophecy as a positive word of hope rather than as a word of condemnation: the quotation from Hosea proves that God calls Gentiles, and the quotation from Isaiah proves that he calls Jews.[69] This reading would also be fully consistent with Paul's use of the remnant motif in Romans 11, where he employs the notion of the remnant to prove that God has *not* rejected his people.

Finally, in Rom. 9:29, Paul echoes the other key term of the Gen. 21:12 quotation, *seed*, by citing another prophecy of Isaiah that draws together the images of remnant and seed: "If the Lord of hosts had not left [*egkatelipen*] us a seed [*sperma*], we would have become like Sodom, and we would have been likened to Gomorrah." This reference to the elect remnant/seed[70] closes an intertextual circle opened in 9:7 and concludes Paul's demonstration from Scripture that the selective operation of God's will is a truth deeply imbedded in Israel's canonical texts. Only the presence of the seed distinguishes Israel from the archetypal targets of God's wrath.

Has God Abandoned His People?

Romans 11 brings to a climax Paul's wrestling with the question of Israel's status before God. The rhetorical question of Rom. 11:1 articulates the anxious concern that has generated the whole argument: "I say then, has God abandoned his people?" Paul curiously warrants his emphatic denial of this possibility (*mē genoito* [by no means!]) with autobiographical information ("I also am an Israelite, from the seed of Abraham, the tribe of Benjamin"). One would not suppose that Paul's ethnic affiliation could prevent God from abandoning his people; presumably, the implication is that Paul, as a Jew, should never be suspected of suggesting such an appalling idea. (Perhaps he is also anticipating the argument of the following verses by putting himself forward as a notable representative of the "remnant chosen by grace" [Rom. 11:5].) Then, more substantively, he resorts to the language of Scripture to make his point: "God has not abandoned his people [*ouk apōsato ho theos ton laon autou*] whom he foreknew" (Rom. 11:2a). Because Paul supports this climactic affirmation by appealing directly to the story of Elijah (Rom. 11:2b–5), it is easy to overlook that the affirmation is itself an echo of two other scriptural passages, whose original contexts frame Romans 11 instructively.

In 1 Samuel 12, the people, having incurred Samuel's disapproval by asking for a king, implore him to intercede for them: "Pray for your servants to the Lord your God, that we may not die; for we have added to all our sins this evil,[71] to ask for ourselves a king" (1 Sam. 12:19). Samuel responds with a speech that would sound strangely apropos if it were found in Paul's mouth addressing his Jewish kin:

> Fear not; you have done all this evil, yet do not turn aside from following the Lord, but serve the Lord with all your heart. . . . For the Lord will not cast away his people [*ouk apōsetai kyrios ton laon autou*], for his great name's sake, because the Lord has gently received [*proselabeto;* cf. Rom. 14:3, 15:7] you as a people for himself. Moreover, as for me, far be it from me that I should sin against the Lord by ceasing to pray for you [cf. Rom. 9:3, 10:1]. (1 Sam. 12:20–23)

Does Samuel's speech sound in sympathetic harmony behind Rom. 11:2? If so, Paul has changed *kyrios* to *theos*, to make it clear that he is speaking of Yahweh, the God of Israel, not of Kyrios Christos, and he has shifted Samuel's future tense verb into the aorist ("has not cast off," rather than "will not cast off"), to make it clear that he is speaking of an accomplished not-abandonment rather than an anticipated one.

"God will not cast off his people." Exactly the same sentence is found in Ps. 94:14 (93:14 LXX). Here no narrative context is indicated, but the following lines play the theme of which Romans 9–11 is a variation:

> For the Lord will not cast off his people
> [*ouk apōsetai kyrios ton laon autou*],
> And he will not leave [*egkataleipsei*] his heritage,
> Until righteousness [*dikaiosynē*] returns for judgment.

The verb *egkataleipō*,[72] appearing in the line immediately following the psalm line that Paul echoes in Rom. 11:2, is the same verb that occurs in

Isa. 1:9, quoted in Rom. 9:29, and it is etymologically connected with the verb *kataleipō* and the noun *leimma*, used in Rom. 11:4–5 to describe the remnant left by God's elective grace. The interplay of these words can be approximated in English only through recourse to a metaphor from the book trade: "God will not *remainder* his heritage. . . . He has caused seven thousand[73] to *remain* who have not bowed the knee to Baal. . . . So too at the present time there is a *remnant*." Paul's allusion in Rom. 11:2a to Psalm 94 adumbrates the remnant theme that appears in the following sentences. This foreshadowing effect is formally identical to the pattern observed with regard to the use of Psalm 143 in Rom. 3:20 (see pp. 51–52 above): an unvoiced element of the explicitly cited text subliminally generates the next movement of the discourse.

It is difficult to say whether Paul intended to create resonances with 1 Sam. 12:22 and Ps. 94:14 when he wrote straightforwardly that "God has not cast off his people." But whether he intended it or not, the language through which his trust in God found voice was the language of Scripture. It would be inadequate to say that Scripture was *langue* and Paul's discourse *parole*, as though Scripture were merely a pool of lexemes from which Paul draws; rather, Scripture's poetry and narratives materially govern his confession. Scripture's *parole*, already spoken, rebounds and is heard once again in Paul's discourse. Consequently, Paul's sentences carry the weight of meanings acquired through earlier narrative and liturgical utterance. This allusive evocation of earlier declarations of God's faithfulness to Israel covertly undergirds the burden of Paul's overt argument.

Rejoice, Gentiles, with His People

The reading of Romans that has emerged from our examination of the letter's scriptural echoes is confirmed by the conclusion of the letter-body in Rom. 15:7–13, a passage that functions as a *peroratio*, a summation of the letter's themes.

> Receive one another, therefore, just as Christ has received [*proselabeto;* cf. 1 Sam. 12:22] you, for the glory of God. For I am saying that Christ became a servant of the circumcision for the sake of the truthfulness of God [*hyper alētheias theou;* cf. Rom. 3:4,7], in order to confirm the promises given to the fathers [cf. Rom. 4:16] and in order that the Gentiles might glorify God for his mercy,[74] just as it is written,
>
>> Therefore I will praise you among the Gentiles,
>> and I will sing to your name.[Ps. 18:49, 2 Sam. 22:50]

And again he says,

Rejoice, Gentiles, with his people. [Deut. 32:43]

And again,

Praise the Lord, all you Gentiles,
And let all peoples praise him. [Ps. 117:1]

And again Isaiah says,
There shall be a root of Jesse,
And one who rises to rule the Gentiles;
Upon him Gentiles shall hope. [Isa. 11:10]

May the God of hope fill you with all joy and peace in believing, in order that you might abound in hope in the power of the Holy Spirit.

Why does Paul place this florilegium at the end of his letter to the Romans? Clearly, he has saved his clinchers for the end. After much allusive and labored argumentation, Paul finally draws back the curtain and reveals a collection of passages that explicitly embody his vision for a church composed of Jews and Gentiles glorifying God together. Commentators often note that Paul has offered here one quotation from the Pentateuch, one from the Prophets, and two from the Writings, all strung together by the catchword *ethnē*, all pointing to the eschatological consummation in which Gentiles join in the worship of Israel's God: truly the Law and the Prophets are brought forward here as witnesses. As Käsemann remarks, "The Old Testament foreshadowed this message. The recipients of the letter must recognize this agreement with Scripture. An apology could hardly have a more magnificent conclusion."[75] There is no sleight of hand here: Paul rests his case on the claim that his churches, in which Gentiles do in fact join Jews in praising God, must be the eschatological fulfillment of the scriptural vision. If so, then God's Gentile-embracing righteousness, proclaimed in Paul's gospel, really is "promised beforehand through his prophets in holy texts" (Rom. 1:2), and Paul has successfully made his case in defense of the justice of God. That is why these particular quotations are a fitting culmination of the letter's argument.

Even here, however, where the significance of the passages for Paul's case is evident, we will miss important intertextual echoes if we ignore the loci from which the quotations originate. Both of the psalm passages refer not only to Gentiles, but also to God's mercy (*eleos;* Ps. 17:51 LXX, Ps. 116:2 LXX), the attribute for which the Gentiles are said in Rom. 15:9 to glorify God. In neither instance does Paul quote the part of the text that mentions mercy, but the appearance of the word in these passages is hardly a case of blind luck. Paul has presumably selected these passages precisely because they bring references to God's mercy into conjunction with references to praise of God among the Gentiles. In all likelihood, Paul's own discursive formulation in Rom. 15:9a is influenced directly by the Psalm vocabulary. One way of putting this point is to say that Rom. 15:9a is an allusion to the passages quoted in 15:9b and 15:11, an allusion to an original context slightly wider than the explicit quotations.

Ps. 18:49–50, in addition to its references to Gentiles and mercy, voices other themes that echo tantalizingly in Romans. In verse 50, God is described as

> Magnifying the saving deeds [sotērias] of his king
> And performing mercy [eleos] for his Messiah [Christō],
> For David and his seed [spermati] forever.

A reader who remembered these phrases would hear in them an echo creating a satisfying *inclusio* with the letter's opening proclamation about God's son, who was promised in holy texts, "who came from the seed [spermatos] of David, . . . Jesus Messiah [Christou]," who commissioned Paul to preach the obedience of faith among all the Gentiles (Rom. 1:3–5). Indeed, given a messianic reading of the psalm, it is hard to avoid the impression that the "I" who speaks in the verse that Paul quotes must be the Messiah himself,[76] whom Paul would of course identify as Jesus, who now is pictured as praising God among the Gentiles. The quotation, after all, is introduced as a supporting prooftext for a description of something that Christ did (Rom. 15:8), and Paul has just quoted in Rom. 15:3 another psalm (69:9) in which he understands Christ to be the speaker: "The reproaches of those who reproached you fell upon me." Thus, the picture evoked by Paul's quotation of Psalm 18 is very much like the picture painted in Heb. 2:10–13: Jesus stands amidst the congregation of his brothers, singing praise to God. Paul, of course, emphasizes for his purposes not the solidarity of Jesus with the congregation but the fact that the congregation is made up of Gentiles.

The quotation from Deut. 32:43, then, adds a crucial element to the portrait. "Rejoice, Gentiles, *with his people*." The Gentiles do not stand alone around Christ; they are being summoned to join *with* Israel in rejoicing. Here Paul's agreement with the LXX is crucial. The Hebrew text reads, "Gentiles, praise his people," an admonition very different from what Paul finds in the LXX. For Paul's purposes it is wonderfully useful to find a text in which Moses, in his great climactic song at the end of Deuteronomy, includes Gentiles in the company of the people of God.

Similarly, the final text in Paul's catena also envisions a gathering of Gentiles and Jews around the Messiah. The full force of Paul's citation of Isa. 11:10 becomes apparent only when the reader recollects Isa. 11:11–12: "And it shall be in that day that the Lord will purpose to show his hand to be zealous for the remnant of the people that is left [*to kataleiphthen hypoloipon tou laou*] . . . . And he will lift up a sign for the Gentiles, and he will gather the lost ones of Israel, and he will gather the dispersed ones of Judah from the four corners of the earth." Paul quotes only an excerpt that prophesies Gentiles placing their hope in the "root of Jesse," but the quotation also works as an allusion to Isaiah's vision of God's eschatological kingdom in which the lost ones of Israel rejoin these Gentiles in being gathered at the feet of the one whom God has raised up. This allusion in turn forges an intertextual link back to the remnant theme of Romans 11.

As in Romans 9–11, these scriptures project an inversion of the order suggested by Paul's earlier claim that the gospel is the power of salvation to the Jew first and then subsequently to the Greek. Here the Gentiles seem to come in first; that is the anomaly that Paul must explain. Isaiah sings in the background, however. If Gentiles come, can Israel be far behind?

"THE RIGHTEOUSNESS FROM FAITH SAYS"

In surveying the scriptural texts that sound within Paul's discourse in Romans, we have observed an extraordinary—indeed, almost monotonous—thematic consistency. In Romans, Paul cites Scripture not as a repository of miscellaneous wisdom on various topics but as an insistent witness of one great truth: God's righteousness, which has now embraced Gentiles among the people of God, includes the promise of God's unbroken faithfulness to Israel. Virtually every text that Paul cites or alludes to is made to circle around this one theme. It is as though the letter were a great parabola that picks up echoes of Scripture and reflects them all onto a single focal point.

Only after we have followed the trajectory of these echoes and concentrated our attention on the theme to which they incessantly lead can we hope to make some sense out of Rom. 10:5–10, the baffling text with which we began our inquiry in the previous chapter. In an apparently capricious act of interpretation, the reader will recall, Paul seizes Moses' admonition to Israel, warning them to obey the Law without rationalization or excuse (Deut. 30:11–14), and turns it into an utterance of The

Righteousness from Faith, a character who contravenes the manifest sense of Moses' words by transmuting them into a cryptic prophecy of the Christian gospel as preached by Paul.

Such a reading looks on the face of it like a wild and disingenuous piece of exegesis, so much so that embarrassed Christian commentators have with surprising frequency—and perhaps not without a certain disingenuousness of their own—attempted to deny that Paul is actually interpreting Scripture at all. For example, W. Sanday and A. C. Headlam, in their Romans commentary in the International Critical Commentary series—throughout much of the twentieth century the most influential English-language commentary on Romans—argue that "the Apostle does not intend to base any argument on the quotation from the O.T., but only selects the language as being familiar, suitable, and proverbial, in order to express what he wishes to say."[77] More recent critical opinion, however, has tended to acknowledge that Paul is indeed interpreting Scripture; most studies of the passage have either sought to establish some historical background against which Paul's reading looks intelligible[78]—or to explain on theological grounds why Paul's use of the text is legitimate.[79] These studies have turned up some helpful insights, which may be most usefully integrated if we reexamine Romans 10 in light of our foregoing observations about the effects of intertextual echo in Romans.

The Place of Rom. 9:30–10:21 within the Argument

The movement of the discourse through Romans 9–11 is, as we have previously indicated, easy to chart in broad outline. After first expressing dismay over his own people's evident unbelief in the gospel message, which they ought by rights to embrace (9:1–5), Paul argues that their unbelief is not to be construed as evidence that God's word has failed, because God has always dealt with humanity through a dialectic of rejection and election (9:6–29). In 9:30–10:21, Paul gives a fuller account of the anomaly that gives rise to these reflections: "Gentiles who did not pursue righteousness have grasped[80] righteousness, the righteousness from faith, but Israel, pursuing a Law of righteousness, did not attain to the Law" (9:30–31). The remainder of this section of the discourse (9:32–10:21) elaborates this paradox, reflecting on how it came to be, explaining what went wrong. This phase of the argument ends by recapitulating the paradox through Paul's remarkable misreading of Isa. 65:1–2: he splits the oracle down the middle, interpreting the first verse ("I have been found by those who did not seek me; I have become manifest to those who did not ask for me") innova.'vely as a reference to Gentile Christians, and the second verse ("All day long I have stretched out my hands to a disobedient and contrary people"), quite properly, as a reference to Israel.[81] The image of God's persistently outstretched hands, however, foreshadows the final turn of Paul's dialectic, in which God's grace has the last word.[82] In chapter 11, Paul affirms that God remains faithful to his people Israel despite their unbelief and that he will in the end effect their eschatological redemption as he had always promised. In short, Rom. 9:30–10:21 has a parenthetical place in the logic of the argument. While Rom. 9:6–29 and 11:1–32 affirm the unshakeable efficacy of God's word and God's elective will, Rom. 9:30–10:21 pauses in midcourse to describe how Israel has temporarily swerved off the track during an anomalous interval preceding the consummation of God's plan.

Paul's strange interpretation of Deut. 30:12–14 must fit somehow into this train of thought. In other words, this text must for Paul somehow support an explanation—or at least a description—of how Israel and the Gentiles came to switch roles in the drama of election, how Israel, despite its advantages and its intentional pursuit of the "Law of righteousness," failed to grasp the Law's real message. In order to see how Paul's reading of Deuteronomy serves this purpose, it is necessary to set the quotation in context with some care.

The Telos of the Law

In Rom. 9:31–32 Paul describes Israel as failing to attain the Law, despite their concern for works. One hoary interpretive tradition in Christian theology holds that they failed to attain the Law in the sense that they were unable to perform all the commandments perfectly. In the present discussion, however, Paul makes no such claim. The problem is not that they are unable to do what the Law requires: the problem is that they pursue obedience not *ek pisteōs* (through faith) but *ex ergōn* (through works). This suggests that the aim of the Law is actually not perfect performance of works at all, but something else.

Paul contends that his Jewish brothers and sisters have zeal for God, but it is poorly informed zeal. They seek to establish their own righteousness because they are ignorant of the righteousness of God (which, of course, equals the righteousness of faith; cf. 9:30), to which they do not submit—understandably, since they do not know about it (Rom. 10:1–3). But what is this righteousness of God? The answer is given in Rom. 10:4: "For Christ is the *telos* of the Law, for righteousness to everyone who believes." The conjunction *gar* (for) in 10:4 is a crucial logical connective.

This sentence explains what was said in the foregoing sentence: the real aim of the Law, the righteousness of God, *is* Jesus Christ. Strongly established Christian tradition, especially in the Reformation churches, has construed this statement to mean that Christ is the termination of the Law, but this interpretation makes no sense at all in the context of Romans.[83] Paul has already written that the Law and the Prophets bear witness to the righteousness of God (3:21) and that his gospel of righteousness through faith confirms rather than abolishes the Law (3:31), demonstrating through the story of Abraham (Romans 4) that the Law teaches faith-righteousness. What more could he say to make his point clear? The sum and substance of the Torah, according to the whole argument of this letter, is righteousness through faith. That is what Israel failed to grasp, and that is what God's act in Christ now makes evident— to Paul—beyond all possible doubt.

Therefore, Rom. 10:5 and 10:6 must not stand in antithesis to one another. Paul is not playing "the righteousness from the Law" (10:5) off against "the righteousness from faith" (10:6). He is using these terms synonymously, quoting Moses in both verses to support his interpretation.[84] The quotation from Lev. 18:5 ("The person who does these things shall live by them") appears in the argument not because Paul wants to disparage "doing"; indeed, Paul has already argued a few paragraphs earlier (8:1–11) that those who receive the Spirit through Jesus Christ are now enabled to fulfill the righteous intent (*dikaiōma*) of the Law (8:4) and to submit (*hypotassō*) to God's Law.[85] The quotation from Lev. 18:5 appears because of its promise of life for those who heed the Law, a promise fully consonant with the message of Deuteronomy 30 (see especially Deut. 30:15). The efforts of some commentators to drive a wedge between these two texts as though they represented radically different conceptions of righteousness[86] have wrought disastrous consequences for Christian theology.[87]

The exegetical debate is technical and convoluted, but a paraphrase of the passage (Rom. 10:1–6a, 8–9, omitting for the moment the strange comments in 6b–7) can clarify the interpretation proposed here:

> Brothers, the desire of my heart and my prayer to God for the sake of the Jewish people is that they may be saved. For I bear them witness that they have zeal for God, though it is ill-informed. For, because they are ignorant of the righteousness of God and because they seek to establish their own righteousness, they do not submit to the righteousness of God. What is it that they do not know about the righteousness of God? Just this: that Christ is the *telos* of the Torah, for

righteousness to everyone who believes. How can I say that Christ is the *telos* of the Torah? Let me prove it by citing two passages from Torah. Moses writes concerning the righteousness that is from the Torah, that "The person who does these things will live by them" [Lev. 18:5]. What things does he mean? In another place, as Moses writes, this righteousness from faith [equivalent to righteousness from Torah equivalent to righteousness of God] speaks like this: . . . "The word is near you, in your mouth and in your heart" [Deut. 30:14]. What "word" does Moses mean? He is referring to the word of faith, which we also now preach, because if you confess with *your mouth* that Jesus is Lord and believe *in your heart* that God raised him from the dead, you will be saved, i.e., you will find life, just as Moses promised in Lev. 18:5, because you will be obeying the true message of the Law.

Only when the passage is interpreted in this way does its coherence become clear.[88]

There is a sad irony here. Paul agonized over the fact that his Jewish contemporaries failed to understand that Israel's Law pointed to the righteousness of faith; now, Christians make the same tragic error when they fail to acknowledge that the Law and the Prophets bear witness to the righteousness of God and when they think that Torah and Christ are antithetical. It is the same hermeneutical mistake, viewed from the two different sides of the schism that it created.

"In Your Mouth and in Your Heart"

All of this preliminary discussion was necessary in order to establish the conceptual framework within which Paul's peculiar handling of Deut. 30:12–14 must be understood. Paul's fundamental claim is that the Torah proclaims the Christian kerygma. We have seen throughout our consideration of Romans that he reads Israel's Scripture under the guidance of this hermeneutical presupposition, and that his readings of the text frequently achieve their effects through an intricate play of intertextual echoes. Nowhere is this peculiarly poetic mode of interpretation more boldly evident than in Rom. 10:5–10.

When Paul places his Deuteronomy quotation in the mouth of The Righteousness from Faith, he has already provided the decisive clue to his understanding of the text: he is reading Deuteronomy in light of the same hermeneutical framework developed through his interpretations of Hab. 2:4 ("The righteous one shall live by faith") and Gen. 15:6 ("Abra-

ham believed God, and it was reckoned to him for righteousness").
Moses' speech in Deuteronomy, no less than these other biblical texts,
will be read as an expression of faith-righteousness.[89]

In contrast to the Habakkuk and Genesis passages, however, there is
no reference to faith or to righteousness in Deuteronomy 30. How then
does Paul achieve the reading that he proposes? He does it through
tinkering with the text in order to create an impressionistic textual triple-
exposure.

First, he opens the quotation with a phrase extracted from Deut. 8:17,
9:4: "Do not say in your heart." This simple formulation replaces Deut.
30:11, which emphasizes a point uncongenial to Paul, the fact that Moses
is speaking about the accessibility of the commandments of the Law[90]:
"This commandment which I am commanding you today is not grievous,
nor is it far from you. It is not in heaven." Paul tacitly omits these words
and replaces them with the briefer formula from earlier in the text of
Deuteronomy.

This textual substitution does not, however, merely serve the negative purpose of deleting material uncongenial to Paul's case; it also at the
same time introduces echoes that ring in harmony with the positive position that he is developing. Both Deut. 8:17 and 9:4, recalling God's gracious deliverance of them from Egypt and his provision for them in the
wilderness, admonish Israel against complacency after they enter the
land.[91] The former text reads (in the LXX), "Do not say in your heart, 'My
strength and the might of my hand have accomplished for me this great
mighty deed.' You shall remember the Lord your God, for he gives you
the strength to do a mighty deed, even in order that he might establish his
covenant, which the Lord swore with your fathers, as today" (Deut. 8:17–
18). The second text, occurring just a few sentences later, stirs even more
echoes for the reader who listens carefully:

> Do not say in your heart, when the Lord your God drives these na-
> tions [ethnē] out before you, "Because of my righteousness[92] the
> Lord has brought me in to inherit this good land." . . . Not on ac-
> count of your righteousness nor on account of the holiness of your
> heart will you go in to inherit their land, but on account of the im-
> piety of these nations the Lord will destroy them from before you,
> even in order that he might establish his covenant, which he swore
> with your fathers, Abraham and Isaac and Jacob. And you shall
> know today that not on account of your righteousness is the Lord
> your God giving you this good land to inherit, because you are a
> stiffnecked people. (Deut. 9:4–6)

Paul, it seems, has deftly chosen the words "Do not say in your heart" to introduce the discourse of The Righteousness from Faith because these words evoke an earlier word of God to Israel, in which the Lord God warns them against the presumption of their own righteousness and reminds these "stiffnecked" people that the initiative in deliverance and covenant-making is his, not theirs. The message is so apt for Paul's argument in Romans that we are left wondering why he did not go ahead and quote these words rather than delving into his problematical exegesis of Deut. 30:12–14. In fact, however, he leaves his readers only the subtlest allusion to Deuteronomy 8 and 9. Any reader who knows where the words come from will surely smile in recognition of the point; most readers will miss the point altogether.

Perhaps Paul passed up the shot because it was too easy. To make his case by quoting "Do not say in your heart, 'It is because of my righteousness' " would be to end the argument prematurely. He spins a more complex effect by citing the tag phrase from Deut. 9:4—perhaps counting on the reader to finish the sentence—but then shifting ground to a new text in which he also hears faith-righteousness speaking.

The choice of Deut. 30:12–14, with its blunt insistence on doing the commandments, is daring and perhaps deliberately provocative. It would not be easy to find another text in the Old Testament that looks less promising for Paul's purposes. In Deuteronomy, the questions, "Who will go up into heaven for us and receive it for us?" and "Who will cross for us to the other side of the sea and receive it for us?" serve as foils for Moses' assertion of the nearness of the Law. It has already been given to Israel "in the book of this Law" (Deut. 30:10), so there is no need for speculative excurses and inquiries. Yet even here, Paul argues, the speaker is The Righteousness from Faith.[93] His subversive exegesis commands our attention for several reasons.

Adopting an uncharacteristic exegetical format, Paul offers a running line-by-line pesher commentary on the passage. Formally, the method is similar to the exegesis found in the Qumran biblical commentaries (e.g., lQpHab), where the biblical text is treated as a cryptically encoded allegory of the community's own history, apocalyptically interpreted. Materially, however, the commentary in Rom. 10:6–7 takes a distinctive turn as Paul fancifully supposes that the imaginary questers are looking high and low for Christ. They may suppose that they are looking for "the commandment" of the Law (Deut. 30:11), but since Christ is the *telos* of the Law, Paul portrays them as looking for Christ, whether they know it or not. The absurdity of the undertaking is stressed: Christ has already come down from heaven, already been raised up from the dead.[94] God has already done the work in Christ's incarnation and resurrection and needs no help from well-intentioned spiritual questers. The futility of the undertaking mirrors the futility of Israel's seeking to establish their own righteousness and not submitting to God's.

As all commentators notice, Paul's citation of Deut. 30:13 diverges widely from any known textual tradition. Whereas both the MT and the LXX speak of crossing the sea to find the commandment, Paul's citation reads, "Who will go down into the abyss?" This is the sort of divergence from the scriptural text that encouraged Sanday and Headlam to venture the opinion that Paul was not really interpreting Deuteronomy 30. In fact, however, this deviant quotation is not just a careless Pauline paraphrase; it is the third layer of the triple exposure that I mentioned earlier, a textual overlay that is decidedly interpretive in effect. M. Jack Suggs has demonstrated convincingly that Paul's formulation reflects conventions associated with the personified figure of Sophia in Jewish Wisdom tradition.[95] Suggs adduces a number of texts in which heaven and the abyss are symbols of the inaccessibility of Wisdom. For example, in Sir. 24:5 Sophia speaks:

> Alone I have made the circuit of the vault of heaven
> And have walked in the depths of the abyss.

This same tradition appears tellingly in Bar. 3:29–30, which allusively transfers the language of Deut. 30:12–14 onto the figure of Wisdom:

> Who has gone up into heaven and taken her,
> and brought her down from the clouds?
> Who has gone over the sea and found her,
> and will buy her for pure gold?

Paul's filtered citation of Deuteronomy echoes these Wisdom traditions, in which Wisdom is identified with Israel's Torah (cf. Bar. 4:1). Paul's variation on Deut. 30:13 signals to the reader that the text must be heard not only in polyphony with Deut. 8:17 and 9:4 but also with Bar. 3:29–30 and other traditional texts about elusive Wisdom (cf. Job 28:12–14). Suggs is probably correct to suggest that this intertextual fusion serves Paul's christological interpretation of Deut. 30:12–14: "The tension between Gospel and Law is resolved by the identification of Christ with Wisdom-Torah. The apostle hopes in this way to rescue his gospel from the stigma of absolute opposition to the law. . . . The righteousness based on faith does not annul the law but brings it to its true goal, for 'the word of faith which we preach' is Jesus Christ, incarnate wisdom, *telos nomou*." The only trouble with Suggs' insightful argument is that he underplays the allusive character of Paul's textual transformation: he assumes that Paul's transmutation of the Deuteronomy text would have a self-evident argumentative force in the defense of his gospel. In fact, however, only a very subtle reader would make the connections that Suggs makes and draw the appropriate theological conclusions. Paul does not explicitly argue that Christ is to be identified with Wisdom and therefore also with Torah. This fusion occurs in the cave of echo, not at the overt discursive level.

Paul centers his reading of Deut. 30:12–14 on the theme of the *nearness* of the word, rather than on the imperative to do the commandments. He omits from his quotation not only the introductory sentence (Deut. 30:11) but also the last clause of Deut. 30:14: "so that you can do it." With these strategic excisions, his reading of the text drives toward a climax in Rom. 10:8. After the comical portrayal of questers who fret about where to find Christ, Paul states positively what The Righteousness from Faith actually does say: "But what does it say? '*Near* you is the word, in your mouth and in your heart'; that is, the word of faith which we preach." Thus, Paul provocatively reads Deuteronomy 30:11–14 not as a summons to do what the plain superficial sense of the Law requires, but as a summons to discern the true content of the word (*rēma* [that which God has spoken]), which has always been the word of the righteousness of faith. The word that was near to Israel in the Law is identical with the word that is now near in the Christian kerygma.

This revisionary reading of Deut. 30:14, employing the pesher style, treats each phrase of the precursor text as a shorthand cipher for an element of the Christian confession. Paul works out his interpretation in Rom. 10:8–9 by expanding each key term of Deut. 30:14. The result can be diagrammed as follows:

(Rom. 10:8a, quoting Deut. 30:14)	(Rom. 10:8b–9:)
But what does it say?	That is
The word is near you,	the *word* of faith which we preach.
	Because if you confess
in your *mouth*	with your *mouth*
	that Jesus is Lord,
	and if you believe
and in your *heart*	in your *heart*
	that God raised him from the dead,
	you will be saved.

Paul is not merely echoing Deuteronomy. This is an instance of line-by-line rereading, asserting explicitly that the latent sense of the Torah text is now expressed overtly in the gospel.

Thus, Paul's interpretation presupposes what it argues and argues what it presupposes: that the real meaning of Deuteronomy 30 is disclosed not in lawkeeping but in Christian preaching. The argument, at its explicit level, rests on sheer force of assertion. Implicitly, however, the intertextual echoes created by Paul's evocation of Deut. 9:4 and of the Wisdom tradition suggest hauntingly that Paul's reading is less arbitrary than it sounds. From Deuteronomy, Paul echoes the idea that the covenant depends on grace from start to finish rather than on Israel's own righteousness. Echoing Job, Baruch, and Sirach, Paul hints at the notion that the word of God spoken in the Law is identical with the Wisdom of God, who "appeared upon earth and lived among men" (Bar. 3:37)–not as Torah, as Israel's sages affirmed, but in the person of Jesus Messiah.

The Word as Metaphor

> Where shall the word be found, where will the word
> Resound? Not here, there is not enough silence.
> —T. S. ELIOT, "ASH WEDNESDAY"

This account of the effects of intertextual echo in Rom. 10:5–10 should not be read as a defense of Paul's exegesis. It is, rather, an account of the devices whereby a historically outrageous reading gains poetic plausibility. (Whether this intertextual plausibility ought, normatively speaking, to confer upon the reading theological legitimacy is a question beyond the scope of our present deliberations. Readers interested in this issue are referred to the final chapter of this book.) What Paul has in fact done is, simply, to read the text of Deuteronomy 30 as a *metaphor* for Christian proclamation. This particular metaphorical reading seems especially jarring to modern historically sensitive readers. Paul's interpretation of this passage, however, is neither more nor less fanciful than many other scriptural interpretations in Romans. When Paul reads Habakkuk as a proclaimer of justification by faith or interprets Hosea's prophecy to the northern kingdom of Israel as an adumbration of God's calling of Gentiles, the same sort of metaphorical shift takes place: Paul is reading the ancient scriptural text as a trope, which speaks by indirection about his own message and ministry. Romans 10 differs from other cases only in articulating more explicitly the hermeneutical warrant that implicitly authorizes all of Paul's intertextual excursions: the word of God, now present in the Christian gospel, is the same word of God that was always present to Israel in Torah. It was so close to them that they had no need to go looking for it; yet they were unable to hear it.

The function, then, of Rom. 10:5–10 is to intensify the paradox of Israel's unbelief. Paul exposits Deuteronomy in such a way that its latent sense is alleged to be identical with the manifest claims of his own proclamation. The nearness of the word stands in ironic juxtaposition to Israel's deafness. The same people of Israel to whom Moses proclaims the nearness of the word, whose hearts God promises to circumcise (Deut. 30:6), are also the "perverse generation" (Deut. 32:20) who so stir God's anger that Moses pronounces on them the judgment cited by Paul in Rom. 10:19:

> I will make you jealous of those who are not a nation;
> With a senseless nation I will make you angry.

Paul later explains his hope that even this stirring of the Jews to jealousy against Gentile converts will be subsumed into God's design for saving Israel (11:11–14, where the verb *parazēloun* should be heard as an echo of Deut. 32:21). In Romans 10, however, Paul meditates on the mystery of Israel's culpable unresponsiveness to the word in their midst. Behind the quotation of Deut. 32:21 in Rom. 10:19 lingers the—metaleptically suppressed—echo of God's verdict on Israel in Deut. 32:20 (LXX):

> I will turn my face away from them,
> And I will show what will happen to them
> in the last times [*ep' eschatōn*].
> Because they are a perverse generation,
> Sons in whom there is no faith [*pistis*].

CHAPTER THREE

Children of Promise

ECCLESIOCENTRIC HERMENEUTICS

Paul's interpretive strategies, as we have seen throughout his letter to the Romans, refract Scripture in such a way that the church—composed of Jews and Gentiles together—comes into focus as the goal of God's redemptive action. On reflection, however, this account of Paul's hermeneutical procedure might seem to omit a crucial factor: what about the *christological* interpretation of Scripture? After all, Paul's interpretations of the Old Testament are often described as *christocentric*.[1] According to this view, Paul read Scripture as a coded message about Jesus Christ, whose coming was promised by the Law and the Prophets, whose death and resurrection occurred "according to the Scriptures" (1 Cor. 15:3–4). To read Scripture as Paul read it, then, would be to decode its cryptic figurations so as to discover in Jesus Christ the secret meaning of Israel's sacred text. When the evidence is carefully examined, however, remarkably little of his interpretive practice bears a christocentric stamp.

Certainly Paul does sometimes discover christological figurations in Scripture. In 1 Cor. 15:25–27, for example, he alludes to Ps. 110:1 and Ps. 8:6 as prophecies of Christ's enthronement at the right hand of God and ultimate authority over all creation. Thus, Paul offers the earliest documentation of a christological exegesis of these psalms, which seems to have been widely influential in the early church (cf. Mark 12:35–37 and parallels; Acts 2:33–36; Heb. 1:13, 2:5–9; Eph. 1:20–22). The allusive character of Paul's reference to these texts makes it difficult to determine whether he is the originator of this christological reading or whether he is appealing to an already established tradition; the latter is perhaps more likely.

Another notorious instance of christocentric exegesis appears in Gal. 3:16, where Paul insists that the grammatically singular *seed* of Gen. 13:15 (cf. Gen. 17:8, 22:18, 24:7) can refer only to Christ. This exegesis is less perverse than it might appear, depending as it surely does on the linkage of the catchword *seed* to God's promise to David in 2 Sam. 7:12–14: "I will raise up your seed after you, who shall come forth from your body, and I will establish his kingdom. He shall build a house for my name, and I will establish the throne of his kingdom forever. I will be his father, and he shall be my son." This passage treats the singular noun *seed* not as a collective term, but as a reference to a specific royal successor to David; thus, it bears evident potential for messianic interpretation—as attested by its inclusion in a florilegium of messianic prophecies discovered among the Dead Sea Scrolls[2]—and it authorizes, by means of the device of *gezerah shawah,* a messianic reading of other promissory texts in which the key word *seed* appears.[3] Paul can therefore interpret the promise to Abraham's seed as a promise made to the Messiah (*Christos*), who is to be the heir of God's promised blessing.

The same scriptural promise from 2 Sam. 7:12–14 is echoed by the confessional formula in Rom. 1:2–4, which proclaims that the "gospel of God" was promised beforehand in prophetic writings that speak of one who comes from the *seed of David* and is established as *Son of God* by being *raised up* from the dead. Thus, the usual preference of commentators for connecting the prepositional phrase *peri tou huiou autou* (concerning his Son [v. 3]) with the noun *euaggelion* (gospel [v. 1]) is probably erroneous. The phrase should be connected instead with the words that immediately precede it, *graphais hagiais* (holy writings [v. 2]), yielding the translation "the gospel of God, which he promised beforehand through his prophets in holy writings about his Son." By placing this formula, perhaps a fragment of pre-Pauline tradition,[4] in a prominent position at the beginning of Romans, Paul creates the expectation of a christocentric exposition of Scripture. Nonetheless, despite this impressive formal declaration and despite other scattered examples that could be cited (e.g., Rom. 15:3), the letter to the Romans does not carry through this implied program of christological exegesis.

Indeed, in contrast to other early Christian writers, Paul shows relatively little interest in messianic prooftexts. A comparison of the use of Scripture in Romans to the use of Scripture in the Gospel of Matthew or the Gospel of John reveals striking differences on this point. Matthew repeatedly claims—in a sententious formulaic manner—that particular events in the story of Jesus are fulfillments of prophetic predictions: "this all happened to fulfill what the Lord had spoken by the prophet."[5] Simi-

larly, John's relentlessly christocentric Gospel portrays Jesus as the fulfillment of all manner of scriptural symbols, especially those associated with
Israel's worship and festivals: Jesus *is* the Passover lamb, the true temple,
the bread from heaven. By contrast, we rarely find Paul using Scripture to
define the identity of Jesus Christ or to reflect theologically about it.

Perhaps the genre of Paul's surviving writings obviates overt attention to christological prophecy: he writes pastoral letters to Christian
communities, not evangelistic or apologetic treatises. Paul's readers do
not need to be convinced that Jesus was and is the Messiah. In that case,
the messianic exegesis of Scripture might be assumed as the presupposi-
tional background to Paul's interpretations.[6] However, the claim that
Paul's exegetical work is materially governed by a christocentric hermeneutic seems to cut against the grain of much evidence in the letters;
his hermeneutical procedures do not ordinarily produce christological
interpretations of particular Old Testament texts.

Let us ask ourselves a sweeping but simple diagnostic question: when
Paul reads the Bible, what does he find there? On the basis of the evidence
actually supplied by the Pauline letters, what is the characteristic central
theme that comes to expression through Paul's activity of scriptural interpretation? To state the question crudely, if Paul did not use Scripture to
prove that Jesus was the Messiah, what did he use it for?

What Paul finds in Scripture, above all else, is a prefiguration of the
church as the people of God. (By *church*, I mean, of course, not the institu-
tional hierarchy that took shape over time but the community of people
who confess that Jesus Christ is Lord.) This way of reading is not just a
contingent effect of the problems addressed in Romans. In the other
letters also, Paul uses Scripture primarily to shape his understanding of
the community of faith; conversely, Paul's experience of the Christian
community—composed of Jews and Gentiles together—shapes his reading of Scripture. In short, Paul operates with an *ecclesiocentric* hermeneutic.[7]

Gal. 4:21–31, for example, reveals the unexpected working of this
ecclesiocentric hermeneutic. When Paul announces that the story of
Abraham, Sarah, and Hagar is an allegory (4:24a), the reader, conditioned by Paul's earlier adamant identification of Abraham's seed with
Christ (3:16), expects a christological reading of the patriarchal narrative.
But Paul's allegorical reading fails to execute the anticipated identification
of Isaac—Abraham's seed who was offered up as a sacrifice—with Jesus
Christ.[8] Instead, Paul reads Isaac as a prefiguration of the church: "Now
we,[9] brethren, like Isaac, are children of promise" (4:28). The Christian
community, as "children of the free woman" (4:31), constitutes the anti-

type, the fulfillment of the figure, the true meaning of Scripture. Christ is not even mentioned in Paul's interpretation.[10] What are we to make of this state of affairs? I contend that this Galatians allegory is no anomaly; rather, it discloses an essential aspect of Paul's approach to Scripture.

In the following pages I explore selected passages in which Paul finds Scripture to prefigure the eschatological community. I begin with a consideration of two texts in which he posits a typological correlation between the church and Israel's wilderness generation (2 Cor. 8:8–15, 1 Cor. 10:1–22). Then, after examining Paul's treatment of the Abraham story in Gal. 3:6–14, I return for a closer look at the puzzles posed by the allegory of Gal. 4:21–31. These samples of ecclesiocentric reading pose two questions of considerable theological gravity.

First, what does Paul's use of the scriptural texts suggest about his understanding of the relation between the church and Israel? If Paul's hermeneutic is ecclesiocentric, how does he come to terms with the fact that the Old Testament writings describe and address Israel? Does he think of the church as organically continuous with Israel or as having superseded it? We saw in Romans that he argued passionately for organic continuity. Was this a late development, a concession elicited by Jewish challenges to his Gentile mission?[11] Or was it a commitment structurally imbedded in his use of Scripture from the first? Here we must take into account not only Paul's explicit assertions about this problem but also the implications of his exegetical methods. For example, does typological interpretation of Scripture highlight the abiding theological importance of Israel's history, or does the antitype in a promise/fulfillment scheme effectually annihilate the type?

Second, what is the relation of Paul's ecclesiocentric hermeneutical practice to his christological beliefs? Is Paul's reading strategy incongruous with fundamental elements of his own kerygma? Or is there an overarching theological structure that reconciles them?

ISRAEL IN THE WILDERNESS

Paul has a disconcerting habit of adducing scriptural prooftexts whose pertinence to his argument is not immediately evident. In some cases the logic of the quotation depends on a preexisting conceptual/theological structure, presupposed both by Paul and by his intended readers but not explained in the text. The convention of reading the lament psalms as prophetic anticipations of the Messiah's suffering provides a good illustration of this phenomenon (e.g., Rom. 15:3, quoting Ps. 68:10 LXX). In other cases, however, he appeals abruptly—and apparently spontaneously—to a text whose supportive function in his argument can be discerned only by a reader who follows Paul's intuitive leap; he suggests a correspondence but does not sketch it in, leaving that task to the reader. The mode of discourse is not merely elliptical (requiring the reader to fill in some obvious missing steps) but metaleptic: the figurative effect of the quotation is to establish a resonant interplay of significations between Scripture and the text that Paul is creating, in such a way that crucial elements of the precursor text are hushed rather than voiced. An instance of this interplay of significations is found in Paul's citation of Exodus 16:18 in 2 Cor. 8:15.

He Who Gathered Little Had No Lack

In 2 Corinthians 8, Paul appeals for generous contribution to his relief-offering to the Jerusalem church: the Corinthians, out of their material abundance, should supply the want of others so that there might be equality. This exhortation is capped by an abrupt citation of a prooftext from Exod. 16:18: "As it is written, 'He who gathered much had nothing over, and he who gathered little had no lack' " (2 Cor. 8:15). The intertextual reference calls attention to itself ("As it is written") and cries out for interpretation. How exactly does the Exodus quotation support Paul's argument?

Opinions of the critics have ranged from Lietzmann's dismissive view[12] that Paul is superficially interested in the wording (*Wortlaut*) of the text without reference to its original meaning to A. T. Hanson's oversubtle opinion that Paul finds a cryptic christological typology in the quotation (the manna incident is "a type of God's self-giving in grace").[13] Hanson's interpretation, in effect a reading of 2 Cor. 8:15 through lenses colored by John 6, illustrates the lengths to which interpreters will go to maintain the hypothesis of Paul's consistently christological hermeneutic. Most, however, are content to take the "bottom-line" interpretive approach exemplified by Plummer, who finds the point of the analogy in the simple maxim, loosely illustrated by the manna story, that God intends equality among his people: "The quotation hardly illustrates more than the idea of equality of some sort."[14]

The apparent logical difficulty with the prooftext, as Plummer notes, is that the Exodus story neither commands nor narrates any sharing of goods among the people: the equality is imposed through God's miraculous dispensation. Indeed, one might use the same story to argue a position diametrically opposed to Paul's. Why worry about sharing goods if God will provide miraculously for those in need? Thus, a literalistic objector could protest that Paul's appeal to the story is unpersuasive and illogical: how can Paul turn an account of supernatural divine grace into an authorization for mutual sharing in the church? Consequently, some commentators have defended Paul by downplaying the connection of the Exodus quotation to the narrative from which it is taken.

In order to make sense of Paul's handling of the quotation of Exod. 16:18, however, greater, not less, attention to the original narrative—along with its subsequent interpretation in Deuteronomy—is required. In Exodus 16 the manna story already contains a definite, though implicit, hortatory element. Moses tells the people that they are to gather only as much of the manna as they can eat on a daily basis; they are not to keep any of it overnight. Some, apparently trying to plan prudently for the future, disregard Moses and try to save some of the manna. The result: "it bred worms and became foul, and Moses was angry with them" (Exod. 16:20). Moreover, in Exod. 16:4–5 and 16:22–30 we learn that the prohibition on gathering more than a single day's supply is suspended for the day before the Sabbath. In order to permit punctilious Sabbath observance, God permits gathering a double portion on the sixth day and miraculously allows the perishable manna to last an extra day. Those who go out on the Sabbath looking for manna find none and receive Moses' scolding. Thus, the whole story becomes—within the text of Exodus—a legendary example story that seeks to reinforce Sabbath observance.

The Deuteronomist's reminiscence of the story (Deut. 8:2–3) generalizes from the specific point about the Sabbath to the inference that the wilderness experience was not only God's test of Israel's obedience (cf. Exod. 16:4) but also a divine pedagogical device:

> And you shall remember all the way which the Lord your God has led you these forty years in the wilderness, that he might humble you, testing you to know what was in your heart, whether you would keep his commandments or not. And he humbled you and let you hunger and fed you with manna, which you did not know, nor did your fathers know; that he might make you know that man does not live by bread alone, but that man lives by everything that proceeds out of the mouth of the Lord.

Thus Deuteronomy, interpreting manna as a metaphor for the word of God, reads the story as a lesson about Israel's absolute dependence on God, which above all else ought to be acknowledged through absolute obedience to Torah.[15]

Paul, extending Deuteronomy's interpretive trajectory, ignores the theme of Torah observance but develops new inferences from the theme of dependence. One way of putting this point would be to say that Paul interprets the story of Exod. 16:14–21 without reference to the covenantal nomism in which the story is framed both in Exodus and Deuteronomy. Nor does he adopt the strategy of Philo, who allegorizes the story by treating manna as a figure of divine wisdom, or of the Gospel of John, which interprets Exodus 16 christocentrically, reading manna as a typological prefiguration of "the true bread that comes down from heaven," Jesus.[16]

Instead, Paul sees in this manna story an economic parable whose moral is that God provides for those who rely on him for their daily bread, taking no thought for the morrow. Hoarding is both unnecessary and an affront to God, who is perfectly capable of providing abundantly for those who trust him (cf. Paul's explicit development of this theme in 2 Cor. 9:8– 12). The narrative, without direct exhortation to the reader, posits and commends a value system in which radical dependence on God is good and stockpiling goods is bad. Consequently, Paul can use the manna story to good effect in depicting the Corinthians' material "abundance" (2 Cor. 8:14) as a superfluous store that could and should be made available to supply "the wants of the saints." (Cf. the warning in Deut. 8:11–20 about the dangers of complacency that can accompany material prosperity.) Thus, his application of the story taps and draws out hermeneutic potential that is already fairly oozing out of the Exodus narrative—or, more precisely, Paul taps Exodus 16 and then walks away, leaving the reader to draw out the sap. If we as readers demand our significations drawn, processed, and canned for sale, we will miss the sweetness here.

The trouble with cautious interpretations like Plummer's is that they fail to register the full range of resonant significations evoked by Paul's metaleptic use of quotation. It is certainly true that Paul uses Exod. 16:18 as an illustration of God's intention for equality among his people; however, the impact of the story can hardly be reduced to a bare maxim. The quotation does not just state a principle of equality; rather, by implicitly likening the Gentile Corinthian church to Israel in the wilderness, it suggests an extensive series of suppressed correspondences—silent echoes—that Paul chooses to leave unexplored here. Israel redeemed and graced, Israel as pilgrim people, Israel grumbling and unfaithful: here is the original story that is now played out again in the experience of the church. Elsewhere, Paul pursues and develops the figure (cf. 1 Cor. 10:1–13); here in 2 Cor. 8:15 his pithy quotation, without even mentioning Moses or manna or Israel, rings like a tuning fork struck and balanced on a sounding surface. Little is said, much suggested: this is the trans-umptive imagination at work. Paul gathers little of the text of Exodus, but he comes away with no lack of significance.

Shall We Provoke the Lord to Jealousy?

Of course, not all of Paul's references to Scripture work in such a subtly suggestive fashion. An interesting contrast to the metaleptic use of quotation in 2 Cor. 8:15 is provided by the cognate passage 1 Cor. 10:1–13. (Indeed, the allusive technique of 2 Cor. 8:15 is rendered feasible as a rhetorical strategy by Paul's explicit elaboration of the Israel/church ty-pology in the earlier letter.)[17] There, explicitly declaring that Israel's expe-riences in the wilderness happened "as types" (*typikōs*) for the instruction of his own generation of Christians ("upon whom the ends of the ages have come"), Paul fancifully explores the figurative possibilities inherent in the imaginative act of reading Exodus as metaphor for early Christian experience: the Israelites were "baptized into Moses in the cloud and in the sea" (an imaginative construction on the analogy of Christian baptism into Christ in water and Spirit),[18] they consumed "spiritual" (*pneu-matikon*) food and drink (thus prefiguring the Christian Eucharist), and they were followed by a "spiritual rock," which Paul—in a startling stroke—identifies with Christ.

Here again the argumentative purpose is deliberative, seeking to per-suade the readers to action: the fanciful analogies allow Paul to make the serious point that participation in spectacular spiritual experiences does not relieve the people of God from ethical responsibility (vv. 6–13). In contrast to the allusive 2 Corinthians passage, however, the rhetorical strategy is entirely different: in 1 Corinthians 10 we find the sort of "re-lentless pursuit of further figuration" that Hollander observes in the metaphysical conceit.[19] Rather than sprinkling his readers with echoes and whispers, Paul immerses them in explicit and startling figurative claims; the effect of the passage is achieved through an outpouring of explicit figurations. Each of these figurations, however, considered indi-vidually, bears only slight "assertorial weight."[20] Paul's metaphors should not be pressed. He does not mean, at the level of literal statement, that Moses passed out baptismal certificates or that theologians should debate whether Christ was igneous, metamorphic, or sedimentary.

While the figurative elaboration is explicit, however, the actual use of scriptural quotation is not extensive. The only direct quotation in the argument is the citation in verse 7 of Exod. 32:6: "The people sat down to eat and drink and rose up to play." The other wilderness episodes are evoked by Paul's summarizing allusions. This observation should remind us how inadequate it is to restrict consideration of Paul's use of Scripture to the passages that he quotes explicitly. Israel's story, as told in Scripture, so comprehensively constitutes the symbolic universe of Paul's discourse that he can recall the elements of that story for himself and his readers with the sorts of subtle gestures that pass between members of an interpretive family.[21]

Why, then, does Paul cite this single verse from Exodus when his allusions to Israel's wilderness experience have already set the stage clearly? And why quote a passage from Exodus when the incidents described in the catalogue of errors in verses 6–10 seem otherwise to allude to the narrative of Numbers? (See Num. 14:26–35, 25:1–9, 26:62, 21:5–9, 16:41–50.) Wayne Meeks has proposed that the Exodus quotation, taken from the golden calf episode, is actually the foundation ("midrashic basis") on which the "homily" of verses 1–13 has been constructed.[22] The eating and drinking are interpreted—with ironic effect—not as a reference to the feasting that accompanied Israel's idolatrous worship of the golden calf (this is of course the meaning of the text in the immediate narrative setting of Exodus 32) but as a retrospective allusion to the eating and drinking of the manna and water that God had supplied in the desert. Thus 1 Cor. 10:1–4 elaborates on the first clause ("The people sat down to eat and drink"), and verses 6–10 elaborate on the second ("and rose up to play"). Meeks labors to demonstrate how the verb *paizein* (play) can be construed within the conventions of midrash to include all the sins listed in verses 6–10, but he does not remark on the rhetorical effect created by Paul's referential transference of the first clause.[23] The slap-in-the-face audacity of the people's idolatry is underscored by Paul's device of reading the eating and drinking as a reminiscence of the earlier narrative of God's gracious provision.

Paul's quotation from Exodus, by coaxing the reader to recall the golden calf story, links the present Corinthian dilemma (whether to eat meat offered to idols) to the larger and older story of Israel in the wilderness. This metaphorical act creates the imaginative framework within which Paul judges—and invites his readers to judge—the proper ethical response to the problem at hand. Of course, this rhetorical strategy depends on the reader's acquiescence to the fitness of the elaborate Israel/church correspondence created by the metaphor, a point to which we shall return shortly. The Exodus quotation anchors the discourse at the point of its central concern (idolatry) and does so in a way that permits the poetic expansion of Paul's germinal metaphorical intuition into a metaphysical conceit, spanning the experiences of Israel and church with multiplex analogies.

The Israel/church conceit continues to play through Paul's direct pastoral exhortations in verses 14–22.[24] In verse 14, he pointedly states the lesson to be drawn from the typology of verses 1–13: "Therefore, my beloved, shun the worship of idols." But this summarizing exhortation does not signal an end to Paul's development of the figure. In verse 18, he summons it again, inviting the Corinthians to cast their minds back over his account of the wilderness story: "Look at Israel according to the flesh." The rhetorical questions and answers in verses 18b–20a, with their present tense verbs, not only generalize the application of the figure but also project the action of the golden calf worshippers onto the screen of present experience: "Are not those who eat the sacrifices partners in the altar? What am I saying? That idol meat is anything or that an idol is anything? No, I am saying that what they sacrifice they offer to demons and not to God." The last sentence echoes the song of Moses in Deut. 32:17: "They sacrificed to demons and not to God, to gods whom they had not known." Thus, Paul sees the Corinthian controversy about idol meat (v. 19) in double exposure with Israel's wilderness idolatry.

Paul's intertextual figuration proved opaque to many subsequent Christian readers. Failing to recognize the allusion to Deut. 32:17, some scribes tried to clarify the sense of 1 Cor. 10:20 by supplying the words *ta ethnē* as subject of the clause. These words ultimately gained a place in the Textus Receptus and are still found in the RSV rendering: "what *pagans* sacrifice they offer to demons and not to God." This clarification, however, muffles the wit of Paul's trope. Happily, recent critical editions of the Greek text have rectified the matter by dropping the gloss from the text.[25]

A similar double-exposure use of the golden calf episode as a metaphor for pagan idolatry appears in Rom. 1:23 ("They became fools and exchanged the glory of God for images resembling mortal man or birds or animals or reptiles"),[26] this time through an echo of Ps. 106:19–20:

> They made a calf in Horeb
> and worshiped a molten image.
> They exchanged the glory of God
> for the image of an ox that eats grass.

Here the double exposure plays a strategic role in Paul's argument: by describing the spiritual blindness of Gentiles in language borrowed from the psalmist's account of Israel's wilderness idolatry, Paul cocks the spring of the rhetorical trap that he will spring in Rom. 2:1–3:20.[27] Jews have no excuse for judging pagans, because Jews as well as Gentiles stand under God's just sentence of universal condemnation; there is no distinction. Because there is no distinction, the golden calf story becomes a parable of the human condition apart from the gospel, a condition of self-destructive idolatry.[28]

The culmination of Paul's artful development of the wilderness conceit appears in 1 Cor. 10:22: "Shall we provoke the Lord to jealousy [parazēloumen]? Are we stronger than he?" Still echoing here is Moses' song, which presents God saying: "They provoked me to jealousy [parazēlōsan] with what is no god; they angered me with their idols" (Deut. 32:21).[29] Thus, Paul seizes on Deuteronomy 32 to round off the discussion, because its reminiscence of the wilderness tradition already drives in the direction of hortatory application of the story. There is nothing distinctively Christian in the lessons that Paul draws from the Scripture that he cites here. Deuteronomy has already performed the imaginative act of turning the exodus into a paradigm for Israel's future experience; consequently, Paul's typological reading of the story is nothing other than a fresh performance within Israel's long-established poetic-theological tradition.

If indeed Paul is reading the wilderness story through the lens of Deuteronomy 32,[30] one puzzling feature of his conceit turns out to be more explicable. Why does he identify the rock with Christ? The Hebrew text of Deuteronomy 32 repeatedly ascribes to God the title "the Rock" (vv. 4, 15, 18, 30, 31). Though the LXX—regrettably for Paul's purposes—eliminates the metaphor, translating each of these references with the generic theos, Paul surely knows the tradition.[31] However, since he is writing to Greek readers who would not know the Hebrew text, he cannot quote Deuteronomy 32 to support his assertion. To explain to the Corinthians the difference between their Greek Bible and its Hebrew Vorlage would interrupt Paul's argument.[32] In any case, the identification of the rock with Christ is a parenthetical remark, an embellishment of the Israel/church trope. Consequently, rather than digressing to explain the grounds for his imaginative leap, he just leaps.

The leap creates an extraordinarily interesting case of metalepsis: the trope of 1 Cor. 10:4 is fully intelligible only as a transformed echo of a text cited later in the chapter; moreover, even if the text were explicitly quoted in the language known to Paul's readers, the echo effect would still not be audible. In this case, it is doubtful that Paul's readers could have traced the image back to its source in Deuteronomy 32. The Rock echo lies entombed in a Hebrew subtext.

THE ISRAEL/CHURCH TYPOLOGY

Paul's linking of church and Israel in 1 Corinthians 10 is a locus classicus for the discussion of typology not only in Christian theology but also in the Western literary tradition. Indeed, Paul's use of the terms *typoi* and *typikōs* in this passage (cf. also Rom. 5:14)—terms not bearing a standard technical sense in Greco-Roman rhetorical theory[33]—laid the foundation on which later tradition constructed a distinction between typology and allegory as modes of figurative reading. Recognizing that typology was probably not a rhetorical category known to Paul, some scholars have interpreted the term *typoi* in this passage to mean "warnings"; indeed it is so translated by the RSV.[34] This translation, however, fails to take into account not only Paul's use of the same term in Rom. 5:14—which surely does not mean that Adam is a "warning" of Christ—but also the character of the correspondence posited by the metaphors of 1 Cor. 10:1–4. The admonitory function of the passage depends upon the imaginative device of reading Israel's story not just as an instructive example but as a prefiguration of the Christian church with its sacraments.

This hermeneutical strategy of typology, however, appears to introduce grave theological difficulties. If Israel's story is a metaphor for Christian experience, has Paul so usurped the meaning and claims of the precursor story that he has in effect annihilated it, deprived it of a right to independent existence? The comments of Herbert Marks describe the problem: "The Israelites, 'baptized into Moses' but still liable to destruction, are important only insofar as readers of scripture are capable of seeing in their predicament a prefiguration of their own situation. . . . [Paul] suggests, more boldly than the *pesharim* or their New Testament counterparts, that the biblical events were recorded in their written form for the specific purpose of eliciting the interpretation he gives them."[35] Does the Pauline Israel/church typology annihilate Israel and subordinate Scripture to Paul's own belated conceptions? Does Paul's ecclesiocentric hermeneutic finally—whether intentionally or not—wrest the Scriptures from Israel?

These Things Happened as Types

Paul introduces the typology by addressing the Corinthians as "brethren" and calling their attention to the experiences of "our fathers."[36] In what sense are the Israelites of the exodus the fathers of the Gentile Corinthians? The oddity of the idea has sometimes been used to buttress a hypothesis that the opening verses of 1 Corinthians 10 are a preformed unit of Jewish Christian midrash inserted by Paul at this point in the letter.[37] Even if that doubtful theory should be correct—indeed, *especially* if it is correct—Paul's use of the midrash in this pastoral situation executes a crucial rhetorical maneuver by addressing his Gentile Corinthians as children of Israel.

That this is a matter of theological conviction for Paul, not just an unreflective use of an early Jewish Christian tradition, is suggested by an unguarded turn of phrase two chapters later, as he opens a new topic of discussion: "Now concerning spiritual gifts, brethren, I do not want you to be uninformed. You know that when you were Gentiles [*hote ethnē ēte*], you were led astray to dumb idols, however you may have been moved" (12:1–2). The casual imperfect tense of his description (*ēte*) indicates that Paul thinks of the Corinthian Christians as Gentiles no longer; they have been incorporated into Israel. Exactly the same pattern of thought operates here as in the grafting metaphor of Rom. 11:17–24: Gentile Christians are branches grafted on "to share in the richness of the olive tree" (Israel). The incorporation has occurred, of course, not through their becoming Jewish proselytes, which would entail adopting the praxis of Torah observance, but through faith and baptism.

Elsewhere, where the relation of Jew and Gentile in Christ is the point at issue, Paul will insist that uncircumcised Gentile believers participate by faith along with Jewish believers as true children of Abraham (cf. Romans 4 and Gal. 3:6–14). Furthermore, he can say that in Christ the distinction between Jew and Gentile has been overcome (Gal. 3:28, 1 Cor. 12:13; for a later and more explicit outworking of this insight, see Eph. 2:11–22). But the division has been overcome in a way that claims for his Gentile churches a fundamental continuity with Israel and its story. That is why Paul can describe this new community of Gentile and Jewish believers as "the Israel of God" (Gal. 6:16).

But what of Paul's reference to *Israēl kata sarka* (1 Cor. 10:18)? Does this imply that the old fleshly Israel has been replaced by a new spiritual Israel? By no means. First Corinthians 10 should not be read as unqualified deprecation of the historical Israel. The description of Israel as fleshly appears in the context of Paul's specific allusion to the golden calf story: he is discussing Israel's fall into idolatry at a particular point in the narrative. Does Paul think that the church is now a new Israel *kata pneuma* that could never fall into such errors?[38] If so, the warnings of 1 Corinthians 10 would be entirely superfluous. Indeed, in 1 Cor. 3:1–4 he specifically castigates the Corinthians for being fleshly—an *ekklēsia kata sarka*. It is no accident that Paul never uses expressions such as "new Israel" or "spiritual Israel." There always has been and always will be only one

Israel. Into that one Israel Gentile Christians such as the Corinthians have now been absorbed.

For that reason, Paul can deploy the words of Deut. 17:7 (LXX) as a direct word of exhortation to the Corinthians to guard the purity of their community: "Drive out the evil person from among you" (1 Cor. 5:13).[39] No introductory formula intrudes between Moses and the Corinthians, no conjunction weakens the command to a simile. Paul could have written, "Just as Moses commanded Israel to drive out the evil person, so you too should practice church discipline by breaking off table fellowship with flagrant offenders." But he did not write in this way. The scriptural command is treated as a self-evidently valid word addressed immediately to these Gentiles, who are thereby encouraged to assume an extraordinarily daring hermeneutical posture: they are to stand with Israel and join in the covenant confession: "The Lord our God made a covenant with us in Horeb. Not with our fathers did the Lord make this covenant, but with us, who are all of us here alive this day" (Deut. 5:2–3). Only for readers who stand within this covenant community does the immediacy of Paul's appeal to Deut. 17:7 make sense. Of course, in the absence of overt signals of citation, the actual readers at Corinth might well overlook a quotation so seamlessly joined to Paul's pastoral directives. Paul's admonition is clear even for a reader who has never heard of Deuteronomy and who has no inkling of belonging to Israel. In this instance, direct quotation becomes an allusive trope: only the reader who recognizes the source of the words will grasp the bold theological proposal implied by Paul's metaphorical act of addressing Corinthian Gentiles as children of the covenant.

The implicit claim of 1 Cor. 5:13 is made explicit in the metaphorical structure of the typology in 1 Cor. 10:1–22: the relation between Israel and church is one of positive correspondence, not antithesis. Paul does not point to Israel's unfaithfulness in order to gloat over it; rather, he warns his readers that they stand in precisely the same situation. Nowhere in the text is there a hint of a claim that the church stands in some relation of superiority to the wilderness generation, or that the church has superseded Israel. Indeed, such notions would undermine precisely the point that the typology is designed to serve.

That is surely one reason for Paul's fanciful reading of Christ back into the exodus: if Christ was present to Israel in grace and judgment just as he is now present to the church, the Corinthians have no remaining ground for supposing themselves to possess an immunity from judgment that Israel did not possess. There is no distinction: just as Israel in the wilderness was tempted to worship the golden calf, so the Corinthians are tempted to participate in pagan temple feasts. In both cases, Christ is present; in both cases, those who tempt the Lord will incur wrath. Paul's entire reading of the exodus story is metaphorical; to extend the conceit by a metaphorical equation (stimulated by Deuteronomy 32) of the rock with Christ sharpens the admonitory force of the typology by rendering its analogies more comprehensive.[40]

If this analysis of the relation between parenesis and poiesis is correct, it confirms the hypothesis that Paul's hermeneutic is not christocentric in this passage. He does not begin with the postulate that the rock is Christ and then infer a typological correspondence between Israel and the church. Rather, the Israel/church metaphor is the generative poetic insight from which the identification of the rock with Christ is an imaginative inference.

These observations must be underscored because so much commentary on typology—among literary critics and biblical critics alike—has veered in a very different direction, as exemplified by Eric Auerbach, whose learned essay "Figura" has often defined the terms of the discussion. While acknowledging that Paul shares with other "Judaeo-Christians" an interest in discovering "prefigurations and confirmations of Jesus in the Old Testament," Auerbach thinks that in Paul

> these Jewish conceptions were combined with a pronounced hostility to the ideas of the Judaeo-Christians. . . . Those passages in the Pauline Epistles which contain figural interpretations were almost all written in the course of Paul's bitter struggle in behalf of his mission among the Gentiles; many are answers to the attacks and persecutions of Judaeo-Christians; nearly all are intended to strip the Old Testament of its normative character and show that it is merely a shadow of things to come. His whole figural interpretation was subordinated to the basic Pauline theme of grace versus law, faith versus works: the old Law is annulled; it is shadow and *typos*.[41]

The telling detail in this extraordinary caricature of Paul is that Auerbach's key image of the Old Testament as "shadow of things to come" is derived not from Paul, but from Hebrews (Heb. 10:1), which he apparently regards as a Pauline Epistle!

Indeed, the typological strategy in the Letter to the Hebrews is relentlessly christocentric and relentlessly supersessionist. Consider the following samples:

> [Jesus] was faithful to him who appointed him, just as Moses also was faithful in God's house. Yet Jesus has been counted worthy of as much

more glory than Moses as the builder of a house has more honor than the house. (Heb. 3:2–3)

But as it is, Christ has obtained a ministry which is as much more excellent than the old as the covenant he mediates is better, since it is enacted on better promises. For if that first covenant had been fault-less, there would have been no occasion for a second. (Heb. 8:6–7)

See that you do not refuse him who is speaking. For if they [i.e., the Israelites at Sinai] did not escape when they refused him who warned them on earth, much less shall we escape if we reject him who warns from heaven. (Heb. 12:25)

The Letter to the Hebrews builds its typology on the rhetorical ground structure of inference from the lesser to the greater. The above quotations illustrate the phenomenon of escalation or heightening, often described as a defining characteristic of typology.[42] The antitype is much greater than the type; it "fulfills and annuls" the work of the "precursor."[43]

A comparison of these ideas to 1 Corinthians 10, however, shows how strikingly absent all such notions are from Paul's text. Here there is no hint that the Christian sacraments are greater or more spiritual than the spiritual food and drink of Israel in the wilderness. There is no hint that Israel's idolatry was a consequence of some flaw in the forms whereby God's grace was mediated to them. There is no hint that the Corinthians' knowledge of God in Christ places them in a better or more secure posi-tion, nor that their defiance of God's greater grace will produce a fate still more ghastly. To the contrary—let it be said again—the point of Paul's metaphor depends on seeing Israel and church as pilgrim people who stand in different times, different chapters of the same story, but in identical relation to the same gracious and righteous God.

This interpretation does not, however, dissolve all distinction be-tween ancient Israel and the church of Paul's time. The clue that forces us to maintain a distinction appears in 1 Cor. 10:11: "Now these things happened to them *typikōs*, but they were written for our instruction, upon whom the ends of the ages have arrived." Paul could not write this sentence if he were still operating within the Deuteronomic symbol struc-ture that treats the exodus as definitive paradigm for Israel's continuing life. Does this dictum mean, then, as Marks contends, that Israel's story has been swallowed up by Paul's revisionary interpretation of it? If so, then Paul's hermeneutic would be supersessionist after all. If 1 Cor. 10:11 is a statement of hermeneutical principle, how are we to balance its claim of privileged perspective against our foregoing exegetical argument that established the fundamental identity between church and Israel?

We must give due weight to the apocalyptic perspective of Paul's hermeneutical dictum. He does believe himself to be living in the final age toward which the eternal purpose of God has been aiming from the beginning of time. To return to the story/book metaphor, we might say that Paul sees himself and his churches enacting the events of the final chapter, whose conclusion, the parousia, can be no more than a few pages away. His perspective from within this final chapter allows him to read the story whole from the standpoint of its ending, thus perceiving correspondences and narrative unities that would have been hidden from characters in the earlier chapters of the story, as well as from even the most perceptive readers before the climactic peripeteia of the crucifixion and resurrection of Jesus Messiah. This astonishing event, completely unpredictable on the basis of the story's plot development, is nonetheless now seen as the supremely fitting narrative culmination, providing unforeseen closure to dangling narrative themes and demanding a reconfiguration of the *dianoia*, the reader's grasp of "what the story is all about."[44] The rapidly unfolding denouement of this story finds Paul carrying forward the paradoxical message of the crucified Messiah in such a way that a correspondingly paradoxical result follows: through trusting in Christ, Gentiles come to worship the God of Israel.

None of this, however, implies that the events of earlier chapters, such as the Exodus, are insignificant or meaningless in their own right. If later events disclose foundational patterns, of which the earlier events may now be seen as anticipations, this means that the earlier events are themselves more rather than less laden with significance. The exodus events happened, Paul asserts, to the fathers in the wilderness in such a way that they can aptly serve as instruction for later generations, as Deuteronomy also proclaims. This does not mean that their significance is derivative from the later events. The earlier events were in themselves authentic disclosures of grace, not mere shadows or pointers to future realities. But the full theological significance of the whole story arises from the metaphorical act of grasping together past (Israel) and present (church).

This brings us to the heart of the matter. Typology is before all else a trope, an act of imaginative correlation. If one pole of the typological correlation annihilates the other, the metaphorical tension disappears, and the trope collapses. The viability of the Israel/church typology depends, for Paul's purposes, on maintaining the separate integrity of both poles. The church discovers its true identity only in relation to the sacred story of Israel, and the sacred story of Israel discovers its full significance—so Paul passionately believed—only in relation to God's unfold-ing design for salvation of the Gentiles in the church.[45]

If typologies are tropes, then surely typological correlations can be of various kinds, as Paul's own practice indicates. To classify a rhetor-ical figure such as 1 Cor. 10:1–13 as typology does not fully define the relation between the metaphorically linked elements; we have to ask what Paul is doing with the typology in each particular case. Some ty-pologies create antithetical correlations, such as the Adam/Christ typolo-gy, and others create positive correlations, such as the Israel/church ty-pology. These broad characterizations can only be matters of degree, since all typologies, being metaphorical, spring from a perception of likeness between dissimilar entities. Thus, even the most antithetical typology must contain elements of likeness, and even the most positive typology must contain elements of contrast. Otherwise, the figure would not work at all.

Within each typological pair the corresponding elements will assume differing weights, and one or the other will become the center of gravity for meaning. In each instance, the interpreter must ask which event provides the foundational paradigm in relation to which the other is read, while recognizing, of course, that in every metaphor semantic trans-ference between the elements will occur. In the case of Joshua 3–4, for example, the Red Sea crossing narrative provides the paradigm that structures the narrative of Israel's crossing the Jordan to enter the prom-ised land.[46] This is a good example of a typology that establishes a positive correlation, like 1 Cor. 10:1–22; however, in Joshua the later event is based on the earlier and primary salvation event. Lest we dull readers miss the point, the Lord tells Joshua, "This day I will begin to exalt you in the sight of all Israel, that they may know that, as I was with Moses, so I will be with you" (Josh. 3:7). The pattern is established by Moses at the Red Sea; Joshua derives glory and dignity by participating in a reenactment of the pattern laid down by his precursor.

This example illuminates Paul's contrasting strategy in 1 Corinthians 10. For Paul, Jesus Christ is emphatically *not* a new Moses. Although Luke later portrays Jesus as "prophet like Moses" (cf. Acts 3:17–26), Paul conspicuously avoids this typological possibility by identifying Christ with the rock. Furthermore, for Paul the foundational paradigm in the typological correlation is given not by the exodus events but by the Chris-tian experience of salvation. As Hans Conzelmann notes in his comment on 1 Cor. 10:2, "[Paul's] thought moves back to the Old Testament from the present datum, baptism, and certainly does not vice versa derive baptism from the Old Testament."[47] That is why Paul's hermeneutic must be called ecclesiocentric: he makes the biblical text pass through the filter of his experience of God's action of forming the church. The full meaning of God's eschatological redemptive purpose is now definitively enacted in the Christian community. Consequently, the Christian sacraments provide the categories with reference to which the Exodus narrative is interpreted: the phrase "baptized into Moses" reveals where the center of gravity lies. Thus, Marks is fully justified in remarking that "Paul, having appropriated the scriptural figure, incorporates it as part of a dramatic sequence in which he and his contemporaries are the ultimate term."[48] Against Marks, however, we must stress that the particular eschatological logic of the Pauline "dramatic sequence" does not entail the annulment or supersession of Israel's Scripture or of Israel's election. On the contrary, Paul's rhetorical strategy in 1 Corinthians 10 presupposes the same conviction that is defended explicitly by the argument of Romans 9–11: the experience of the Christian community stands in continuity with the story of Israel, not in contradiction to it.

Their Storie Pennes and Sets Us Down

One more comparison—this time to a much later Christian text that echoes Paul's typology—highlights the ecclesiocentric character of Paul's hermeneutic in the passages that we have been considering. George Herbert's poem, "The Bunch of Grapes," employs the same exodus metaphor that Paul elaborates, but plays out the conceit in different ways[49]:

The bunch of grapes

Joy, I did lock thee up: but some bad man
Hath let thee out again:
And now, me thinks, I am where I began
Sev'n years ago: one vogue and vein,
One aire of thoughts usurps my brain.
I did toward Canaan draw; but now I am
Brought back to the Red sea, the sea of shame.

For as the Jews of old by Gods command
Travell'd, and saw no town:
So now each Christian hath his journeys spann'd:
Their storie pennes and sets us down.
A single deed is small renown.

> Gods works are wide and let in future times;
> His ancient justice overflows our crimes.
>
> Then have we too our guardian fires and clouds;
> Our Scripture-dew drops fast:
> We have our sands and serpents, tents and shrowds;
> Alas! our murmurings come not last.
> But where's the cluster? where's the taste
> Of mine inheritance? Lord, if I must borrow,
> Let me as well take up their joy, as sorrow.
>
> But can he want the grape, who hath the wine?
> I have their fruit and more.
> Blessed be God, who prosper'd Noah's vine,
>
> And made it bring forth grapes good store.
> But much more him I must adore,
> Who of the laws sowre juice sweet wine doth make,
> Ev'n God himself, being pressed for my sake.

Without undertaking a full exploration of the contrasts between the poetic handling of the Exodus conceit by Paul and Herbert,[50] let us note three key points of difference.

First, Herbert employs the Exodus story as a metaphor for his individual spiritual journey.[51] This is particularly evident in the first stanza, but the same device sustains the poem throughout, as demonstrated by the recurrence of the pronoun *I*. By contrast, Paul's pronouns are predominantly first person plural: "types of us . . . for our instruction. . . . We must not put the Lord to the test. . . . Shall we provoke the Lord to jealousy." Paul relates the Exodus story to the corporate experience of the church, not to the pilgrimage of the individual soul. In this regard, Herbert's trope swerves closer to the traditional preserve of allegorists from Philo to Bunyan who have construed biblical narrative as an encoded account of individual spiritual formation.

Second, formally, Herbert uses the Exodus narrative as the foundational paradigm in the typological correlation, especially in the second and third stanzas: "Their storie pennes and sets us down." In contrast to Paul's description of Israel as "baptized into Moses," Herbert says of Christians, "Then have we too our guardian fires and clouds," and so forth. In these stanzas, the logic of the typology is "Israelocentric" rather than ecclesiocentric. Indeed, the last three lines of the third stanza complain that Herbert, the Christian, lacks even the foretaste of joy that Israel experienced in the sign of the cluster of grapes brought back by the scouts from Canaan (Num. 13:17–24). Through the first three stanzas, the poem exploits a reversal of Christian convention: Israel's salvation, far from being a transient thing superseded by the glories of the new covenant, is portrayed as the more palpable and enviable condition.

Third, the final stanza, however, executes a reversal of the reversal. The poet, who has the "wine" of Christ, can suddenly declare, "I have their fruit, and more." The logic of supersession sets in, as in the reference to "the laws sowre juice," and the poem culminates not just with an allusion to the eucharist but with a christological affirmation: "God himself, being pressed for my sake." One possible reading of the poem would stress the eucharistic interpretation of the final stanza and observe that, in light of the poet's earlier declarations of unfulfillment, the proleptic character of the eucharist is in view, read metaphorically in conjunction with the grapes that signify a promised land not yet entered. This interpretation would move the poem more closely into agreement with Paul's use of the Israel/church typology. The final stanza, however, contains too many indications of joyous supersession to overlook: the Christian poet "hath the wine" of "God himself being pressed for my sake." The climactic position of this assertion forces us to read the poem's imagery as spiraling in around a christological hermeneutic center. The climactic reversal gives Herbert's christological symbolism a weight much greater than the weight of Paul's parenthetical association of the rock with Christ.

I propose these contrasts not to criticize Herbert's exquisite poem—which is, after all, only ringing changes on a conventional Christian reading of the Exodus story—but to highlight the interpretive moves that Paul does *not* make in his imaginative play upon the Exodus story. He does not focus on individual experience, he does not treat the Exodus imagery as metaphorical paradigm for Christian experience (rather the reverse), and he does not resolve the typology into a christological allegory.

What he does do is to use Christian experience in the church as a hermeneutical paradigm for reading Scripture, from which he is then able to draw material for the guidance of his community. This necessarily circular procedure is authorized by his conviction that his churches, in which Jews and Gentiles together offer up praise to the God of Israel, are an eschatological sign and fulfillment of the promises woven into the fabric of Israel's history and enunciated in the word of Scripture. Anyone who rereads Scripture in light of such convictions is operating with an ecclesiocentric hermeneutic.

SCRIPTURE PREFIGURES THE BLESSING OF GENTILES

From the conviction that Israel's experiences were written down "for our instruction" (1 Cor. 10:11), it is only a small step to the inference that Christian experience must be *prefigured* in Scripture, that Scripture speaks not only to the church but also about it. If the ends of the ages have come upon Paul and his readers, then all God's dealing with Israel in the past— as recounted in Scripture—must have pointed toward the present apocalyptic moment. If God was authoring the sacred story, then all the story's narrative patterns must foreshadow the experience of the community that has now encountered the apocalypse of God's grace.

The hermeneutical consequences of such an understanding of Scripture are played out explicitly in Paul's Letter to the Galatians, in which Paul employs biblical texts not allusively (the rhetorical strategy of this broadside does not permit such delicacy) but directly in service of a vigorous argument against the demand for circumcision of his Gentile converts. Of special interest for our purposes are two passages (Gal. 3:1–14 and 4:21–31) at the beginning and end of the letter's central argumentative section,[52] both discovering in the story of Abraham a prefiguration of the church.

Scripture Prepreached the Gospel to Abraham

The ecclesiocentric interpretive program of Galatians 3 and 4 comes into focus if we bear in mind the fundamental concern of the argument: Paul is contending that Gentile believers in Jesus need not—indeed, must not— become Torah observers.[53] In order to support his contention, he must argue that Scripture already proclaims and authorizes a Law-free community of God's people, that is, a church in which Jews and Gentiles stand on common ground. With characteristic chutzpah, Paul is not content to argue that such a development is merely permissible; rather, he intends to show that it is the real meaning of Scripture, God's ultimate purpose to which Scripture has pointed all along.

That is why, in an affirmation crucial to the logic of his argument, he emphasizes the proleptic character of the promise to Abraham: "Scripture, *foreseeing* [*proïdousa*] that God justifies the Gentiles through faith [*ek pisteōs*], *prepreached the gospel* [*proeuēngelisato*] to Abraham: 'In you all the Gentiles shall be blessed'" (Gal. 3:8). The role ascribed to Scripture in Gal. 3:8 illuminates Paul's use of Scripture throughout the letter; in order to appreciate the nuances of Paul's discussion, we must mark three features of this key declaration.

First, the substantive *content* of the gospel message that Scripture prepreached to Abraham is said to be that "all the Gentiles" (*panta ta ethnē*) will be blessed in him. In contrast to the Johannine notion that Moses and Isaiah saw Christ and wrote about him (e.g., John 5:46, 12:41), nothing is said here about a revelation to Abraham of the crucified and risen Christ; rather, the preproclaimed gospel is a promise of God's intent to bless all nations. This way of formulating the content of the message has two clear advantages for Paul: it serves the immediate purpose of his pastoral letter to the Galatians by emphasizing the inclusion of *Gentiles* in the blessing,[54] and it does not require him to impose a labored christological exegesis on the Genesis texts. The LXX texts in fact say exactly what Paul wants them to, though he does take the liberty of conflating Gen. 12:3 ("In you all the tribes of the earth will be blessed") with Gen. 22:18 ("In your seed all the Gentiles [nations] of the earth will be blessed" [cf. Gen. 18:18, 26:4]). The underlying Hebrew text means, "All tribes of the earth will bless themselves by you," that is, Abraham will become a proverbial byword exemplifying God's favor so that people will say to one another, "May we be as blessed as Abraham." Paul, however, reads the *en soi* of the LXX in an instrumental—or even locative—sense: through or in Abraham and his seed, Gentiles will be enabled to receive the promised blessing.[55] Thus, the gospel sneak preview granted to Abraham is ecclesial rather than christological in content: it concerns the inclusive scope of the promise rather than the means whereby the promise is to be fulfilled. The message preproclaimed to Abraham is a gospel about God's people rather than about a Messiah.

Second, the agent that does the preproclaiming to Abraham is Scripture, quasi-personified. It is easy enough to give a rationalistic explanation of Paul's phrase: he really means that God proclaimed the gospel to Abraham,[56] or he means that Scripture, in the story of the promise to Abraham, foreshadows the gospel. But these explanations are reductive. Paul thinks of *Graphē* (Scripture) as alive and active; for instance, it "locked up all things under sin" (3:22). It has a voice, and it speaks[57]—not only to readers like Paul but also to characters within the story that it narrates, such as Abraham and Pharaoh (cf. Rom. 9:17). (The detail is telling; Paul thinks of Abraham less as a figure of the historical past than as a character inscribed within a narrated text.) In this case, *Graphē* speaks as it does to Abraham because it "foresees" the subsequent unfolding of God's purposes in the drama. Elsewhere in Galatians, Scripture also is depicted as a voice that speaks directly to the Galatians (4:30; see discussion below).

This time-spanning speech of the text is a crucial attribute; the text is reckoned as a knowing voice that has the power to address the present out of the past—or to address the past about the present, in such a way that readers, overhearing, may reconceive the present.

Third, the meaning of Scripture's preproclamation must be understood retrospectively in light of its fulfillment in the church. Before the present time, in which the mystery of God's action of justifying Gentiles *ek pisteōs* is revealed, the sense of the gospel that Scripture preached to Abraham remained opaque. The verb *proeuēngelisato* ("prepreached or preproclaimed the gospel") is a New Testament *hapax legomenon*,[58] but this is just one of a number of instances in which Paul uses the prefix *pro* before verbs of writing, promising, or proclaiming in order to assert the temporal priority of the scriptural word to the contemporary events in which Paul discerns God's salvific action. (See, e.g., Rom. 1:2, 15:4, cf. also the use of *egraphē* in Rom. 4:23–24; 1 Cor. 9:9–10, 10:11.) In each case, the temporally prior promise or event is read through the filter of its gospel fulfillment, so that its true meaning can be discerned only retrospectively.

With Gal. 3:8 as a hermeneutical guideline, then, let us turn to a reading of Gal. 3:1–14, the first of the two major passages in Galatians where the story of Abraham figures prominently.

Paul marks the beginning of the letter's central section with a sharp rhetorical interrogation of his readers: "O foolish Galatians, who has bewitched you, before whose eyes Jesus Christ was portrayed [*proegraphē*] as crucified?" Commentators have usually debated whether the verb *proegraphē* in this sentence refers to some sort of literal public display—even if only through vivid dramatic description of the crucifixion of Jesus—or whether it means, less specifically, "proclaimed publicly."[59] In either case, the reference must be to Paul's original telling of the gospel story to the Galatians.[60] After this initial allusion to a (christocentric) gospel proclamation, Paul takes a different tack in verses 2–5, focusing on the Galatians' own experience in response to the proclaimed gospel. The appeal to their experience of the Spirit is presented rhetorically as a decisive argument: "Let me ask you only this."[61] The community's corporate experience of the Spirit and of the miracles wrought in their midst (3:5)—all prior to their flirtation with the Law—ought to convince them beyond any doubt that God's blessing operates through the proclaimed word and does not depend on obedience to Torah.

Paul turns next in verses 6–9 to an argument from Scripture, appealing to the story of Abraham. But before delving into that story, we are bound to ask a question suggested by the order of Paul's presentation:

what is the relation between the argument from experience and the argument from Scripture? Does the latter simply confirm the former? Of course, Paul thinks that it does; the weight of his arguments is cumulative. The conjunction *kathōs* (just as), introducing the quotation of Gen. 15:6, posits a direct analogy between the story of Abraham and the Galatians' experience.[62] But does the experience of the Spirit have a *hermeneutical* function? To state the issue broadly, is the scriptural text to be illuminated in the light of Spirit-experience, or is Spirit-experience to be measured by normative constraints laid down by the text? This is the fundamental question at issue between Paul and the teachers who were influencing the Galatians.[63]

Paul's unflinching answer, to the dismay of his more cautious kinsmen then and now, is to opt for the hermeneutical priority of Spirit-experience. This choice leads him, to be sure, not to a rejection of Scripture but to a charismatic rereading, whose persuasive power will rest precariously on his ability to demonstrate a congruence between the scriptural text and the community summoned and shaped by his proclamation.

The rereading begins in verse 6 with the citation of Gen. 15:6 ("Abraham believed God, and it was reckoned to him for righteousness"), followed by a bold interpretive pronouncement: "Know, therefore, that those who live by faith [*hoi ek pisteōs*] are the sons of Abraham" (3:7). By fiat, Paul forges the decisive link between the scriptural character Abraham and the contemporary faith-community, on the basis of the family resemblance implicit in the verb *believed*. The odd expression *hoi ek pisteōs* (literally, "those out of faith") is a *Vorklang* of Hab. 2:4, *ho dikaios ek pisteōs zēsetai* (the righteous one shall live by faith), not yet cited in the discussion, but soon to appear in 3:11.[64]

Lest the claim of Gal. 3:7 appear ungrounded, Paul supports it in verse 8 with a citation spliced together from Gen. 12:3 and Gen. 22:18: "In you all the Gentiles shall be blessed." (The original narrative contexts of these words are noteworthy: Gen. 12:3 is the climax of God's initial call of Abraham away from his country and kindred, and Gen. 22:18 concludes God's benediction upon Abraham for his obedience in offering up his "only son" Isaac. Paul's departure from his own kindred and his sacrifice of a putatively God-given Law-righteousness [cf. Phil. 3:4–11] bear deep structural correspondences to these aspects of the Abraham narrative.) As we have seen, this quotation is presented as a word addressed to Abraham by Scripture, which speaks with prophetic assurance on the basis of its foreknowledge of God's plan to justify Gentiles *ek pisteōs*. In other words, the promise to Abraham is deemed possible and intelligible only in light of the present reality of the Christian mission to Gentiles. Gal. 3:9, then, offers Paul's exegetical gloss on the text just quoted: the blessing pronounced in Genesis on "the faithful Abraham" encompasses all "those who live by faith" (including Gentiles as well as Jews).

The linkage between Gentiles and *hoi ek pisteōs* is strictly Paul's interpretive act. Nowhere does the text of Genesis say that those Gentiles who believe as Abraham did will be blessed along with him, or any such thing. Paul's reading of the blessing pronounced on Abraham is implicitly but decisively shaped by the empirical datum of his Gentile congregations who have come to believe in Israel's God without accepting a requirement of circumcision. The fulfillment precedes the promise,[65] hermeneutically speaking: only because he sees in the Christian community the fulfillment of the promised blessing does Paul venture a retrospective interpretation of its latent sense.

This does not mean, however, that Paul's reading is supersessionist in character. Rather than denying the truth or abiding validity of the promises to Abraham, Paul incorporates them into a wider narrative framework that simultaneously affirms and transmutes them.[66] Indeed, Paul's rhetorical strategy in Galatians depends in part on the claim that he is reasserting the efficacy of a divine promise even older than the Sinai Law (Gal. 3:15–18). His eschatologically privileged hermeneutical perspective, however, allows him to acknowledge the truth of God's revelation to Israel while at the same time discovering new dimensions of meaning in that revelation that were necessarily concealed from readers in all prior generations. It is a complex intertextual strategy that permits him to read Abraham as a metaphor for the Christian community.

To trace the uses of Scripture in Gal. 3:10–12, a notoriously vexing passage, would take us far afield from the Abraham story and into quagmires of exegetical controversy. For the purpose of the present discussion, we can be satisfied to observe that Paul employs citations from Deut. 27:26, Hab. 2:4, and Lev. 18:5 to drive a wedge between Law and Faith as means to righteousness and life. In verse 13, Christ (mentioned here for the first time since 3:1) is said to have redeemed us from the curse pronounced by the Law by taking it on himself in order that the blessing pronounced on Abraham—here, in verse 14, Paul picks up the main thread of his argument again—might come upon the Gentiles. The curse-blessing polarity in verses 13–14 echoes both Gen. 12:3 (quoted in Gal. 3:8) and the curses and blessings of the Deuteronomic covenant, as set forth in Deuteronomy 27 and 28 (quoted in Gal. 3:10). Indeed, though Paul quotes only the blessing from Gen. 12:3, the blessing-curse opposition in that subtext subliminally smoothes the otherwise abrupt transition from Gal. 3:9 to 3:10. The compressed narrative logic of the scenario of redemption in Gal. 3:13–14 is a little obscure,[67] but the meaning of the blessing of Abraham is rendered utterly explicit by the final clause of verse 14, which sums up and explicates the result of Christ's redemptive action: "in order that we might receive the promise of the Spirit through faith."

The reference to receiving the Spirit through faith closes the discursive circle that started in 3:2 ("Did you receive the Spirit through works of Law or through the message of faith?") and supplies the argument's heretofore missing premise: the promise made to Abraham finds its fulfillment in the reception of the Holy Spirit, experienced by the Galatians. But, the skeptical reader might protest, there is nothing at all in the Genesis story about the gift of the Spirit: the promises made to Abraham were promises of descendants as numerous as the stars and of the land of Canaan for an everlasting possession.

At this climax of the discussion, the answer to our earlier question emerges clearly: does the Spirit have a hermeneutical function? Indeed it does, so much so that the textually articulated content of the promise in the Genesis narrative—the land and numerous descendants—is supplanted altogether by a new reading of the promise, a reading that has no discernible warrant in the text. Its basis lies exclusively in the experience of the Christian community, now correlated *ex hypothesi* with the promise to Abraham. The unwritten logic of Paul's claim must be something like this: (a) Scripture promises that Gentiles will be blessed in Abraham. (b) Gentile Christian communities, who—like Abraham—have come to believe in Israel's God apart from the Sinai Torah, have experienced the blessing of the Holy Spirit, palpably present in their midst. (c) Therefore, this experienced Spirit must be the promised blessing of which Scripture speaks.

A more radically ecclesiocentric hermeneutic could hardly be conceived: not only is Abraham's story read as a prefiguration of the church, but the material content of the promise to Abraham is subsumed entirely into categories supplied by the church's experience of the Spirit.[68] So self-evident does this rereading appear to Paul that he does not even bother to justify it. One could imagine an elaborate allegorical interpretation that would provide point-for-point spiritual equivalents for the land of Canaan, the numerous progeny, and so forth. (Philo, for instance, interprets God's promise to make Abraham into "a great nation" as a promise of "progress in the principles of virtue," and he interprets the "blessing"—on the basis of a whimsical deconstructive etymology of *eulogein*—as "excellent reason.")[69] Paul, however, offers no such interpretation. The explanatory power of his reading seems to Paul self-justifying. The hermeneutical function of the Spirit is to generate an inspired reading that discloses the secret truth to which the story of Abraham points: God will grant the eschatological Spirit to a community of Gentiles, who will thereby become recognizable as Abraham's true promised children.[70]

Abraham Had Two Sons

Against the background of such a reading of the Abraham story, Paul presents the allegory of Abraham's two sons in Gal. 4:21–31. Enough evidence has already been adduced to secure the thesis proposed at the beginning of this chapter: this rigorously ecclesiocentric allegory is not an anomaly but a heightened expression of themes that repeatedly surface when Paul turns to interpreting Scripture. Indeed, his conviction that Scripture points to the church as its essential meaning is so firm that he risks a fancifully subversive ecclesiocentric reading of Genesis 21, the very text that might threaten to undo his mission to the Gentiles.

C. K. Barrett has proposed that Gen. 21:1–10 may have been cited triumphantly by Paul's opponents as the definitive refutation of Paul's anticircumcision gospel.[71] Ishmael, Abraham's son by the slave woman Hagar, represents Abraham's Gentile progeny; in accordance with Gen. 21:10 he "shall not be heir" with Isaac, Sarah's son, who—as father of Jacob/Israel—represents the Jewish people. Precisely such a reading of the story is illustrated by Jub. 16:17–18:

> All the seed of [Abraham's] sons should be Gentiles, and be reckoned with the Gentiles; but from the sons of Isaac one should become a holy seed, and should not be reckoned among the Gentiles. For he should become the portion of the Most High, and all his seed had fallen into the possession of God, that it should be unto the Lord a people for [his] possession above all nations and that it should become a kingdom of priests and a holy nation.[72]

Only Isaac, whom Abraham circumcised when he was eight days old "as God had commanded him" (Gen. 21:4), is the legitimate heir of the promised blessing. The Jewish Christian teachers in Galatia would have insisted that the Gentile Galatians be circumcised in order to legitimize themselves and to regularize their status as recipients of salvation. After all, even Ishmael was circumcised when he was thirteen years old (Gen. 17:25).

If Barrett's proposal is correct, we see Paul in Gal. 4:21–31 practicing hermeneutical jujitsu. He not only deflects the force of the charge but also turns it to his own advantage. "Tell me, you who desire to be under the Law, do you not hear the Law?" (Gal. 4:21). The claim that Torah, rightly read, warrants the *rejection* of lawkeeping is, on its face, outrageous. No sane reader could appeal, without some flicker of irony, to the Law in order to nullify circumcision as the definitive sign of covenant relation with God. Unless we suppose that Paul was an insane (or duplicitous) reader, we must credit him with some ironic sensibility as he flips the story on its back.

The audacity of the maneuver contributes to its rhetorical effect. Like Elijah dousing the sacrifice with water before calling down fire from heaven to consume it, Paul takes on the most difficult case and provocatively raises the stakes. Invoking a hermeneutical miracle calculated to end the argument by leaving his audience agape,[73] he executes a counterreading that reverses the terms of the discussion, claiming the putatively hostile evidence for his own case.[74]

Paul's interpretation of the story drives toward and centers on his quotation in verse 30 of Gen. 21:10, which he conforms subtly to the thematic focus of his counterreading.[75] This quotation, Paul's only direct citation of the Pentateuchal text under discussion, anchors the discourse in a juxtaposition between slavery and freedom. The anchoring effect, however, is enhanced by certain modifications in the wording of the quotation. He follows the LXX text with only minor differences (e.g., adapting the quotation from its original narrative context to his application of it by omitting the demonstrative pronoun *this* before the word *slavegirl*) until the end of the sentence, but he tailors its conclusion to correspond to the slave/free dichotomy around which he has organized his allegory.

> Cast out this slavegirl and her son
> for the son of this slavegirl shall not inherit
> with my son Isaac. (Gen. 21:10 LXX)

> Cast out the slavegirl and her son,
> for the son of the slavegirl shall not inherit
> with the son of the freewoman. (Gal. 4:30)

This adjustment of the quotation highlights the slave/free contrast and thus emphasizes its application to the decision confronting Paul's readers, which Paul has already categorized as a choice between slavery and freedom (cf. Gal. 4:1–11). He makes this parenetic point—implicit in the Genesis quotation—fully explicit in the transitional sentence that follows his allegorical interpretation: "For freedom Christ has set us free; stand fast, then, and do not again submit to a yoke of slavery" (5:1).

Once we recognize the telos of the argument, we can begin to discern how Paul has staged his narration to lead the reader to the desired inferences. He usually employs the expression "it is written" (*gegraptai*) to introduce a direct quotation. In Gal. 4:22, however, it introduces an allusive summary of the narrative about Abraham's children: "Abraham had two sons, one by a slavegirl [*paidiskē*] and one by a freewoman [*eleuthera*]."[76] Though the summary looks concise and neutral, Paul has already framed the categories within which his counterreading will proceed. The two sons are marked not by their circumcised or uncircumcised status but by the slave/free polarity that distinguishes their mothers. This polarity, however, is a hermeneutical device introduced by Paul, highlighting a minor feature of the Genesis narrative. In Genesis (LXX), Hagar is repeatedly described as a *paidiskē*, but Sarah is never called *eleuthera*. The emphasis on her free status, crucial for Paul's reading, is brought to the story by Paul himself.

Paul reemphasizes the importance of the slave/free markers in Gal. 4:23, continuing to allude to Ishmael and Isaac not by name but as the progeny of the two women: "But the one by the slavegirl [*ho ek tēs paidiskēs*] was born according to the flesh, the one by the freewoman [*ho ek tēs eleutheras*] through promise." (The apparent incongruity of the flesh/promise dichotomy—where we might expect a flesh/spirit contrast—results from Paul's attentiveness to the contours of the Genesis narrative, which says nothing about the Spirit but which does contrast the natural expedient whereby Ishmael was conceived to the miraculous conception of Isaac in accordance with God's earlier words of promise. Up to this point, Paul is merely recapitulating the scriptural story; he reserves the flesh/spirit pairing for his interpretive comment in v. 29.) Thus, Paul's economical sketch in verses 22–23 of the story of Abraham's sons establishes polarities that will play themselves out in his allegorical reading: Ishmael-slave-flesh over against Isaac-free-promise.

When Paul announces that these narrative entities are to be interpreted allegorically (v. 24), no one should be surprised. Even the conventional Jewish interpretation offered in Jubilees is allegorical,[77] with its symbolic identification of Ishmael and Isaac as representatives of Gentiles and Jews. (The wider canonical context of the patriarchal narrative supports the Jubilees reading, of course; it will become evident that Paul can construe the Abraham story as he does only by placing it within a new and allegedly more comprehensive narrative structure.) The hermeneutical surprise pops out when, momentarily ignoring the two sons, he asserts that the two women are two *covenants* and that Hagar represents the covenant "from Mount Sinai, giving birth into slavery." Although the allegorical interpretation of Sarah and Hagar as symbols for different covenants has no direct parallel in Jewish exegetical traditions, such a notion is easily conceivable once their sons are read as symbols of the Jew/Gentile dichotomy. The shocking reversal executed by Paul, however, is that he associates the Hagar-Ishmael-slavery symbolic complex not with the Gentiles but with Sinai and the Law.

What Jewish thinker could propound such an equation? Only one convinced, as Paul was, that the Law of Moses was an interim arrangement designed to keep the people of God in protective custody until the promised "Seed" of Abraham should come (see Gal. 3:19–25). Within Judaism, of course, the covenant with Abraham was characteristically seen as anticipatory of the Sinai covenant; the rabbis even depicted Abraham—in a playful anachronism—as the great exemplar of Torah-obedience.[78] The antiquity of this tradition is demonstrated by Sir. 44:19–20:

> Abraham was the great father of a multitude of nations,
> and no one has been found like him in glory;
> He kept the Law of the Most High,
> and was taken into covenant with him;
> he established the covenant in his flesh,
> and when he was tested he was found faithful.

Paul, however, shifts all the narrative valences by setting Abraham and Moses in antithesis to one another and emphasizing the priority of the promises to Abraham over the covenant given to Moses (Gal. 3:15–18).[79] God's blessing is thus pegged securely to God's elective grace (promise) rather than conditioned on the performance of commandments (law). "For if the inheritance were by law, it would be no longer by promise. But God graced Abraham by promise" (Gal. 3:18).

The payoff of this innovative interpretive strategy is that it allows Paul to link the Abrahamic covenant to the present reality of his Gentile churches, leaping over and negating the Sinai covenant.[80] This is another place where later Christian readers, influenced by the Letter to the Hebrews and by Christian conventions of speaking about the "Old Testament" and the "New Testament," stand in danger of misconstruing Paul's allegorical polarities. The "two covenants" of Gal. 4:24 are *not* the old covenant at Sinai and the new covenant in Christ. Rather, the contrast is drawn between the old covenant at Sinai and the older covenant with Abraham, which turns out in Paul's rereading to find its true meaning in

Christ. In Paul's scheme, the freedom and inheritance rights of the Gentile Christian communities are not novelties but older truths that were always implicit in Isaac, in the promise to Abraham.[81]

In relation to the symbolic grammar of Judaism, Paul's association of the Law with slavery is offensive and heretical; the Sinai Torah was given precisely as the covenant sealing God's liberation of Israel from slavery in Egypt. How then can Paul interpret the slavegirl Hagar as an allegorical symbol for the Law? The notoriously obscure explanation of Gal. 4:25a ("Now Hagar is Mount Sinai in Arabia"), which has attracted numerous emendations in the textual tradition and countless quizzical comments by critics,[82] is actually nothing other than a puff of rhetorical smoke that distracts the audience from noticing the naked assertion (Gal. 4:25b) on which Paul's strong misreading actually depends, the assertion of a phenomenological correspondence between Law and slavery: "she corresponds to the present Jerusalem, for she is in slavery with her children." Within Galatians, Paul has already laid the groundwork for this allegorical reversal by associating the Law with curse (3:10), confinement (3:23–24),[83] and slavery (4:1–11).

Significantly, Paul presents these associations as retrospective judgments on the Law, grounded upon a new communal experience of freedom in the power of the Holy Spirit, as he affirms in 4:4–7.

> But when the fullness of time came
> God sent forth his son,
> born of a woman,
> born under Law,
> in order that he might liberate those under Law from slavery,[84]
> in order that we might receive adoption.
> And because you are sons,
> God sent forth the Spirit of his son into our hearts,
> crying, "Abba, Father."
> Thus, you are no longer a slave, but a son;
> and if a son, also an heir through God.

Gentiles once deemed Ishmaels have now been adopted by God's free elective grace so that they are no longer slaves. Because of the palpable grace of the Spirit among these Gentile Galatians, Paul dares to address them as "children of promise, according to Isaac" (4:28), fully legitimate heirs of the promise to Abraham who are "children not of the slavegirl but of the freewoman" (4:31).

Paul has not merely made a case for admitting the Gentiles into membership among the people of God; he has argued that the Genesis narrative is a veiled prefiguration of precisely the historical development that has now come to pass in the Gentile church. That is why some commentators[85] insist that this passage, despite Paul's use of the word *allēgoroumena*, ought to be classified as typology rather than allegory: it deals with correspondences between figures past and present rather than with timeless spiritual truths. Unlike Philo, who interprets the same story as an allegory of the soul's choice between wisdom (Isaac) and sophistry (Ishmael),[86] Paul finds the completed meaning of the tale in particular redemptive actions of God in history. The distinction between typology and allegory, however, though it may seem important to us, is not one that Paul himself recognizes, as the present passage demonstrates. When he says of the story of Abraham's sons that "these things are to be interpreted as allegories," he means simply that they are not to be taken at face value—we might say they are to be read neither merely as history nor as self-enclosed fictional narrative—but that their meaning must be sought in a latent sense of some sort.[87] In this particular case, the latent sense is disclosed, according to Paul, only when the narrative is correlated with the present experience of the community of those whom Paul now addresses as "brothers" (vv. 28, 31)—that is, the church. The story of Abraham, Sarah, Hagar, Isaac, and Ishmael is a figurative portrayal whose meaning can only be understood with reference to the pastoral and theological issues that Paul is now addressing.

That is why the voice of Scripture must be heard as a voice directed to the present moment. It is no accident that Paul's only direct quotation here from Genesis 21 is Sarah's demand to Abraham: "Cast out the slavegirl and her son; for the son of the slavegirl shall not inherit with the son of the freewoman." This is the climax of Paul's argument, drawing together in a single fertile sentence the motifs of slavery, freedom, sonship, and inheritance, and calling on the reader to act on the demand. In quoting Gen. 21:10 (LXX), Paul effaces all hints that these are the words of Sarah. They become the words of *Graphē* (Scripture), whose second person singular imperative ("Cast out") is now directed to the reader of the letter. That is why Paul changes the wording from "shall not inherit with my son"—a formulation that could readily have been transformed into a declaration of God about the exclusive inheritance rights of Christ, if Paul were interested in christological allegory—to "shall not inherit with the son of the freewoman." No longer do we hear Sarah speaking to Abraham[88]; instead, we hear *Graphē* echoing Sarah's words, at last uttering the words at their divinely foreordained targets, the readers of Paul's letter, who are thereby exhorted to expel the advocates of circumcision from their midst in Galatia.[89] The message was suspended in time and text, awaiting the activating spark created by contact between the story and the church. Now in the *ekklēsia* the story can be read aright for the first time: the meaning of the story is found in the church, and the identity of the church is found in the story.

As confirmation of this ecclesiocentric reading, Paul adduces a further correspondence between Scripture and present experience: "Just as then the one born according to the flesh persecuted the one born according to the spirit, so it is also now" (Gal. 4:29). Galatians offers several intimations concerning the persecution of Christians by Jews, beginning with Paul's references to his own activity of persecuting the church of God (Gal. 1:13, 23) before his apostolic call and ending with his suggestion that at present he finds himself persecuted precisely because he is no longer preaching circumcision (5:11). While the character and extent of these persecutions of Christians by Jews is an important historical question, the actual evidence provided here is scanty. Paul's readers presumably knew what he was alluding to. He could make his strange reading of the text appear more convincing by pointing out that it was Torah advocates who were persecuting non-Torah-observant Christians rather than the other way around. Thus, if Ishmael is the persecutor of Isaac, then the very persecuting activity of the Torah advocates aligns them with the slave offspring rather than with the child of promise. (Parenthetically, one might ask what the theological implications of this argument are for readers who have inherited a history stained by relentless Christian persecution of Jews. Who now is Ishmael?)

The argument is clever, except for one problem: the text of Genesis does not say that Ishmael persecuted Isaac. Indeed, most modern readers of Genesis 21 would surely suppose that it was the freewoman Sarah who, on behalf of Isaac, instigated a persecution of the innocent and powerless Hagar and Ishmael. No doubt Paul's argument presupposes a longstanding Jewish tradition of exonerating Sarah's apparently vicious jealousy by supplying a provocation on the basis of Gen. 21:9: "Sarah saw the son of Hagar the Egyptian, whom she had borne to Abraham, playing" (*měṣaḥeq;* LXX adds, "with her son Isaac"). Into the single word *playing,* later rabbinic commentators read all manner of mischief, including mockery, idolatry, child molestation, and attacks with bow and arrow (cf. Gen. 21:20).[90] Even if Paul knew such traditions—he does not tell us how Ishmael persecuted Isaac or where the account of such persecution is to be found—his use of the persecution motif illustrates once again that his allegorical reading of the text is shaped significantly by the empirical situation of the church in his own time. The fact is that Torah advocates are persecuting those who carry out the Law-free mission to the Gentiles;

consequently, given the way Paul has set up the allegory, the text must be read in a way that portrays Ishmael as the persecutor. Thus, the church's experience of persecution generates a fanciful expansion of a minor obscurity in the scriptural narrative, and, in circular fashion, the correspondence between interpretive expansion and present experience is adduced as proof of the truth of Paul's reading.

Many Are the Children of the Desolate One

One peculiar feature of Paul's allegorical interpretation has not yet been examined in the foregoing discussion. Besides Gen. 21:10, the one other scriptural passage explicitly adduced in Paul's interpretation is Isa. 54:1:

> Rejoice, O barren one that does not bear;
> break forth and shout, you who are not in labor;
> for many are the children of the desolate one,
> more than of her that has a husband.

Why does Paul appeal to this text, and how does it fit into his allegory?

Paul has cited the text in verbatim agreement with the LXX, but the aptness of the quotation is not immediately evident. Aside from its reference to a "barren one"—an epithet appropriate to Sarah before the conception of Isaac—there is no apparent connection between the Isaianic prophecy and the story of Abraham's two sons. Isaiah is apostrophizing Zion, not Sarah; and there is no hint of a reference to Hagar. Isaiah's contrast between "the desolate one" and "her that has a husband" fits awkwardly into Paul's allegorical Sarah/Hagar juxtaposition: Sarah, after all, is the one who was married to Abraham. How then does the Isaiah passage serve Paul's purposes?

First of all, the quotation is introduced after Paul has already identified Hagar with "the present Jerusalem" and Sarah with "the Jerusalem above" (vv. 25–26). The juxtaposition seems slightly askew: we would expect the *"future* Jerusalem" to be the dialectical opposite of the present one, but Paul appears to be alluding to a conventional notion of Jewish apocalyptic that the eschatological Jerusalem already exists in heaven, awaiting the time when it will come down to earth. (Theologically, this image suggests that the hope of Israel rests in God's transcendent grace rather than in the results of a human historical process.) The idea appears in Rev. 21:2 in a form closely related to Paul's use of it here: "And I saw the holy city, new Jerusalem, coming down out of heaven from God, prepared as a bride adorned for her husband." When Paul claims this heavenly Jerusalem as "our mother," he is in effect asserting that he and his Christian readers already belong to the new age; their identity receives its definition from the *polis* redeemed by God.

Once Paul has allegorically identified Christian believers as children of the eschatological Jerusalem, his use of Isaiah's prophecy follows without undue difficulty, because the prophecy's words of consolation are spoken to Jerusalem after the exile.[91] Though Jerusalem is not explicitly mentioned in the passage that Paul quotes, a reader familiar with this section of Deutero-Isaiah would immediately recognize that Jerusalem is being addressed here, not only in Isaiah 54, where verses 11–14 particularly reveal that the barren/afflicted one whom the prophet comforts is the city itself, but also throughout the wider context, extending back at least to Isa. 51:17 (cf. also especially Isa. 52:1–10). Thus, to grasp the sense of the quotation, the reader must recover its original scriptural context; Gal. 4:27 is one of the very few passages in this otherwise blunt letter where Paul employs Scripture in an allusive, echo-laden manner.

How widely do the echoes of Isa. 54:1 spread before they disperse into silence? As Isaiah's prophetic paraclesis sounds in Paul's letter, a sympathetic harmony answers from Isa. 51:1–3:

> Hearken to me, you who pursue deliverance,
> you who seek the Lord;
> look to the rock from which you were hewn,
> and to the quarry from which you were digged.
> Look to Abraham your father
> and to Sarah who bore you;
> for when he was but one I called him,
> and I blessed him and made him many.
> For the Lord will comfort Zion
> . . . .
> joy and gladness will be found in her,
> thanksgiving and the voice of song.

Is the "voice of song" from Zion the same voice summoned forth in Gal. 4:27-Isa. 54:1?

The prophet's reminiscence of "Sarah who bore you" is the only passage in Paul's Bible that refers back to her story in Genesis. Isa. 51:1–3 represents Sarah as the mother of Jerusalem and assures the readers of deliverance by reminding them of their true parents, who were blessed and greatly multiplied by God; thus, Isaiah's description in 54:1 of Jerusalem as a "barren one" creates an internal echo hinting at the correspondence between the city in its exilic desolation and the condition of Sarah before Isaac's birth, a correspondence that also implies the promise of subsequent blessing. Consequently, Paul's link between Sarah and a redeemed Jerusalem surely presupposes Isa. 51:2, even though the text is not quoted in Galatians 4. It is Isaiah's metaphorical linkage of Abraham and Sarah with an eschatologically restored Jerusalem that warrants Paul's use of Isa. 54:1. The effect of Paul's allusive use of the quotation, however, can be better described the other way around: the citation of Isa. 54:1 metaleptically evokes the whole rippling pool of promise found in the latter chapters of that prophetic book.[92] The promises found there include, as we have noted in our earlier discussion of Romans, the conviction that the eschatological blessing of Israel will be the instrument for extending God's saving righteousness to the Gentiles, who are to be included—in Paul's interpretation—in the "many children of the desolate one."

Of course, by reading Isa. 54:1 as a word addressed to a Gentile church, Paul has wrought a major transformation in the sense of the text. Isaiah's prophecy envisions a literal restoration of the city of Jerusalem as a manifestation of God's justice and faithfulness to his own people. When Paul works this prophecy into his allegory as supporting evidence for his claim that God's blessing of uncircumcised Gentiles is prefigured in Scripture and actualized in the church, an extraordinary hermeneutical inversion has taken place before our eyes. The case is precisely analogous to that of Rom. 9:25–26, in which Paul reads Hosea's promise of Israel's restored relationship to God as a promise that God will call those who are "not my people," that is, Gentiles. In both instances, Paul extends the logic of reversal at work in the text well beyond the referential sense envisioned in the original. If God is a God who reaches out to call those who are not his people, if God causes the barren to sing by granting children where they are least to be expected, then the inclusion of the Gentiles as recipients of the promise to Abraham is an act thoroughly consistent with the character and purposes of the God to whom prophetic Scripture bears witness. The "many children" of Isa. 54:1 are to be found precisely in the Gentile churches, in which the surprising grace of God is made manifest; thus Paul's ecclesiocentric hermeneutic claims and reconstrues the scriptural text in a manner that would confound a Torah-centered Jewish reader and elude a Christian reader searching for christological prooftexts.

If we ask ourselves how Paul could have developed such an interpretive approach, the role of christology as a theological presupposition for Paul's innovative reading procedures emerges into the light: christology is the foundation on which his ecclesiocentric counterreadings are constructed. In Gal. 3:16, Paul claims—for reasons explained at the beginning of this chapter—that Christ is the one "seed" who is the rightful heir of the promise to Abraham. How then can Gentile Galatians also be numbered among the children of promise? The missing term in the chain of argument is supplied by Gal. 3:29: "If you [*hymeis*, (plural)] are Christ's, then you are Abraham's seed, heirs according to promise." Because the Gentile believers have "put on Christ" in baptism (Gal. 3:27), they have become united with him in a way that allows them to participate—vicariously—in his inheritance and his destiny.

Thus, Gal. 3:29 finally unlocks the riddle of the relation between Paul's ecclesiocentric hermeneutic and his christological convictions. Galatians demonstrates more clearly than any other Pauline letter how these aspects of Paul's thought are complementary rather than contradictory: Paul's understanding of Jesus Christ as the one true heir of the promise to Abraham is the essential theological presupposition for his hermeneutical strategies, though these strategies are not in themselves christocentric. His readings of the scriptural texts rarely seek to excavate messianic prophecies. Instead, his prevailing concern is to show how the church is prefigured and guided by Scripture: that is why he reads Isaac not as a type of Christ but a symbol for the Christian community. Paul can treat Scripture as a word for and about Gentile Christians only because these Gentiles have become—in a remarkable metonymic transfer— Abraham's seed, heirs of God's word to Israel, as a result of God's act in Jesus Christ, "who became a curse for us . . . in order that the blessing of Abraham might come to the Gentiles" (Gal. 3:13–14). With this christological warrant firmly in place, Paul can proceed to read Israel's Scripture as a mysterious prefiguration of the church, a story in which Christ's Gentile adherents can find their own story prewritten.

In the texts explored in this chapter, Paul reads the Bible in light of a central conviction that he and his readers are those upon whom the ends of the ages have come. They are God's eschatological people who, in receiving the grace of God through Jesus Christ, become a living sign, a privileged clue to the meaning of God's word in Scripture. This hermeneutical conviction demands a fresh reading of Scripture and produces the ecclesiocentric interpretations that we have probed, interpretations that find in Scripture prefigurations of the church and words of grace spoken to those who are "children of promise."

CHAPTER FOUR

A Letter from Christ

Here the Spirit takes on a hermeneutical function.
ERNST KÄSEMANN[1]

The letter-spirit antithesis has nothing to do with Pauline hermeneutics.
STEPHEN WESTERHOLM[2]

NEW COVENANT HERMENEUTICS?

In a burst of retrospective candor, Paul tells the Philippians that he has now come to regard his whole prior religious orientation as "crap."[3] Even with allowances made for hyperbole, the underlying claim is remarkable: Paul, "circumcised on the eighth day, of the people of Israel, of the tribe of Benjamin, a Hebrew of Hebrews, as to the Law a Pharisee," has now suffered the loss of the network of trusts and observances to which he was once passionately committed, seeking instead "to gain Christ and be found in him" (Phil. 3:4–11).

In Philippians, Paul is not writing directly about his transformed understanding of Scripture; however, since the pharisaic Judaism from which he defected was by all accounts a way of life grounded in the conscientious interpretation and application of Israel's sacred texts,[4] Paul's turning to Jesus Christ must have entailed some fundamental reassessment of the meaning and use of these texts. How did he explain in principle to himself and to others the new role played by Scripture in his faith?

If Israel's Scripture was, as we have seen in the foregoing chapters, the grand textual matrix within which Paul's thought took shape, the privileged predecessor with which he wrestled, it is reasonable to ask whether he had a coherent and consciously articulated hermeneutic. The term is an anachronism, of course, but the question is not. Paul was insistent that his message stood in direct continuity with Scripture and, at the same time, equally insistent that his gospel was radically new, a revelation that demanded reassessment of all that was past. Does Paul anywhere offer his readers an extended discussion of this hermeneutical paradox?

In exploring Paul's ecclesiocentric hermeneutic, we have discovered a pervasive implicit hermeneutical strategy. Furthermore, we have already noted certain passages, such as Rom. 15:4 and 1 Cor. 10:11, where Paul explicitly states his conviction that Scripture is rightly read as a word addressed to the eschatological community. These remarks encapsulate a positive judgment about the function of Scripture in and for the church, but they do not address the theoretical problem of continuity and discontinuity, a problem that Christians later came to know as the problem of the relation between the testaments. There is, however, one lengthy passage in Paul's surviving correspondence that has traditionally been read as his definitive reflection on this hermeneutical issue: in 2 Cor. 3:1–4:6 Paul contrasts "the letter" and "the spirit" as hallmarks of the distinction between the old covenant and the new. Any investigation of intertextuality in Paul's letters must come to grips with the hermeneutical implications of this passage.[5]

Unfortunately, 2 Corinthians 3, though squeezed and prodded by generations of interpreters, has remained one of the more inscrutable reflections of a man who had already gained the reputation among his near-contemporaries for writing letters that were "hard to understand" (2 Peter 3:16). It is hard to escape the impression that, to this day, when 2 Corinthians 3 is read a veil lies over our minds. The task of the present chapter will be to investigate whether an avowedly intertextual reading of the passage can provide some insight that will spare us, as ignorant and unstable belated readers, from twisting the text to its detriment, or to our own.

The heart of the matter lies exposed in 2 Cor. 3:6, where Paul asserts that God "has made us competent as ministers of a new covenant, a covenant not of the letter [*gramma*] but of the spirit; for the letter kills, but the spirit gives life." The matter of present concern to us can be formulated in a simple question: does this new-covenant ministry-competence entail a new form of reader-competence?

When God conscripted him as a proclaimer of the gospel, did Paul find himself given new eyes to read Scripture in a new way? Everything that we have seen of Paul's innovative reading of the Bible would lead us to expect an affirmative answer to this question. Indeed, in 2 Cor. 3:12–18

Paul goes on to contrast himself and other Christians to "the sons of Israel," who are said to have a "veil" lying over their minds "when Moses is read." In Christ, however, the veil is taken away, so that the truth can be perceived and proclaimed clearly (cf. 4:2). The image certainly suggests that a new reader-competence is born in the Christian convert. The presence of these motifs in 2 Corinthians 3 encouraged Ernst Käsemann to find evidence here of an explicitly developed "approach to a theological hermeneutic"—an approach which "implies a critical interpretation of scripture and of all tradition in general"[6]—and Koch is willing to speak of the passage as "a fundamental reflection of Paul about the understanding of Scripture *en Christo.*"[7]

Despite the presence of these themes in the context, numerous other commentators have insisted that the letter-spirit antithesis in 2 Cor. 3:6 ought not to be read as a hermeneutical principle. The reason for their demurral is stated succinctly by Plummer: "We must not be misled by the common contrast in English between 'letter' and 'spirit,' which means the contrast between the literal sense and the spiritual or inward sense of one and the same document or authority. By *gramma* and *pneuma* Paul means two different authorities; *gramma* is the written code of the Law, *pneuma* is the operation of the Spirit in producing and promulgating the Gospel."[8] Granting Plummer's point, however, we can still ask whether for Paul "the operation of the Spirit in producing and promulgating the Gospel" does not include preeminently the inspiration of the apostle as interpreter of the Torah.

The concern to exclude the interpretation of 2 Cor. 3:6 as a hermeneutical guideline arises partly as a backlash against certain traditions within Christian theology. At least since the time of Origen, some Christians have appealed to this passage as the definitive warrant for a mode of exegesis that discarded the literal sense of the biblical text in favor of esoteric allegorical readings.[9] Where such charismatic readings are practiced, where biblical narratives are construed as coded figurations, the specters of Gnosticism and arbitrariness lurk. The interpretation of 2 Cor. 3:6 that haunts the commentators is articulated by Robert M. Grant: "By 'letter' Paul seems to mean the literal, verbal meaning of scripture. . . . [T]he only way to understand the Old Testament is under the guidance of the Holy Spirit, who removes the veil of literal legalism from the minds of believers. This Spirit gives exegetical freedom. He destroys the tyranny of words. He makes possible a Christian exegesis of the Old Testament, intuitive rather than based on words."[10]

Against such a reading of the letter-spirit antithesis, protest is certainly justified. Paul is writing an apologia for his ministry, not an excursus on hermeneutical method. He attributes Israel's failure to understand the true import of Scripture neither to their neglect of allegorical techniques nor to a fixation on the outward and visible over the inward and spiritual. By no means is this epistle writer, for whom the power of the word was so palpable, conducting a polemic against "the tyranny of words." However, once we strip away the anachronisms, what remains? If Paul is neither a philosophical idealist nor an apologist for the Alexandrian brand of Platonizing allegory, what does he mean by his distinction between *gramma* and *pneuma*, and why does his contrast between the old and new covenants turn into a discussion of minds veiled and unveiled when Scripture is read?

Questions such as these are best addressed through a fresh reading of the text. My reading seeks to take the three factors below into account.

First, justice must be done to the exegetical foundations on which both the hermeneutical and nonhermeneutical readings rest. Where learned critics divide over the interpretation of a passage, it is a reasonable working hypothesis that the roots of the divergent readings must lie buried within the text itself. It is possible that subsequent interpreters have created dichotomies where Paul saw dialectical unity.

Second, we should pay attention not only to what the text says about the interpretation of Scripture but also to how the text uses Scripture. If the text does offer a hermeneutic, it is reasonable to expect Paul's practice to exemplify—and therefore to illuminate—the theory that he espouses. (Of course, it is possible that the theory and practice might be at odds; if so, critical inquiry will expose the inconsistency.)

Finally, a corollary of the above point: though most discussions of the use of Scripture in 2 Corinthians 3 focus on Paul's alleged midrash on Exod. 34:29–35, a sensitive reading of the passage will give due attention to other scriptural texts echoed in the chapter.[11] The semantic effects of the passage are achieved in part through an interplay of allusions. My reading seeks to unveil Paul's metaphorical moves as he evokes scriptural figurations, deforms them, and fuses them with other figurations.

2 COR. 3:1–4:6—A READING

The Tablets of Fleshy Hearts

Second Cor. 3:1–4:6 is a part of Paul's defense of the legitimacy of his apostolic ministry.[12] Though Paul had founded the Corinthian church, rivals had come on the scene after his departure from Corinth, questioning his credentials and his version of the gospel. Paul derisively labels them as "superapostles" who preach "another Jesus than the one we preached" (2 Cor. 11:4–5). Apparently these superapostles emphasized their Jewish heritage (see 2 Cor. 11:22) and their wisdom and eloquence. Judging from 2 Cor. 3:1–3, we can surmise that they brought with them letters of recommendation (a common practice in antiquity)[13] from other churches, perhaps from Jerusalem, and asked why Paul had not presented similar authenticating documents. Paul finds himself, awkwardly, forced into defending himself and contrasting his ministry to that of his detractors.

The third chapter of 2 Corinthians is framed by Paul's thinly veiled counteraccusations that his opponents are "hucksters" (2:17) who "adulterate the word of God," crafty operators with hidden motives (4:2).[14] Thus, although these rivals are nowhere directly mentioned in 2 Corinthians 3, the contrast that Paul develops in 3:7–18 between his own ministry and the ministry of Moses must play a role in his response to the awkward polemical situation that he is addressing.[15]

Many scholars have attempted to read between the lines of Paul's bitterly ironic response in order to create a detailed conjectural reconstruction of the opponents' teachings and their charges against Paul. Dieter Georgi's ingenious monograph on *The Opponents of Paul in Second Corinthians* presses this sort of analysis to its limits—and perhaps beyond—by treating 2 Cor. 3:7–18 as the *opponents'* interpretation of Exodus 34, into which Paul has interpolated his own critical remarks.[16] In fact, any such reconstruction is necessarily speculative. In the absence of further evidence, it cannot be ascertained whether Paul's rivals had already somehow identified their own ministry with the glory of Moses or whether, on the contrary, Paul's juxtaposition of himself and Moses is of his own devising, spontaneously generated out of rhetorical momentum. Whatever his opponents may have taught, Paul's discourse in this chapter has its own internal metaphorical logic, which can be described in terms of its unfolding intertextual tropes, without recourse to hypotheses about external sources or influences on the discourse.[17] Therefore, employing no historical construction beyond the above brief sketch of the situation, I propose to examine the scriptural allusions and commentary that stand at the heart of 2 Corinthians 3, asking how Scripture functions within Paul's argument and how he weaves it into the extraordinarily complex trope that concludes the chapter.

In 2 Cor. 3:1–3, Paul plaintively rejects the demand for letters of recommendation. Rather than flatly asserting his claim to authority, however, he turns the notion of the letter of recommendation (*epistolē sys-*

tatikē) into a metaphor that shifts attention from his own qualifications to the Corinthian community itself as the visible fruit of his apostolic labor. "You are our letter, inscribed on our hearts, known and read by all people. You show that you are a letter from Christ, carried by us, inscribed not with ink but by the Spirit of the living God, not on stone tablets but on the tablets of fleshy hearts." The argument is a potent one: the very existence of the church at Corinth is manifest evidence of the efficacy of Paul's apostleship. They cannot question the legitimacy of his ministry without simultaneously questioning the legitimacy of their own origins as a community.

Once Paul has coined the metaphor, he starts to play with its ramifications. The community—as a living letter—is better than a mere human letter of recommendation because it comes from a higher authority; no less than Christ himself must be the author. This claim, here expressed metaphorically, is no casual fancy: Paul thinks of the church as an eschatological community actually brought into being through the agency of Jesus Christ, not through merely human efforts. But if Christ is the author, how does Paul fit into the figure? He is not only the person recommended by the letter but also its bearer. (That is probably the reason for the somewhat odd notion that the letter is "inscribed on *our*[18] hearts": Paul carries around with him in his own heart the attestation that the Corinthians seek, because he bears *them* in heart and memory. The turn of phrase is a little confusing because it makes two points at once; it emphasizes both Paul's love for the Corinthians and the fact that they themselves are the proof of Paul's legitimacy.) Of course, because it would have been common practice for a person to carry his own letters of recommendation with him, Paul's self-portrayal as both recommended person and letter courier stays within the bounds of the metaphor. Slightly unusual, however, is his use of the participle *diakonētheisa* in 2 Cor. 3:3, describing the letter, literally, as *"ministered* by us." This verb choice anticipates the subsequent discussion of the ministry (*diakonia*) of the Spirit/righteousness (vv. 8–9) and of Paul's role as minister (*diakonos*) of a new covenant (v. 6). Thus, in verse 3, the verb works on metaphorical and nonmetaphorical levels simultaneously: it images the courier's careful handling of the letter and, at the same time, reminds the Corinthians of Paul's ministry among them.

Paul's witty troping of the "recommendation letter" motif, superficially an ad hoc response to the Corinthians' request, gains gravity by evoking echoes of a series of scriptural texts. The reader who follows these echoes will be led back into a thesaurus of narrative and promise; only there, in the company of Moses and Jeremiah and Ezekiel, does

Paul's metaphor of the Corinthians as a "letter from Christ" disclose its true wealth.

The first clue that biblical echoes might linger about the text appears in Paul's affirmation that the Corinthians are a letter "written on our hearts" (v. 2). The phrase recalls God's striking promise of a "new covenant" in Jer. 38:33 (LXX, 31:33 MT): "I will give my laws in their mind, and upon their heart I will write them."[19] Since Paul is referring here to a commendatory epistle written on the heart, rather than to the Law of God, the echo might be dismissed as peripheral, were it not for the fact that the motif of the new covenant, a motif distinctive to Jeremiah, appears explicitly in the next sentence (v. 6).[20] Once this intertextual link is secured, the careful reader is led on to ask what the relation might be between Paul's letter of Christ and Jeremiah's new covenant. Some points of correspondence are evident. In both cases, God writes on the heart. In both, God claims a new people for himself (cf. Jer. 38:33c [31:33c MT]: "I will be their God and they shall be my people"), a people whose life constitutes a visible sign of God's grace.

At this point, Paul has not yet drawn a negative comparison between the old covenant and the new. Instead, he has pointed to the consistent authorial activity of God as one who writes on the hearts of his people, both in Jeremiah's prophecy and in the Corinthians' experience. The phrase, "inscribed not with ink but by the Spirit of the living God" (v. 3) probably echoes the language of yet another scriptural passage in which God is depicted as a covenant writer: Exod. 31:18 (cf. Deut. 9:10–11) describes the stone tables (*plakas lithinas*) of the covenant given to Moses as "written by the finger of God [*gegrammenas tō daktylō tou theou*]."[21] If this echo of Exodus, however, creates the expectation of a positive correlation between the Mosaic covenant and the new covenant—in Jeremiah, such a correlation is surely indicated by the figure of the new covenant[22]—that expectation is immediately disturbed by the last phrase of 2 Cor. 3:3: "not on stone tablets [*en plaxin lithinais*] but on the tablets of fleshy hearts [*en plaxin kardiais sarkinais*]." The negative contrast between stone and flesh echoes Ezek. 36:26: "And I will give you a new heart [*kardian kainēn*], and a new spirit [*pneuma kainon*] I will give among you, and I will take away the stone heart [*tēn kardian tēn lithinēn*] out of your flesh, and I will give you a fleshy heart [*kardian sarkinēn*]." The paraphrastic RSV translation of 2 Cor. 3:3, "not on tablets of stone but on tablets of *human* hearts" unfortunately suppresses the allusion to Ezekiel. The allusion was kept close to the surface by the King James Version (KJV), which retained the adjective *fleshy* but misplaced it, reading it as a modifier of *plaxin*, rather than of *kardiais*: "fleshy tables of the heart."

The effect of these clashing echoes is to set up an implicit dissonance in 2 Cor. 3:1–3 between the Mosaic covenant and the new covenant, though neither has yet actually been mentioned. Paul's allusions gather and meld the prophetic images of Jer. 38:33 (God will write on the heart) and Ezek. 36:26 (fleshy hearts replace stone); the Ezekiel text, though present only allusively, is the pivotal point of the contrast between old and new, because its pejorative reference to stone hearts becomes the ground of intertextual plausibility for Paul's daring interpretive act of imputing negative connotations to the stone tablets on which God once wrote at Sinai. It is hardly mere coincidence that Paul, rather than referring to Ezekiel's stone hearts, uses the very phrase (*plakas lithinas*) that describes the tables of the Law in Exodus and Deuteronomy, and sets these "stone tablets" in antithesis to Christ's letter written on fleshy hearts. The juxtaposition of allusions foreshadows the radical claims that will follow about the contrasting character of the old and new covenants. Paul's intertextual trope hints, in brief, that in the new covenant incarnation eclipses inscription.

By incarnation I mean not the incarnation of the divine Son of God as a human being, but the enfleshment of the message of Jesus Christ in the community of Paul's brothers and sisters at Corinth.[23] That fleshy community is, according to Paul, Christ's letter, which is to be recognized and read by all people (v. 2b). The prophetic promises of Jeremiah and Ezekiel envision the consummation of God's redemptive purposes in terms of the creation of a living community of people who have God's spirit in their midst ("I will give my Spirit in your midst" [Ezek. 36:27]), who require no admonition to "know the Lord" because "they shall all know me, from the least of them to the greatest" (Jer. 38:34 [31:34 MT]). In this eschatological community of the new covenant, scribes and professors will be useless, because *texts* will no longer be needful. Scripture will have become a "self-consuming artifact"; the power of the word will have subsumed itself into the life of the community, embodied itself without remainder.[24]

Thus, Jeremiah's new covenant, "not like the covenant which I made with their fathers in the day when I took them by the hand to lead them out of the land of Egypt" (Jer. 38:32), differs from the old precisely because it is enfleshed rather than inscribed. Ink and stones and Ezekiel's bones are deathly until God, in accord with Ezekiel's word, breathes the spirit: "Thus says the Lord God to these bones: Behold, I am bringing into you the spirit of life, and I will place sinews upon you, and I will bring flesh upon you, and I will stretch skin upon you, and I will give my spirit into you, and you shall live. And you shall know that I am the Lord"

(Ezek. 37:5–6). That prophecy, Paul believes, finds its fulfillment in the church.

Such claims may seem extravagant when measured against what we know of the empirical reality of the Corinthian community, or of any human community. If they are Christ's letter, has the text become corrupt in transmission? How can Paul write calmly that they *are* a letter from Christ inscribed by the Spirit of the living God?

Should we be surprised if metaphorical equations strain our comprehension? As Thomas Greene remarks while surveying a florilegium of stunning metaphors, "The mind must be very still to begin to register the force of the copula, expressed or unexpressed, that speaks from any *mundus significans* not our own. . . . Beneath its surface limpidity, each 'is' conceals profundities of unreason."[25] So too with Paul's audacious, allusive application of the prophetic vision to the Corinthian community: to read the writing of God on fleshy hearts fastened to dying Gentiles is possible only for those who have been made competent. The offense of the trope is a clue; if we are still enough, we can follow it and begin to plumb the profundities of unreason that lie at the heart of the new covenant's *mundus significans*.

If we have correctly grasped the polyphonic structure of the scriptural allusions in 2 Cor. 3:1–3, the climactic statement in 2 Cor. 3:6 comes neither as a surprise, nor as the solution to a riddle, but as the resolution of a suspension, the cadence for which the preceding measures have prepared us: "God has made us competent as ministers of a new covenant, a covenant not of the script but of the spirit."

My translation of *gramma* as "script"—which should be read as a verbal noun meaning "that which is inscribed"—is an attempt to capture the wordplay that links verse 6 back to verse 3. Just as Christ's epistle is not "inscribed" (*eggegrammenē*) with ink or on stone, but written by the Spirit on hearts, so Paul's ministry of the new covenant is not of the "script" (*gramma*) but of the Spirit.[26] In other words, it is a ministry that centers not on *texts* but on the Spirit-empowered transformation of human community. (*Gramma* should not, however, be equated with Scripture[27]; Paul's word for Scripture is *graphē*, which—as we have seen—he regards not as lifeless text but as living and speaking presence.)[28] The traditional English translation of *gramma* as "letter," based in turn on the Vulgate's *littera*, is an unfortunate one, both because it obscures the echo of verse 3, and because it suggests that Paul is distinguishing between literal and spiritual modes of exegesis. This is the construal against which the advocates of a nonhermeneutical interpretation of 2 Corinthians 3 rightly object. Much better is the RSV's rendering: "not in a written code but in the Spirit." This translation more adequately suggests that for Paul the problem with the old covenant lies precisely in its character as a written thing. Unfortunately, however, the RSV's use of the term *code* has two potentially misleading effects: (1) It weakens the important connection to verses 1–3: Paul is still explaining why he needs no *written* recommendations; (2) The term *code* also might be taken to imply that the problem with the old covenant is its narrow, legalistic character, which is not Paul's point in 2 Corinthians 3. The problem with this old covenant is precisely that it is (only) written, lacking the power to effect the obedience that it demands. Since it has no power to transform the readers, it can only stand as a witness to their condemnation. That is why Paul remarks aphoristically, "The script kills, but the Spirit gives life" (cf. Rom. 7:6–8:4).[29] As Paul's earlier allusion to Ezekiel 36 and 37 indicates, the life-giving power of the Spirit is shown forth precisely in the creation of the enfleshed eschatological community. That is the sense in which the Corinthians are a letter from Christ: they are a breathing instantiation of the word of God. Paul is a minister of the new covenant of the Spirit because he proclaims the message that brings this eschatological community into being.

Thus, the Christian tradition's reading of the letter-spirit dichotomy as an antithesis between the outward and the inward, the manifest and the latent, the body and the soul,[30] turns out to be a dramatic misreading, indeed a complete inversion. For Paul, the Spirit is—scandalously— identified precisely with the outward and palpable, the particular human community of the new covenant, putatively transformed by God's power so as to make Christ's message visible to all. The script, however, remains abstract and dead because it is not embodied.

For that reason, there is more than a grain of truth in Stephen Westerholm's dictum, "The letter-spirit antithesis is . . . the key to Pauline ethics, not Pauline hermeneutics."[31] Westerholm is certainly correct in what he affirms—especially if ethics is understood to refer to the formation of character in a community—but his denial is not equally justified. According to 2 Cor. 3:7–18, when God's Spirit-inscribed people encounter Scripture, a transformation occurs that is fundamentally hermeneutical in character.

Veiled Glory

Having appealed to Jeremiah's prophecy of a new covenant as a warrant for his own ministry, Paul decides to expand on the comparison between the different "ministries" of the two covenants.[32] He conducts the comparison through an extended reflection on a scriptural text already invoked by his mention of stone tablets: the account of Moses' descent from the mountain with "the tablets of the covenant" (Exod. 34:29–35). Interestingly, Jer. 31:31–39 was the *haftarah* correlated with the Torah reading of Exod. 34:27–35 in the Palestinian triennial lectionary cycle.[33] Thus, the linkage of these texts might already have been traditional in the Judaism of Paul's time, though his distinctive interpretation of the texts was certainly far from traditional.

Although 2 Cor. 3:7–18 has often been labeled a midrash by commentators,[34] it stands in a more distant relation to the biblical text than is characteristic of rabbinic midrash.[35] Paul alludes to the story and reflects on it, but he makes little effort to interpret specific details, except in verses 16–17, where he paraphrases Exod. 34:34 and then provides an exegetical gloss. Formally, 2 Cor. 3:7–18 resembles 1 Cor. 10:1–13—an allusive homily based on biblical incidents—more closely than it resembles passages such as Romans 4 or Rom. 9:6–29, which explicitly cite and explicate biblical texts. As in 1 Cor. 10:1–13, Paul assumes his readers' familiarity with the story, on which he comments in an allusive manner, presupposing rather than arguing for a typological reading, and quoting toward the end of his deliberation a single pithy excerpt that focuses the theme he wants to highlight (2 Cor. 3:16). In this passage, in contrast to verses 1–6, there is no complex interplay of subtexts; the single obvious subtext is Exodus 34. Because Paul does not give this text close exegetical scrutiny, it appears to serve merely as a foil for his own reflections, but its role is in fact, as we shall see, a generative one[36]: Exodus 34 becomes for Paul a metaphor that discloses the truth not only about the old covenant but also about the new. To follow the workings of the metaphor within this difficult passage, we must address a number of disputed exegetical issues. Caveat lector: the way to the chapter's climax leads through some heavy undergrowth, but no short cut is possible if we want to arrive at a justifiable and coherent reading.

In verses 7–11, Paul lays out a series of *qal waḥomer* (*a minore ad maius*) contrasts between the covenants. All of the contrasts acknowledge the glory of the ministry of the old covenant, even though this ministry is pejoratively characterized as "the ministry of death" and "the ministry of condemnation." The rhetorical effect of this ambiguous presentation is an unsettling one, because it simultaneously posits and undercuts the glory of Moses' ministry (one recalls Antony's funeral oration). Since Paul is arguing that the ministry of the new covenant outshines the ministry of the old in glory, it serves his purpose to exalt the glory of Moses; at the same time, the grand claims that he wants to make for his own ministry require that the old be denigrated. The paradox reaches its sharpest pitch in verse 10: "For even that which was glorified was not glorified . . . because of the surpassing glory." The oxymoronic clash rings in Paul's Greek, as the sentence struggles against itself: *ou dedoxastai to dedoxasmenon*. In this instance the valence of the typological correlation between old and new covenant cannot be simply categorized. It is neither unambiguously antithetical (like the Adam/Christ typology) nor unambiguously positive (like the Israel/church typology); it can only be described as dialectical.

As in the case of his capsule summary of the story of Abraham, Sarah, and Hagar (Gal. 4:22–23),[37] Paul's allusive recounting of the story of Moses' shining face already stacks the exegetical deck in favor of the interpretation that he plans to give to the narrative. In 2 Cor. 3:7, alluding to Exod. 34:30, he writes: "The sons of Israel could not gaze at the face of Moses because of the transitory[38] glory of his face." This is a summarizing remark rather than a quotation; Exod. 34:30 (LXX) actually says, "Aaron and all the elders of Israel saw Moses and the appearance of the color of his face was glorified, and they were afraid to approach him." Significantly, Paul adds to his account of the story an element that has no evident basis in the Exodus text: he describes the glory of Moses' face as *tēn doxan . . . tēn katargoumenēn*, rendered by the great majority of English translators as "the fading glory."

Of course, if the Exodus story depicts the glory on Moses' face as fading over time, then Paul has at hand an obvious symbol for the impermanence and obsolescence of the old Mosaic covenant. In fact, however, Exodus, chapter 34, neither uses the verb *katargein*, nor says anything about a fading of the glory from Moses' face. Where did this idea come from? Often commentators suppose that Paul himself invented the motif of fading glory to explain why Moses put a veil over his face, since Exodus fails to supply an explicit reason for this mysterious action. Brevard Childs, however, recognizing how unpersuasive such an invention would be in Paul's argumentative situation,[39] hypothesizes that Paul must have been working from an established midrashic tradition, known to his readers, since he does not try to prove that the glory was a fading glory: "He simply made use of a generally accepted interpretation on which to build his own argument."[40] Some such explanation becomes necessary if one understands Paul's phrase *tēn doxan . . . tēn katargoumenēn* to mean that the glory was fading from Moses' face. The difficulty is that there is no direct evidence for the existence of any such tradition within Judaism.[41]

A better explanation, however, lies at hand. The verb *katargein*, which recurs in verses 11, 13, and 14—and therefore turns out to be crucial for the interpretation of the passage—does *not* mean "to fade."[42] It is a word that Paul uses with some regularity, and in his lexicon it always means to nullify, to abrogate, to invalidate, or to render ineffectual. Its semantic field is the realm of legal process rather than of visual images. For example, in Gal. 3:17, he writes: "The law . . . does not annul a covenant previously ratified by God, so as to make the promise void" (*eis to katargēsai tēn epaggelian*). Or again, in Rom. 3:31: "Do we then abrogate [*katargoumen*] the Law through faith?"

The closest Pauline parallel to the use of this verb in 2 Cor. 3:7 appears in 1 Cor. 2:6: "We do speak wisdom among the mature, but it is a wisdom not of this age nor of the rulers of this age who are being nullified" (*tōn archontōn tou aiōnos toutou tōn katargoumenōn*). This use of the verb in its passive participial form is difficult to translate felicitously into English. In my initial rendering of 2 Cor. 3:7, above, I translated it, provisionally, as *transitory*. This translation conveys the idea of impermanence, but it fails to capture the passive verbal force of the participle, which is an important part of the sense here; the participle describes not an innate property of the modified noun but an action performed upon it. In the case of 1 Cor. 2:6, Paul means not only that the wisdom of the rulers of this age is impermanent, but also that it is being doomed, being rendered void and done away, eschatologically, through God's act in Christ. That this is Paul's meaning is made somewhat clearer by his use of the same verb just a few sentences earlier in describing the implications of "the word of the cross": "God chose what is low and despised in the world, even things that are not, to bring to nothing [*hina katargēsē*] things that are" (1 Cor. 1:28).

Similarly, in 2 Cor. 3:7 Paul's formulation means that the glory reflected on Moses' face (i.e., the glory of the old covenant) was a glory that is now, through God's act in Christ, being nullified.[43] This enigmatic statement does not necessarily mean that Paul believed that—within the narrative context of Exodus 34—the glow on Moses' face was fading. If Paul were undertaking a retelling of Exodus 34 in the freely paraphrastic manner of the later Targums—which is not what he is doing here— would he say that the glory was fading from Moses' face? 2 Cor. 3:7–11 gives us no reason to think so. Paul's *katargoumenēn* is not a narrative description but a retrospective theological judgment. Indeed, the meaning of verse 7 is explicated by verse 10: the glory turns out to have been impermanent not because it dwindled away but because it has now been eclipsed by the greater glory of the ministry of the new covenant.

That Paul's thought is moving along these lines is confirmed by verse

11, where he once again employs the present passive participle of *katargein*: "For if the transitory [*to katargoumenon*] came with glory, how much more must the permanent [*to menon*] come with glory." This opposition greatly clarifies the sense of Paul's previous reference to transitory glory. His use of the neuter participle rather than the feminine shows that he is thinking in general theological terms: the (feminine) glory is a symbol for the whole phenomenon of the old covenant and its ministry, which is now synoptically gathered into the neuter participle as "that which is being nullified."

Second Cor. 3:7–11, then, is fully intelligible as a theological comparison between the ministries of the old and new covenants without the dubious assumption that Paul thought of Moses' face as repeatedly losing its radiance in between his audiences with God. The extraordinary staying power of "fading glory" as a symbol for the inferiority of the old covenant is attested by the persistence of this interpretation among Christian readers, despite the fact that neither Exodus nor Paul describes the glory as fading.[44] (If the idea had occurred to Paul, he too might have liked it, but there is no evidence in the text of 2 Corinthians that it ever did.) The participle *katargoumenēn* in verse 7 should be understood, in light of verses 10–11, as Paul's retrospective judgment on that which the radiance on Moses' face symbolized. It is a theological afterthought, just as is his description—in the same sentence—of the old covenant as offering a "ministry of death." (No one supposes that this epithet presupposes some hypothetical midrashic tradition!) This "afterthought" quality of the remark that the radiance was transitory is reflected syntactically by the position of the participle at the end of the sentence, a stylistic feature that is captured nicely by Ralph Martin's translation: "the Israelites were not able to fix their eyes on Moses' face because of his glory, although it was transient."[45] This interpretation should be augmented only by the observation that the old-covenant glory did not just peter out like a battery-powered flashlight; rather it was done away by the greater glory of the new covenant in Christ (cf. v. 10). A paraphrastic rendering will sum up my reading of 2 Cor. 3:7: "But if the ministry of death, chiseled in stone script, came with such glory that the sons of Israel were not able to gaze upon the face of Moses because of the glory of his face (a glory now nullified in Christ), how much more will the ministry of the Spirit come with glory."

All of this has an important bearing on the interpretation of 2 Cor. 3:13, where the participle *katargoumenon* appears again. In contrasting his own boldness to Moses' furtiveness, Paul introduces a feature of the Exodus 34 story that had not previously been mentioned: "Moses used to put a veil on his face so that the sons of Israel did not gaze upon the *telos* of the transitory [*tou katargoumenou*]." This comment, on which the elaborate metaphorical structure of verses 12–18 is built, is one of the most disputed sentences in this puzzling chapter.

The majority view among modern interpreters is that *telos* means "end" in the sense of "termination."[46] On this view, the verse should be interpreted to mean, "Moses put a veil on his face in order to prevent the sons of Israel from seeing the cessation of the fading splendor." This reading of course builds on the assumption that Paul thought of the glory on Moses' face as fading. Interpreters who hold this view often feel compelled to explain why Moses would want to prevent the Israelites from seeing the fading of the glory. All manner of motives are proposed, some of them charitable (e.g., he wanted to spare them the disappointment of seeing the glow fade, or he wanted to keep them from gawking at his face rather than being about the business of heeding God's commandments) some of them not so charitable (e.g., he was enacting a prophetic indictment of Israel's blindness, or he wanted to save face by preventing them from recognizing the impermanence of his ministry). All such explanations, however different, share the belief that the veil concealed from Israel the symbolic evidence of the transitory character of the old covenant.

A minority view among modern commentators, which can, however, claim the support of patristic interpreters such as Augustine and Theodoret, holds that *telos* means "end" in the sense of "goal" or "purpose."[47] On this view, the verse should be interpreted to mean, "Moses put a veil on his face in order that the sons of Israel might not perceive the true aim of the transitory covenant." This reading is fundamentally incompatible with the "fading glory" theory (though not every commentator seems to realize this). Of this interpretation, too, the question is often asked—with even greater urgency—why Moses would want to conceal the true aim of the old covenant from the people. Once again, there are nearly as many proposals as there are critics: for instance, Moses was acting out of obedience to God, who planned all along to conceal the truth from Israel and thus "harden" them (cf. Mark 4:10–12), or Moses was a mystagogue who knew that veiling was an essential pedagogical aid to the spiritual quest. All such explanations, however different, share the belief that the veil concealed from Israel the symbolic evidence of the old covenant's prefiguration of the new.

It would require a monograph to give adequate attention to the history of interpretation of this passage and to address all of the technical exegetical issues that must be resolved in choosing which fork in the road should be followed. Among other things, a choice between the different meanings of *telos* in 2 Cor. 3:13 entails an overall judgment about the role of the Law in Paul's theology and an exegetical resolution of Paul's equally controversial statement in Rom. 10:4 that "Christ is the *telos* of the Law." Rather than entering the exegetical labyrinth, I propose merely to state a conclusion, with a few supporting considerations, and then to show how this interpretation of the verse promotes a coherent reading of the passage's metaphorical logic.

The case for interpreting *telos* as "goal" or "purpose" in 2 Cor. 3:13 is a very strong one. If, as I have contended, the radiance of Moses' face is *not* conceived by Paul as fading, there is really no other possibility. The sense of 2 Cor. 3:12–18 would then be as follows: The veil on Moses' face hid from Israel the glory of God, which Moses beheld at Sinai, a glory that transfigured him. Israel could not bear looking at the transfigured person and concentrated instead on the script that he gave them. That text, too, bears witness (in a more indirect or filtered manner) to the glory, to the person transfigured in the image of God, who is the true aim of the old covenant. For those who are fixated on the text as an end in itself, however, the text remains veiled. But those who turn to the Lord are enabled to see through the text to its *telos,* its true aim. For them, the veil is removed, so that they, like Moses, are transfigured by the glory of God into the image of Jesus Christ, to whom Moses and the Law had always, in veiled fashion, pointed.

In favor of this interpretation, the following considerations may be urged:

(1) The normal meaning of the Greek word *telos* is—pardon the tautology—"teleological"; that is, it refers to purpose, result, or goal, rather than to temporal termination or cessation.[48]

(2) Rom. 10:4 surely must be construed to mean, as I argued in my earlier treatment of Romans, that Christ is the goal and culmination of the Law, the truth to which Moses and the prophets pointed. Despite the references in 2 Cor. 3:7, 9 to Moses' ministry as a ministry of death and condemnation, the witness-bearing function of the Law is never far from Paul's mind, as demonstrated by his use of Scripture within this very passage (especially v. 16).

(3) Patristic interpreters unanimously understood the phrase *to telos tou katargoumenou* as a reference to Christ as the true significance or fulfillment of the old covenant.[49] However uncongenial this interpretation may appear to modern critics troubled by its historical anachronism, this was regarded as the plain sense of the text by generations of expositors whose first language was Greek and who exemplify a range of theological

sensibilities that Paul not only shared but in large measure helped to create.

(4) *Katargoumenon* in verse 13 cannot be read as a reference to fading glory; if Paul were still thinking about the visual image of the glory, he would use the feminine participle *katargoumenē*. Instead, carrying the neuter participle over from verse 11, he repeats his descriptive characterization of the old covenant ministry. The sense would not be materially changed if he had written, "in order that they might not gaze upon the *telos* of the old covenant."

(5) The internal logic of 2 Corinthians 3 favors this reading. If we ask simply, "what is seen when the veil is removed?" the answer, according to 2 Cor. 3:18, is certainly not that those for whom the veil is removed can now see that Moses was a fraudulent pretender or that the old covenant was impermanent. When the veil is removed, what is revealed is the glory of God. Therefore, Moses' veil must conceal not the absence of the glory but its presence. This conclusion can be avoided only if one supposes—as do many commentators—that Paul fails to sustain his metaphor consistently through the passage. That is certainly possible, but I argue in the following pages that the metaphor should be read as contributing coherence rather than confusion to the whole unit.

(6) Interpreters who follow Hans Windisch's influential treatment of verses 7–18 as a preformed midrash not integrally related to its present place in the letter[50] always share Windisch's assumption that Moses was hiding a fading glory; this suggests that the real point of the figure is the obsolescence of the old covenant and the superiority of Christianity to Judaism, themes not readily seen as pertinent to Paul's self-defense against the charges of other Christian apostles. The wider apologetic purpose of the passage is more intelligible, however, if verse 13 is understood in the way I have proposed here. Paul is defending his apostleship by dialectically comparing himself and his ministry to Moses and the ministry of the old covenant. On the negative side, Moses concealed the glory of God, whereas Paul speaks it boldly and openly in the gospel; Moses' old covenant was veiled in script, whereas Paul's new covenant is manifested in the transformation of human community. On the positive side, Moses becomes a metaphor for the person who "turns to the Lord" and sees the glory of God's image, thereby undergoing transformation. These themes make perfect sense as developments of the claims advanced in 3:1–6 and recapitulated in 4:1–6: Paul needs no written proof of his apostolic authority because his open Spirit-empowered proclamation of the gospel has produced, in the transformed Corinthians themselves, empirical proof that God is at work through him.

The remainder of our exposition in this chapter seeks to elucidate and defend the opinions sketched above in points 5 and 6. Before that constructive task is addressed, however, it is necessary to say something about the character of the objections that scholars have raised against interpreting *telos* in 2 Cor. 3:13 as a reference to the goal or purpose of the Law. These can be grouped broadly into the serious objections and the silly ones.

The serious objections all have to do with the viability of a teleological interpretation of the old covenant within the wider context of Paul's theology.[51] Such objections are indeed weighty, and they deserve thoughtful answers. Some have already been addressed in the earlier chapters of this book, some will be addressed in the following pages, and some will have to be left for other times and places.

The silly objections all have to do with the historical implausibility of Moses' hiding Christ, or the true meaning of the Law, from Israel. For example, Plummer writes, "St Paul could not mean that Moses veiled his face to prevent the Israelites from seeing Christ. Nor does *to telos* mean the final cause, the aim and object of the Law. Why should that be concealed from the people, and how would the use of a veil conceal it?"[52] Plummer's protest is cited and amplified by Philip Edgcumbe Hughes.

> [Some interpreters have] understood Paul to mean that Moses veiled his face to prevent the children of Israel perceiving that his dispensation was to have its end or consummation in Christ. This interpretation, however, is consistent neither with the context of Ex. 34:33 nor with good exegesis. Moses' purpose in veiling his face was hardly mystical and eschatological—however significant it now appears in retrospect—but ad hoc, related to the immediate necessity for concealing the divine glory from the eyes of a sinful people. Paul, as Plummer points out, "could not mean that Moses veiled his face to prevent the Israelites from seeing Christ." Had this been his purpose, it would be legitimate to ask, firstly, why the interposition of a piece of material should have been thought adequate to interrupt an essentially spiritual and eschatological vision, and secondly, why Moses should have wished to prevent their enjoying so praiseworthy and desirable a perspective.[53]

Reading through this paragraph, one grows progressively more embarrassed for the author. Hughes seems to have forfeited all sense that Paul is an ancient writer offering a symbolic interpretation of a biblical text; rather, he seems to assume that Paul is writing as a historical critic concerned about "good exegesis" and attempting to explain what in fact happened in the wilderness, *wie es eigentlich gewesen ist*, when Moses emerged from his meetings with God. Hughes is, if we may put it this way, interpreting Paul according to the script rather than according to the spirit. As James Kugel remarks in a different context, "literalists of the imagination turn fanciful exegesis into would-be history."[54]

Hughes' enthusiastic exhibition of historicism is rarely recapitulated by more recent critics, but some of the same assumptions infect even very careful analyses of this passage, whenever the question about Moses' motives for concealment is raised as an objection against translating *telos* as "aim." Paul says nothing about Moses' motives for concealing the telos of the old covenant, and it probably did not occur to him to raise the question. The biblical story is a given, and he sees in it a glowing opportunity to coin a metaphor that will reflect the difference between his ministry and that of his opponents. He apparently disregards even the literary-contextual fact that in Exod. 34:32–35 Moses put on the veil only *after* speaking with the people, a detail that disturbs the neatness of his metaphorical reading. The only thing that interests Paul about the story is its compelling image of a masked Moses whose veil is removed when he enters the presence of the Lord. That image becomes for Paul the center and substance of an imaginative interpretation that is—despite Hughes' conscientious efforts to cover it up—mystical and eschatological.

Lifting the Veil

The unit of discourse running from 2 Cor. 3:12 to 4:4 is, formally, a *dissimile*. I borrow the term from George Lord's analysis of "Pretexts and Subtexts in Milton's Renaissance Homer," where he explains that the dissimile is

> a trope developed from Homer in which characters and places, often of exotic and legendary power, are invoked only to be discarded as false or inferior by comparison with Milton's true mythical version. The strategy of expanding the differential ratios of the simile beyond its referential ones is to a large extent dictated by the poet's compelling need throughout *Paradise Lost* to establish the unique truth of his epic in contrast to the impositions of his precursors.[55]

Paul is of course not imitating Homer, but his invocation and discarding of the powerful figure of Moses works toward an analogous end: he is seeking to establish the unique truth of his new covenant ministry in contrast to the imposition of its precursor. "Having therefore such a hope, we employ great boldness, *not like Moses,* who used to put a veil over his face."

The rhetorical effect of such negations is suggestively probed by Jonathan Culler, who observes that in contrast to positive propositions, "negations are much richer in presuppositions."[56] That is, negations of a proposition presuppose rhetorically that someone has affirmed or might affirm it; consequently, the very act of negation suggests some sort of metaphorical truth, or it at least allows the negated statement to open a door into areas of indefinite metaphorical possibility. Culler offers as an illustration a stanza from Baudelaire's "Un Voyage à Cythère," in which the speaker, having glimpsed "an unusual object," comments on it in the following tantalizing manner:

> Ce n'était pas un temple aux ombres bocagères,
> Où la jeune prêtresse, amoureuse des fleurs,
> Allait, le corps brûlé de secrètes chaleurs,
> Entrebaîllant sa robe aux brises passagères.

> [It was not a temple with bosky shades
> Where the young priestess, in love with flowers,
> Passed, her body consumed by secret flames,
> Her robe blowing open in the fleeting breezes.]

The result of this lengthy nondescription, Culler avers, is to make "the whole stanza the negation of an intertextual citation, the negation of something already in place as a discursive supposition."[57] When Culler speaks of "the negation of an intertextual citation," he does not mean that we could necessarily ferret out a particular literary source for Baudelaire's images; he merely means that the rhetoric of the poem treats these images as *"déjà lu,"* part of the intertextual matrix presupposed by the poem.

Sometimes, of course, particular pretexts can be identified with some precision. That is the case in 2 Cor. 3:12–18, as we have already seen. Even so, Paul's strategy of negative indirection leaves the text pulsing with suggestive denials, especially since his dissimile embraces details not found in the precursor text. By saying that he acts "not like Moses" and then ascribing to Moses' self-veiling a consequence of which Exodus tells us nothing, Paul conjures into existence a discursive supposition, an intertextual assumption that may or may not refer to some actual precursor text. The rhetorical efficacy of this device is confirmed by the reading of Childs, who feels compelled to hypothesize such a precursor, and a fortiori by the constructions of Georgi, who fills the intertextual space with elaborate creatures of the imagination.

As with the Miltonic examples that Lord is considering, Paul's dissimile turns out to be a long and complicated one. The foundational point of contrast is that whereas Moses veiled his face to conceal something (we shall presently consider more closely what was concealed), Paul "with unveiled face" proclaims the gospel before all "with the openness of the truth." The closure of this antithesis, first opened up in 2 Cor. 3:12–13a, is postponed until 3:18–4:4. The intervening description in 3:13b–17 of veils and hardening, of reading without understanding, of turning to the Lord and transformation, thickens the texture of the contrast. The more elaborately Paul develops the images spun from Exodus 34, the more the reader begins to wonder why he is telling us all this, if indeed his ministry is really so unlike that of Moses.[58] Rhetorically, the act of positing a dissimile and then lavishly developing it has a backlash effect: by distancing his ministry from Moses, Paul paradoxically appropriates attributes similar to those that he most insistently rejects; connotations bleed over from the denied images to the entity with which they are discompared. Lord describes an analogous effect in *Paradise Lost*, 4.268–87: "Milton repeatedly denies the beauty of countless pagan paradises in comparison with Eden, while tacitly employing their strong legendary associations to enhance and embellish its incomparable perfections."[59] In the same way, the dissimile in 2 Cor. 3:12–4:4 allows Paul to appropriate some of the mythical grandeur associated with the Sinai covenant—particularly the images of glory and transformation—even while he repudiates the linkage of his ministry to that covenant.[60]

In 2 Cor. 3:12–18, then, Paul's dissimile sets in motion dialectical crosscurrents. On the surface, Moses is a figure not like Paul, because he is veiled and mysterious, not disclosing all that he knows. He has numinous encounters, delivers oracular pronouncements, then retreats behind his veil, keeping his wisdom to himself. That is Paul's picture of the ministry of the old covenant: revelatory glimpses of a truth that remains for the most part hidden. By contrast, Paul has nothing to hide (4:1–2). He lays bare the truth, plays no game of revelational striptease. At this surface level, the dissimile serves Paul's apologia by highlighting his candor and appealing for his readers' trust. That is the major overt theme of this segment of the letter.

Below the surface, however, the current flows in the opposite direction, because Moses did, after all, encounter God face to face.[61] Thus, he becomes a symbol of unveiling as well as of veiling. The seductive power of the metaphor exerts so much pressure on Paul's exposition of the figure that in verses 16–18 Paul finds himself writing that he and other Christians are more like Moses than unlike him. Though Paul began by "expanding the differential ratios of the simile beyond its referential ones," the referential ratios reassert themselves in these verses. The crossover point is reached in verse 16: "But whenever he turns to the Lord, the veil is taken away." Moses' act of entering God's presence and removing the veil becomes paradigmatic for the experience of Christian believers ("we all") who "with unveiled face, looking upon the reflected glory of the Lord, are being transformed into the same image, from glory to glory."

Two major differences between the old and new covenants, however, are still implied here. First, Moses' unveiled encounters with the Lord were intermittent, punctuated by times of withdrawal and veiling. Paul's metaphor implies, by contrast, that he and others who have now turned to the Lord through Jesus Christ live in a continuous experience of the presence of the Spirit. The veil has been removed once and for all. Thus, Moses' occasional entry into the presence of God, while paradigmatic, remains only a prefiguration of the experience of Christians.

Second, under the old covenant, Moses alone entered the presence of God and all the other sons of Israel knew God only in mediated form through him (cf. Gal. 3:19–20).[62] That is one of the major issues at stake in Paul's antithesis between script and spirit. Verses 17–18 correspond directly to verse 7: "the sons of Israel" could not even gaze at Moses' face because of the glory (v. 7), but those who turn to the Lord/Spirit (v. 18) behold the glory of the Lord with unveiled face. Under the old covenant, Paul claims, Israel's knowledge of God was dependent on and limited by the mediated (and therefore veiled) written word of Torah; under the new covenant, direct experience of God is immediately given through the Spirit.

That is why Paul mentions the Spirit three times in verses 17–18: The Lord (*kyrios*) to whom Moses turns is identified with the Spirit, who gives freedom. This abrupt identification of *kyrios* and *pneuma*, notoriously unsettling for interpreters who feel constrained to reconcile it with Trinitarian dogma, is to be explained as Paul's exegetical gloss on the text he has just quoted: the *kyrios* in the LXX of Exod. 34:34 is being read by Paul, for his present purposes, as a figure for the Spirit (i.e., the form in which God is regularly experienced in the Christian community), as over against the merely written covenant.[63] The sense is captured precisely by the New English Bible (NEB): "However, as Scripture says of Moses, 'whenever he turns to the Lord the veil is removed.' Now the Lord of whom this passage speaks is the Spirit." Likewise, the final elliptical phrase of verse

18 ("[this comes] from the Lord/Spirit") indicates that the Spirit is the power who is constantly at work (note the present tense of the verb *metamorphoumetha*) in transforming all the members of the community. Paul's strangely compressed formulation (*kathaper apo kyriou pneumatos*) should be read as a contapuntal echo[64] answering to his earlier *ou kathaper Mōysēs* (not like Moses [3:13]) and *ouch hoti aph' heautōn hikanoi esmen* (not that we are competent from ourselves [3:5]).

This transformation of all believers into the likeness of Christ (cf. "the same image" [3:18] and "Christ who is the image of God [4:4]—the key word *eikōn* is used in both places) should be understood as a further clarification of the sense in which Paul can claim that the Corinthians are a letter from Christ that can be known and read by everyone. Because they are being changed into the likeness of Christ, they manifest the life of Jesus in their mortal flesh (cf. 2 Cor. 4:11).[65] Consequently, the deepest paradox of the passage emerges: Paul's reading of the sacred text (Exodus 34) reveals that revelation occurs not primarily in the sacred text but in the transformed community of readers.

If the foregoing analysis of our passage as a dissimile is correct, the Exodus 34 account of Moses has become for Paul a complex parable, figuring forth the tension between ignorance and knowledge, hiddenness and revelation. The parable resists the attempts of interpreters to turn it into an allegory, because its central figure, Moses, bears within himself metaphorical tensions that resist reduction into a one-for-one allegorical scheme. In verses 13–15, the inscrutable masked Moses, played off against Paul as a personification of covert activity, appears to represent the old covenant, but his veil conceals the telos of that covenant, which is—to speak openly at last—the gospel. In verses 16–18, then, the veil is removed and he appears to become a paradigm for all Christian believers, although Paul stops short of saying so; indeed, for the reasons previously indicated, we must not forget that the differential aspects of the dissimile continue to hover over these verses. Moses prefigures Christian experience, but he is not a Christian. He is both the paradigm for the Christian's direct experience of the Spirit and the symbol for the old covenant to which that experience is set in antithesis.

This is not an inadvertent Pauline contradiction or a garbled metaphor; it is a single powerful metaphor that emerges from Paul's parabolic reading of Exodus 34 and expresses succinctly his complex dialectical apprehension of Israel's Torah. Indeed, a coherent reading of 2 Cor. 3:12–18 is possible only if we recognize that in these verses a metaphorical fusion occurs in which Moses *becomes* the Torah. Commentators frequently observe, with varying degrees of rationalistic tolerance, that the veil on Moses' face in verse 13 is abruptly shifted to the minds of Jewish readers in verses 14–15. That is of course correct, but a more fundamental transfiguration underlies this shift: the dreamlike transfiguration of Moses from man into text. In verse 13 Moses is the prophet and lawgiver who veils his own face; in verse 15, Moses is the sacred text read in the synagogue. The single intervening transitional sentence tells us that the veil over the minds of the readers is "the same veil" (*to auto kalymma*) that Moses put on his face. How can that be so? Because Moses the metaphor is both man and text, and the narrative of the man's self-veiling is at the same time a story about the veiling of the text. The single phrase *to auto kalymma* clinches and requires a hermeneutical reading of the passage.

Thus, the symbolic density of 2 Cor. 3:16 gathers to a greatness. We have already noted that this is the moment when the dissimile collapses into a positive metaphor, when the differential ratios cross over into referential ones as Moses becomes paradigm rather than foil. (Or, if Moses is foil, he becomes shook foil from which God's grandeur flames out.) In light of the metaphorical union of Moses and Torah, we can perceive that this sentence is a symbolic nexus that gathers into itself multiple meanings: Moses turns to the Lord and the veil is removed from his face; Israel turns to Christ and the veil is removed from Moses/Torah; the reader of Paul's letter turns to the Spirit and the veil is removed from Moses the metaphor so that all these turnings can be seen with metaphorical simultaneity, in the wink of an eye. These are not merely "different possible interpretations" of the same text; they are multiple senses carried by the one metaphor.[66] And so, Paul says, "we all"—and this *we* must encompass Moses, Israel, Paul, the Corinthians, and all future readers who participate in this turning—experience freedom and begin to be transformed.

Lest some readers of this chapter fear an excess of cleverness in my proposal that the unveiling of verse 16 symbolically encompasses also the hermeneutical transformation that occurs in the reader of Paul's letter at this point, it should be noted that Paul himself shifts the metaphor onto that level and applies it to his readers in 2 Cor. 4:3–4, using language that echoes his earlier remarks about Israel's failure to understand Moses: "And if our gospel is veiled, it is veiled among those who are being destroyed; the God of this age has blinded the minds of the unbelievers, so that they might not see (or: reflect) the illumination of the gospel of the glory of Christ, who is the image of God." Presumably, if they turn to the Lord, the veil will be taken away.

Now, if Paul can use this veil metaphor in these multiple concentric senses, it is not unreasonable to ask once again what is concealed by the veil. As we have already noted, the majority view of New Testament scholars has been that the veil conceals the disappearance of splendor from Moses' face, symbolizing the obsolescence of the old covenant. But if the metaphor is read in the way I have suggested, a different interpretation is necessary. Behind the veil is nothing other than the glory of God, which is made visible in Jesus Christ.[67] Those who look steadily on his face (2 Cor. 4:6) are transformed into his image, because they reflect his glory.[68] That means that the telos of Moses' transitory covenant (which remained hidden from Israel in the wilderness) was the same thing as the true significance of Moses/Torah (which remained hidden from Paul's contemporaries in the synagogue), and both of these in turn are the same as the true aim of Paul's ministry and proclamation (which remains hidden from readers who reject his gospel or fail to comprehend his metaphors).[69] The veiled telos is, if we must express it in a discursive proposition, the glory of God in Jesus Christ that makes itself visible in fleshy communities conformed to Christ's image.[70] This way of translating Paul's point is cumbersome, but all the elements are necessary to express the hermeneutical and ethical significations that are packed into his metaphor.

The foregoing reading suggests, inter alia, that 2 Cor. 3:12–18, though it does not aim at providing hermeneutical guidelines, certainly is a text laden with hermeneutical implications. These implications can be gauged more precisely if we consider how verse 16 operates in the reader who perceives the convergence of metaphorical significations at this point in the discourse.

"But whenever he turns to the Lord, the veil is removed" is a free quotation of Exod. 34:34. In the LXX, the text reads, "But whenever Moses went in before the Lord to speak with him, he removed the veil until he went out."

LXX: *hēnika d' an eiseporeueto Mōysēs enanti kyriou lalein autō periēreito to kalymma heōs tou ekporeuesthai.*

2 Cor. 3:16: *hēnika de ean epistrepsē pros kyrion, periairetai to kalymma.*

Paul has tightened up the sentence by omitting the phrases "to speak with him" and "until he went out," he has omitted specific mention of Moses, and—most significantly, he has replaced the verb *eisporeueto* (went in) with *epistrepsē* (turns to), a word often used to describe conversion, as in 1 Thess. 1:9: "You turned [*epestrepsate*] to God from idols to serve a living and true God." Furthermore, he has shifted the verb's tense and mood from the imperfect indicative to the aorist subjunctive, thus allowing the clause to be read as a statement of a general possibility rather than as a narration of past action; accordingly, he has shifted the verb *removed* from the imperfect to the present tense.[71] These are far-reaching manipulations, and they are systematically calculated to facilitate Paul's metaphorical appropriation of the text, by cutting the sentence loose from its immediate narrative moorings. The changes in wording should not be explained away by appealing to some hypothetical textual tradition not otherwise attested or by saying that Paul was just quoting from memory. Paul's doctored citation simultaneously shows evidence of minute attention to detail and treats the text with great freedom in order to get it to say what he is convinced it means.[72] In short, he is removing the veil from the text, presenting it in a light which will enable his readers to see in it the same metaphorical sense that he sees.

The reader who has followed Paul's metaphorical logic up to this point knows by the end of 2 Cor. 3:15 that Paul has set up the veiled figure of Moses as a foil against which to commend the candor and boldness of his own ministry. Moses' veiling of the telos of the old covenant has collaborated with Israel's own hardness to insure their incomprehension of the true meaning of his ministry. So now "whenever Moses is read, a veil lies on their hearts." The force of the dissimile is weighty, and we expect the sequel to be a blistering condemnation of Moses' cowardice and duplicity, accompanied by a call to renounce the whole benighted Torah religion.

But in verse 16, a swift reversal—a turning—happens. Moses turns to the Lord, and the veil is removed. And with its removal, the reader grasps anew the purpose of the veil as metaphor. Exodus 34 is troped: no longer is it only an account of Moses' evasiveness and Israel's timid incomprehension. Suddenly the story has become a parable of grace, promising that Moses' turning and unveiling to see the glory of God can be read as a prefiguration of the truth to which the gospel also points.

The rhetorical effect of 2 Cor. 3:16 is exquisite because it enacts an unveiling commensurate with the unveiling of which it speaks. The text performs its trope in the reader no less than in the story. And—the final elegant touch—the trope is performed precisely through a citation of Moses. Moses' words are taken out of Exod. 34:34, unveiled, and released into a new semantic world where immediately they shine and speak on several metaphorical levels at once. Thus, rather than merely stating a hermeneutical theory about the role of Scripture in the new covenant, 2 Cor. 3:12–18 enacts and exemplifies the transfigured reading that is the result of reading with the aid of the Spirit. It is a deft turning. Koch comments,

Dass Paulus seinen Exkurs über das nur "in Christus" gegebene sachgemässe Verstehen der Schrift so gestaltet, dass die Spitzenaussage selbst ein Zitat der Schrift ist, ist nicht nur eine darstellerische Geschicklichkeit, sondern entspricht dem von Paulus hier dargelegten Sachverhalt: Mit der von Paulus behaupteten Verstehensmöglichkeit *en Christō* ist fur ihn kein fremder Sachsgesichtspunkt an die Schrift herangetragen, sondern dies ist in der Schrift selbst vorgegeben. Zugleich ist nicht zu übersehen, dass sich Paulus mit der Verwendung des Zitats von Ex 34,34a in einem hermeneutischen Zirkel bewegt: Die Anführung dieses Zitats für die von Paulus vorgetragene These von dem nur *en Christō* gegebenen sachgemässen Verstehen der Schrift ist nur möglich, weil er das Zitat seinerseits bereits *"en Christō"* interpretiert hat.[73]

[That Paul shapes his excursus, which argues that the appropriate understanding of Scripture is given only "in Christ," in such a way that the climactic statement is itself a citation of Scripture, is not merely a serendipity of presentation; rather, it corresponds to the state of affairs expounded here by Paul: for him, with the possibility (affirmed here by Paul) of understanding in Christ, no foreign point of view is imported to Scripture; rather, this point of view is already given in Scripture itself. At the same time, it should not be overlooked that Paul moves in a hermeneutical circle with the citation of Exod. 34:34a: it is possible for Paul to adduce this citation in favor of the thesis that he proposes here—that Scripture can be understood appropriately only in Christ—only because he, for his part, has already interpreted the citation "in Christ."]

Certain important conclusions follow from these observations. In the new covenant according to Paul, true reading both presupposes and produces the transformation of readers. Only readers made competent by the Spirit can throw back the veil and perceive the sense of Scripture; those who have not turned to the Lord who is Spirit are necessarily trapped in the script, with minds hardened and veiled. At the same time, readers who do by the aid of the Spirit discover the glory of God in Scripture are necessarily transformed by the experience. They cannot merely treat allegorical reading as an entertaining pastime or sit back to write learned and dispassionate books on hermeneutics. Those who have seen the glory of God behind the veil are necessarily caught up into the ministry of the new covenant, which means that they must, like Paul, give their lives over to "the ministry of reconciliation." Under the conditions of a sinful age, that ministry requires "always being given up to death for Jesus' sake, so that the life of Jesus may be manifested in our mortal flesh" (2 Cor. 4:11). This is the theme toward which Paul's hermeneutical reflection relentlessly drives (the passage presently under consideration leads on into 2 Cor. 4:7–15), and no one who draws back from such service can claim to have understood Moses in the sense that Paul envisions. The glory that Moses saw, the "illumination of the knowledge of the glory of God in the face of Jesus Christ" (4:6) is revealed in the face of a crucified Lord who calls his people to be conformed to his cruciform image.[74] That is the price of new covenant reader competence.

Those who pay the price, however, enter into a new freedom, which includes—if Paul's example signifies anything—hermeneutical freedom. Scripture must not be read slavishly according to the *gramma*. It must be read (I write these words in mortal terror of having them quoted back at me by students rebelling against exegesis paper assignments) under the guidance of the Spirit as a witness to the gospel. This means, ultimately, that Scripture becomes—in Paul's reading—a metaphor, a vast trope that signifies and illuminates the gospel of Jesus Christ. And, since the character of this gospel is such that it must be written on human hearts rather than in texts, the community of the church becomes the place where the meaning of Israel's Scripture is enfleshed. With that observation we have come full circle back to 2 Cor. 3:1–3.

THE TEXT TRANSFIGURED

We return to the questions that provoked our investigation of 2 Corinthians 3, to see whether our reading of the text has suggested new ways of addressing the problems. Does Paul articulate an explicit hermeneutical agenda? Are *gramma* and *pneuma* to be construed as hermeneutical principles? Does Paul's ministry of the new covenant require—or produce—distinctive methods of interpretation? These issues have been addressed throughout the foregoing pages, but some summarizing comments draw together our conclusions.

First of all, 2 Corinthians 3 is neither a practical discussion of how to do exegesis nor a theoretical treatise on the problem of continuity and discontinuity between the testaments. (In fact, if we want theoretical reflection on this matter from Paul, a better place to look for it is in Romans.) Instead, it is Paul's apologia, which upholds the legitimacy of his apostleship by expounding a vision of authentic ministry. His radical proposal is to reject all text-bound criteria for discerning authenticity. The new covenant, he insists, is marked and attested by God's writing on hearts, not in script: the ministry of the new covenant is attested by the formation

of communities whose lives, transformed by the Holy Spirit, bear undeniable witness to the truth of God's work in their midst. When Paul
says that the Corinthians are a letter from Christ, he ascribes to the life of
the community the same proclamatory power that Gerard Manley
Hopkins, echoing Paul eighteen centuries later, ascribes to the individual
Christian[75]:

> As kingfishers catch fire, dragonflies draw flame;
> As tumbled over rim in roundy wells
> Stones ring; like each tucked string tells, each hung bell's
> Bow swung finds tongue to fling out broad its name;
> Each mortal thing does one thing and the same:
> Deals out that being indoors each one dwells:
> Selves—goes itself; *myself* it speaks and spells,
> Crying, *What I do is me: for that I came.*
>
> I say more: the just man justices;
> Keeps grace; that keeps all his goings graces;
> Acts in God's eye what in God's eye he is—
> Christ—for Christ plays in ten thousand places,
> Lovely in limbs, and lovely in eyes not his
> To the Father through the features of men's faces.

When Paul's argumentative framework is kept firmly in mind, it becomes evident that *gramma* and *pneuma* are not the names of hermeneutical principles and that the difference between them is not a distinction between two ways of reading texts. So far, the nonhermeneutical
interpreters of the chapter are entirely in the right. When Paul contrasts
Spirit to *gramma,* he is not opposing the basic intent of Scripture to its
specific wording, as in our familiar distinction between "the spirit and the
letter of the law." Nor is he thinking, like Philo or Origen, about a mystical latent sense concealed beneath the text's external form. The Spirit
that Paul is talking about is the Holy Spirit, who is palpably present in the
community as an experienced reality, manifest in spiritual gifts such as
tongues and prophecy (cf. 1 Corinthians 12–14), transforming lives and
empowering the work of ministry. *Spirit* is not an essence or an abstract
theological concept. It is the daily experienced mode of God's powerful
presence in the community of faith.[76]

Thus, when Paul says that his ministry of the new covenant is a
ministry not of the script but of the Spirit, he means something like, "This
is a ministry that changes people's lives, not a ministry that labors over
written words."[77] Those of us in the academic community who spend our

lives laboring over written words may well find this dichotomy unsettling; indeed, it appears disingenuous in view of Paul's own extensive labors with the written word. If Paul regarded the activity of textual interpretation as deadly *in se*, why did he spend so much energy doing it? Clearly, 2 Cor. 3:6 is a rhetorical flourish that introduces a discourse on the *diakonia tou pneumatos* (ministry of the Spirit [2 Cor. 3:7–4:15]), not the definitive conclusion of a treatment of Pauline hermeneutics.

In explaining this ministry of the Spirit, however, Paul, as we have seen, straightway begins to cite and interpret Scripture. This shows that Paul's rejection of *gramma* is by no means a rejection of *Graphē*. Furthermore, his metaphorical fusion of Moses and Torah-text in verses 12–18 suggests that those who turn to Christ *will* be granted a transformed capacity to perceive the *telos* of Scripture, and his handling of Exodus 34 provides a paradigmatic instance of exactly this sort of transformative, Spirit-inspired reading. Thus, though Paul has not set out to discuss hermeneutics, and although the *gramma/pneuma* distinction is not to be construed as a juxtaposition of hermeneutical methods, the substance of this passage indicates that the *diakonia tou pneumatos* carries with it a radically new orientation toward Israel's Scripture. This new orientation is not systematically defined in 2 Corinthians 3, but it is imaged so vividly that it can be described with some specificity.

The reader who turns to the Lord and finds the veil taken away will return to the reading of Moses to discover that all of Scripture is a vast metaphorical witness to the lived reality of the new community in Christ. This observation is fully consonant with the findings of our previous chapter about the pervasively ecclesiocentric character of Paul's hermeneutic. (To be sure, Paul leaves no possibility for mistaking the focal point of his preaching: "We preach not ourselves but Jesus Christ as Lord, ourselves as your slaves for the sake of Jesus" [2 Cor. 4:5]. The turning to Jesus as Lord makes possible Paul's transformed reading of Scripture, but in 2 Corinthians 3 as in the other texts that we have previously considered, Paul finds the real subject matter of Scripture to be God's gracious action of gathering a redeemed people: that is what Jeremiah's promise of the new covenant meant.) When he interprets Exodus 34, he does not represent Moses as a typological prefiguration of Christ; nor does he read the transfiguration of Moses' face, as the writers of the synoptic gospels were to do a generation later, as foreshadowing an event in the life of Jesus. Instead, for Paul, Moses prefigures the experience of Christian believers. There are obscure hints here that Paul might have thought of Moses as having seen the glory of Christ on Mount Sinai,[78] but if that is what he thinks, he makes curiously little of it. His explicit application of the scriptural narrative moves from Moses and Israel to himself and the church. The community of the church is the place where the real meaning of Exodus 34 now finds expression: "So we all, with unveiled face . . . are being transformed."

The meaning of Scripture is enacted in the Christian community, and only those who participate in the enactment can understand the text. Consequently, the transformation of the community is not only the presupposition but also the result and proof of true interpretation. Where God's spirit is at work, the community ("we all") is being transformed into the image of Christ and liberated to see, when they read Scripture, that the old covenant prefigured precisely this transformation. Where this transformation is not occurring in a community of the faithful, no interpretation, however careful and learned, can penetrate the veil that lies over the text.

Thus, the putative dichotomy between hermeneutics and ethics dissolves, as the text is transfigured into the community. The new covenant's hermeneutic is not a theory of interpretation, not an inventory of interpretive procedures like the rabbinic *middot*. In Paul's new covenant hermeneutic, there is no true reading without moral transformation, and there is no moral transformation without true reading. The daily life of a community that lives with its roots in Scripture is its reading of Scripture, for that daily life "deals out that being indoors each one dwells." The *discrimen*[79] that governs interpretation of Scripture, then, is the metaphor of the eschatological covenant community being transformed by the power of the Spirit into the image of Christ. Any reading of Scripture consonant with this discrimen is a true reading.

The operation of this hermeneutic is illustrated in 2 Cor. 4:6, the final sentence of this section of Paul's argument. "For it is the God who said, 'out of darkness light will shine' who has shone in our hearts for the illumination of the knowledge of the glory of God in the face of Jesus Christ our Lord." The apparent quotation in this passage is actually not a direct quotation from Scripture at all. It is, rather, the sort of intertextual citation that Culler describes, a free creation of the apostle that nonetheless presents itself as *déjà lu*. It is a discursive supposition posited by Paul out of the intertextual matrix of Israel's Scripture.

The citation evokes echoes of two foundational texts. The first, more often noticed by commentators, is Gen. 1:3a: "Let there be light." The RSV, apparently trying to help readers recognize this allusion, idiosyncratically translates Paul's future indicative verb *lampsei* (light will shine) as a third person imperative: "Let light shine." The verb does not appear at all in Genesis 1. Indeed, the only direct verbal contact between 2 Cor.

4:6 and Gen. 1:3–4 is the juxtaposition of the terms *light* and *darkness*. This may seem like a faint echo indeed where such universal symbolic elements are concerned, but the Genesis text is so foundational for the Jewish understanding of creation that the allusion can hardly be missed.[80] The other text echoed here, though verbally closer in formulation to 2 Cor. 4:6, is more often overlooked by readers, though it is equally important to perceiving the force of Paul's intertextual echo. In Isa. 9:2 (9:1 LXX), the prophet writes: "O people who walk in darkness [*skotei*], behold a great light. You who dwell in a land and shadow of death, light will shine [*phōs lampsei*] upon you."[81] Paul's words, quoting neither of these texts but echoing both, fuse Israel's confession of God as creator with Israel's hope of a messianic deliverer, thereby implicitly declaring the present illumination of Paul's faith community to be the action of the God who is both creator and redeemer. The casual freedom with which the biblical text is transformed by Paul's echo allows both of these key scriptural passages to be enlisted together as witnesses of the "new creation" (cf. 2 Cor. 5:17).

The creator-redeemer God is said to shine light "in our hearts," because the new creation is manifest, according to Paul, precisely in the community of faith. This illumination yields knowledge "of the glory of God in the face of Jesus Christ." With that phrase, Paul catches up his foregoing discussion of glory and completes the unveiling of which he spoke in 2 Cor. 3:16–18. Moses covered his face to veil the glory, but his unveiled turning to the Lord is recapitulated in the church, where all "with unveiled face" now gaze upon the glory of the Lord. The imagery of 3:18 paints a picture of the community of faith being transformed as they contemplate a vision of glory, but does not yet show the reader what they are gazing at. The source and character of the radiance remain, as it were, offstage. The progression reaches its consummation in 4:6, as Paul, speaking openly as he had promised to do, declares that it is "the face of Jesus Christ" that manifests the glory. Christ is the glory-bearing *eikōn* into which the community is being transformed, the paradigm for the prosopography of the new covenant. So, because the Christian community at Corinth, Christ's letter, reflects in fleshy faces the same glory that Moses hid, their countenances become the true and definitive interpretation of how Moses should be read.

CHAPTER FIVE

"The Word Is Near You": Hermeneutics in the Eschatological Community

PAUL'S READINGS OF SCRIPTURE

Our account of Paul's reading of Scripture has yielded results that must now be gathered in and assessed. This final chapter will first offer a descriptive summary of our findings concerning Pauline hermeneutics and then, in conclusion, consider Paul's interpretation of Scripture as a normative paradigm for intertextual theological reflection. Our observations about Paul as reader of Scripture can be grouped thematically under five headings: hermeneutical freedom; revision and continuity; hermeneutical methods and constraints; the immediacy of the word; and eschatological hermeneutics. Let us consider each of these topics in turn.

Where the Spirit of the Lord Is, There Is Freedom

"Freedom" (*eleutheria*) stands near the heart of Paul's vision for the life of the people of God (Gal. 5:1, 2 Cor. 3:17); as we have seen, that freedom bears hermeneutical implications. Entering into "the knowledge of the glory of God in the face of Jesus Christ" (2 Cor. 4:6) liberates believers from bondage to a circumscribed reading of the old covenant and empowers them to read it with freedom—more precisely, to live it with freedom—as a witness to the righteousness of God in Jesus Christ. This means above all else that Scripture is construed metaphorically: it signifies far more than it says. Its latent sense is disclosed only to those who "turn to the Lord."

Illuminated by the Spirit, readers who have thus turned spin off readings that are themselves tropes. Paul's readings of Scripture are transformative: by correlating God's word to Israel with the new circumstances of his churches and the content of his kerygma, he generates novel interpretations that nonetheless claim to be the true, eschatologically disclosed sense of the ancient texts. Even passages that might have seemed perspicuous, such as Deut. 30:11–14, turn out to have concealed a meaning manifest only in Paul's inspired reading, a meaning that neither Moses nor Ezra could have guessed and that Paul himself could never have imagined before his own turning. Now, however, that latent meaning turns out to be the hermeneutical key that unlocks all the mysteries of God's revelation in the past. "'The word is near you, in your mouth and in your heart,' (That is, the word of faith which we preach)" (Rom. 10:8). The gospel that Paul preaches is—so he contends—the hidden meaning of the word that was always near to Israel.

If the gospel is hidden in Scripture, Scripture must be understood as richly allusive in character, hinting the kerygma, prefiguring it metaphorically. The biblical text must be read as a vast texture of latent promise, and the promise must be recovered through interpretive strategies that allow the hidden word to become manifest. The extraordinarily interesting feature of Paul's hermeneutical strategy, however, is his reverence for Scripture's own indirect and allusive mode of revelation, which he honors by imitating. Line-by-line decoding of the Bible—practiced in different ways by the Qumran covenanters and by Philo—is not Paul's characteristic style of exposition. Rather, if our analysis is correct, he allows Scripture to echo into the text of his letters in such a way that the echoes suggest patterns of meaning wider than his own overt interpretive claims. Paul's own discourse recapitulates the allusive complexity of his great subtext.

Thus, Paul's intertextual *poiēsis* poses a formidable challenge for those who follow him. The Pauline letters, read as hermeneutical events, are evocative allusive reflections on a text (Scripture) that is in turn deemed allusive rather than overt in its communication strategies. Inevitably, such a complex intertextual matrix proves hospitable to the proliferation of metalepsis. Echoes linger in the air and lure the reader of Paul's letters back into the symbolic world of Scripture. Paul's allusions gesture toward precursors whose words are already heavy with tacit implication. In this literary setting even overt quotation can become a mode of troping: citations allude to their original contexts, and the most significant elements of intertextual correspondence between old context and new can be implicit rather than voiced, perceptible only within the silent space framed by the juncture of two texts. If meaning is the product of such intertextual relations, then it is—to alter the figure—not so much like a relic excavated from an ancient text as it is like a spark struck by the shovel hitting rock.[1]

Consequently, for Paul, original intention is not a primary hermeneutical concern. If Paul's intertextual readings are metaphorical in character, the reader of Paul's letters is assigned the same active responsibility that falls on readers of all figurative discourse: to articulate semantic potentialities generated by the figures in the text. Such potentialities can far exceed the conscious design of the author. The scriptural text as metaphor speaks through the author; whether such speaking occurs with or without the author's knowledge is a matter of little consequence, for Paul's readings of Scripture are not constrained by a historical scrupulousness about the original meaning of the text. Eschatological meaning subsumes original sense. Paul's explicit claim in 2 Corinthians 3 is that he and others who have turned to the Lord now have the veil lifted to perceive a truth that was hidden from all previous readers; the true sense of Exodus 34, for example, is actualized in the community of Paul's readers only as a consequence of the hermeneutical transfiguration wrought intertextually in 2 Cor. 3:7–18. True interpretation depends neither on historical inquiry nor on erudite literary analysis but on attentiveness to the promptings of the Spirit, who reveals the gospel through Scripture in surprising ways. In such interpretations, there is an element of playfulness, but the freedom of intertextual play is grounded in a secure sense of the continuity of God's grace: Paul trusts the same God who spoke through Moses to speak still in his own transformative reading.

"Do We Then Nullify the Law?": Revision and Continuity

Such hermeneutical procedures raise an immediate and urgent difficulty: if Paul's Spirit-led readings treat Scripture as trope, do they in fact overturn it? Is his transformation of the sense of Torah so drastic that it constitutes a de facto subversion? Paul had to face such objections in his own lifetime; his insistence that "we uphold the Law" (Rom. 3:31), however, has convinced few Christians over the centuries—and fewer Jews.[2] Herbert Marks states the issue in the bluntest possible terms: "for Paul interpretation is first and foremost an occasion for the exercise of 'Christian freedom' or *exousia*. . . . Paul's impulse toward spiritual autonomy prompted a deep ambivalence toward the Bible itself, making him not an apologist—dependent on scripture for legitimating testimony—but a dogmatist—affirming the priority of his own conceptions by imposing them on the earlier tradition."[3] Are Paul's readings an expression of authentic continuity with the Torah, or are they, as Marks contends, "a paradigmatic instance of revisionary power realized in the process of overcoming a tyranny of predecession"?[4]

At one level, of course, Paul's construal of Torah is flagrantly revision-ary: he effectively sweeps away the normative significance of the prac-tices of Torah obedience. A man who writes, "neither circumcision nor uncircumcision matters, but new creation" (Gal. 6:15), has moved dra-matically outside the hermeneutical conventions of first-century Judaism and arguably to the periphery of the symbolic world of Israel's Scripture. How then can he persist in claiming that his gospel upholds the Law?[5]

Our investigation has shown that Paul finds the continuity between Torah and gospel through a hermeneutic that reads Scripture primarily as a *narrative* of divine election and promise.[6] God is the protagonist in the story, the one who has formed and sustained Israel from Abraham on-ward, the one whose promise of faithfulness stands eternally firm. Scrip-ture is, then, a story about *dikaiosynē theou*, God's righteousness, and God's righteousness is the ground of the narrative unity between Law and gospel. At this deeper level, Paul can hardly be accused of imposing his own conceptions on the earlier tradition. Rather, he has selected fundamental themes of the biblical story as hermeneutical keys to the meaning of the tradition. The selection of key themes differs in important ways from the selection made in rabbinic Judaism, but Paul's claim of hermeneutical continuity is grounded no less thoroughly in the texts themselves. God's act in Jesus Christ illuminates, Paul contends, a pre-viously uncomprehended narrative unity in Scripture. That is the burden of the argument in Romans 3 and 4: God has shown forth his right-eousness in a new way in Christ, apart from Law, but the Law and Prophets bear witness that this unforeseen act of grace is the supremely fitting climactic action of the same God whose character and purposes are disclosed in the narrative of his past dealings with Israel.

This way of reading the Bible through the lens of a narrative her-meneutic has far-reaching consequences for Paul's weighting and in-terpretation of particular elements in the story: Moses and the Law of Sinai are assigned a temporary supporting role, not the lead, in the drama of God's redemptive purpose. Thus, the Torah is neither superseded nor nullified but transformed into a witness of the gospel. That is why even the letter to the Galatians, which appears to pronounce a relentlessly negative judgment on the Law, can continue to build its arguments on Scripture, interpreting the story of Abraham as a prepreached expression of the gospel.

Within this narrative framework for interpretation, Paul's fragmen-tary references to and echoes of Scripture derive coherence from their common relation to the scriptural story of God's righteousness. Though the quotations appear eclectic and scattered, they usually must be understood as allusive recollections of the wider narrative setting from which they are taken.[7] For example, as we have seen, Paul's citation of Hab. 2:4 in Rom. 1:17 evokes the theodicy question that haunts Habakkuk's prophecy as a whole. Or again, a reference to Isaiah's judgment oracles (e.g., the citation of Isa. 52:5 in Rom. 2:24) can be rightly understood only against canonical Isaiah's depiction of Israel's exile and redemption. Because Paul's allusions conjure up such narratively ordered patterns of connotation, we have seen—especially in Romans—that the intertextual echoes often anticipate the subsequent unfoldings of his dialectic, unifying the argument subliminally.

If, then, Paul's hermeneutical procedures do create fundamental narrative continuities between Scripture and gospel, why does Marks judge the evidence so differently? His reading of Paul is not an idiosyncratic one, merely a more aggressive development of a tradition that Marks himself identifies: the tradition of Marcion and Harnack,[8] a tradition that reads Paul as the Apostle of anti-Judaism, a champion among the slayers of Moses.[9] Marks filters this traditional portrayal of Paul through Harold Bloom's critical theory and projects a Paul riddled by the anxiety of influence, yearning to assert his autonomy from the traditions that nurtured him.

This misreading of Paul is as heavily indebted to Bultmann as to Bloom. The debt becomes evident when Marks attributes to Paul "a profound conviction that what matters most is not the conclusion or content of the interpretation but the occurrence of the interpretive act itself," and buttresses this dubious proposition by citing Bultmann's still stranger opinion that "the history of the nation and the world has lost interest for Paul."[10] For Bultmann, interest in history is replaced by a concern about "the historicity of man," which Marks construes to mean that "man creates his own essence through his personal acts—acts which are necessarily incursions against his own past."[11]

There are two fundamental misprisions here. First, the notion that Paul had lost interest in the history of the nation and the world stands in flat contradiction to the pervasive apocalyptic motifs in Paul's thought and especially to the entire argument of the letter to the Romans, in which the fate of the world (see especially Rom. 8:18–25) and of Israel are matters of the most urgent concern.[12] Second, the notion that Paul was concerned about asserting his individual autonomy over against Israel's tradition is a bizarre anachronism. Paul, after all, (as Bloom says of Shakespeare) "belongs to the giant age before the Flood, before the anxiety of influence became central to poetic consciousness."[13] Paul's great struggle is not a struggle to assert his own authority over Scripture; it is, rather, a

dialectical struggle to maintain the integrity of his proclamation in relation to Scripture and the integrity of Scripture in relation to that proclamation, to justify his startling claims about what the God of Israel had elected
to do in Jesus Christ.

The "new creation" to which circumcision is subordinated in Gal. 6:15
is not, as Marks apparently supposes,[14] a reference to the fruits of Paul's
own autonomous hermeneutical creativity; it is an allusion to Isa. 65:17–
25, a pointer to the hope of God's eschatological restoration of the fallen
creation and of Israel:

> For behold, I create new heavens and a new earth;
> and the former things shall not be remembered
> or come into mind.
> But be glad and rejoice forever in that which I create;
> for behold, I create Jerusalem a rejoicing,
> and her people a joy.
> I will rejoice in Jerusalem,
> and be glad in my people;
> no more shall be heard in it the sound of weeping
> and the cry of distress.

In view of Paul's explicit invocation of the image of the new eschatological
Jerusalem ("our mother") earlier in the letter (Gal. 4:26–27), the corporate
aspect of the new creation should be abundantly clear,[15] and above all
else, it should be unmistakable that the new creation depends on an
eschatological act of God's power,[16] not on Paul's hermeneutical ingenuity.

What Marks has really given us is a faithful (therefore "weak") Bloomian exposition of Bultmann's strong misreading of Paul—and Bultmann's
reading is of course an echoic distortion of Luther's still stronger misreading. (For the moment I leave Harnack and Marcion aside.) The mainstream Western Christian tradition running from Augustine through
Luther (in its Protestant branch) to Bultmann has rendered a reading of
Paul fixated on individual salvation,[17] but it has been able to do so only by
strenuously suppressing the voice of Scripture in Paul's letters, stifling
Paul's own claim to expound a gospel that underscores God's faithfulness
to Israel. Marks has, understandably, relied on Paul's most influential
Protestant expositors; his resultant caricature of Paul is of great heuristic
value because it highlights the distorting tendencies of the lens that he
has used.

Against readings of Paul that ignore his roots in Scripture or highlight
antithetical aspects of his relation to it, our investigation has taken his

uses of Scripture as clues to a different construal of his overall theological perspective, signs of a deep-running continuity. Paul finds in Scripture language and images that allow him to give expression to his kerygma. In reactivating these images, he necessarily (and sometimes artfully) twists them in such a way that new significations arise out of the interplay between the old and the new. Gospel interprets Scripture; Scripture interprets gospel. The product of this fusion of readings—in the text of the Pauline letter—is a new figuration of grace.

Hermeneutical Methods and Constraints in Paul

What methods does Paul employ to achieve this new figuration? Our account of Paul's interpretive activity has discovered no systematic exegetical procedures at work in his reading of Scripture. James Barr's generalization about the New Testament's use of the Old Testament applies fully and accurately to Paul: "The most serious arbitrariness appears when a particular interpretative principle or method is rationalized, i.e. so used as to apply continually and indiscriminately. . . . This type of arbitrariness, the arbitrariness of a reasoned or fixed method steadily used, is absent from the New Testament situation. The arbitrariness which attaches to it is the arbitrariness of creativity in departure from a defined tradition."[18] Philo, expounding Scripture in accordance with "the laws of allegory," exemplifies the use of "a reasoned or fixed method" in ancient biblical exegesis. Paul, by contrast, offers helter-skelter intuitive readings, unpredictable, ungeneralizable. In the few cases where he makes passing remarks that look like hermeneutical pointers (Rom. 4:23–24, Rom. 15:4, 1 Cor. 9:9–10, 1 Cor. 10:11), his comments characteristically emphasize the immediacy of the text's word to the community rather than providing specific rules for reading. He adheres neither to any single exegetical procedure, nor even to a readily specifiable inventory of procedures. Modern biblical scholars fascinated by the heuristic power of their own conception of exegesis as a rule-governed science have frequently sought to retroject such a conception onto Paul by ascertaining the methods that he employed. Longenecker, for example, classifies Paul's exegesis into four types (literalist, midrashic, pesher, and allegory).[19] However useful such classification can be for certain purposes, it suffers from ex post facto artificiality. Paul did not do his work of interpretation with such analytic categories in mind; the modern concern for methodological control in interpretation is foreign to him.[20]

In short, there is no evidence in the letters that Paul—in contrast to other ancient authors such as Philo—ever sat down with the biblical text and tried to figure out what it might mean by applying an exegetical procedure abstractable from the particular text that he was reading. Rather, he seems to have leaped—in moments of metaphorical insight— to intuitive apprehensions of the meanings of texts without the aid or encumbrance of systematic reflection about his own hermeneutics.

This does not mean that Paul's readings are "wild" or aimless. There are constraints on Paul's interpretation of Scripture, but the constraints arise primarily from material (i.e., theological) concerns rather than from formal methodological considerations. The hermeneutical foundation for his reading is the conviction that the Law and the Prophets bear witness to the gospel of God's righteousness, now definitively disclosed in the death and resurrection of Jesus Messiah. For that reason, attempts to account for his interpretations by appealing to the exegetical procedures of rabbinic midrash fall to the ground: the occasional formal parallels that can be noted between Paul and the rabbis usually serve to emphasize how differently they are reading the text with regard to substantive issues.[21] In any case, it is no easier to give a systematic explanation of the methods of midrash than it is to explain Paul's hermeneutical method.[22] When these considerations are coupled with the late dating of the rabbinic material, it becomes evident that midrash provides only an indirect analogy to Paul's reading, calling attention by contrast, for example, to Paul's relatively greater interest in the original narrative context of his scriptural citations.[23]

The finding that Paul's hermeneutic is narratively oriented supports the *communis opinio* that typology is a central feature of his interpretive strategy. Paul reads Scripture under the conviction that its story prefigures the climactic realities of his own time. The sense of divinely plotted time sets his readings apart from the sorts of interpretations that are usually classified as allegory, in which the meaning contained by a text turns out to be an eternal moral or spiritual truth. It is questionable, however, whether typology should be considered a method of interpretation[24]; it is, rather, a framework of literary-historical sensibility that creates the hermeneutical conditions necessary for the metaphorical linkage of scriptural text and contemporary situation. Furthermore, because this linkage is conceived in figurative terms rather than in terms of literal immanent causality, it is also seriously misleading to describe Pauline typology, as some critics have sought to do, as concerned with "historical facts."[25] Typology forges imaginative correlations of events within a narrative sequence; not all narrative sequences, however, are historical.[26]

One of the most arresting results of our investigation has been the recognition that Paul's typological linkages center on the people of God as the culmination of God's redemptive activity rather than on Jesus as the antitypical fulfillment of scriptural figures. This does not mean that Jesus was of secondary importance to Paul or that christology was subordinate to soteriology in his theological scheme. Rather, the ecclesiocentric character of Paul's readings is to be understood as a consequence of the historical contingency of his writings as pastoral letters. For Paul's communities, Jesus' identity was not the contested issue, as it was at a later date for the writer of the Gospel of John, a text that bears the wounds of bitter christological debate between Jews and Christians. Paul, writing to small, newly formed communities composed of Gentile Christians (e.g., in Galatia) or perhaps of mixed Gentile-Jewish composition (e.g., in Rome), was confronted most urgently by questions of communal self-definition. How were such communities to interpret their relation to Israel? How were their lives to be governed in relation to the Law that God gave to Moses? How could Paul justify his proclamation of a Law-free faith that incorporated uncircumcised Gentiles into the covenant community of God's people? These are the controversial questions that drive the letters to the Galatians and Romans. Even where the issue of continuity and discontinuity with Israel's Torah is not the primary problem, as in the Corinthian correspondence, we have seen that Paul's pastoral concern for community formation expresses itself through the metaphorical strategy of reading Israel's story as a prefiguration of the eschatological community.

With such hermeneutical criteria shaping the reading of Scripture, it is not difficult to understand retrospectively the emergence of Paul's de facto canon within the canon. He finds Scripture's hermeneutical center of gravity in the texts that most readily lend themselves as vehicles for his gospel message of God's righteousness. Thus, the four scriptural books most frequently quoted by Paul are Isaiah (twenty-eight citations), Psalms (twenty), Deuteronomy (fifteen), and Genesis (fifteen). No other book is quoted more than five times.[27] Isaiah offers the clearest expression in the Old Testament of a universalistic, eschatological vision in which the restoration of Israel in Zion is accompanied by an ingathering of Gentiles to worship the Lord; that is why this book is both statistically and substantively the most important scriptural source for Paul. Most of the Genesis citations are taken from the Abraham story, which Paul takes to be the paradigmatic prefiguration of God's calling of Jews and Gentiles alike to covenant relation through faith. The high incidence of psalms is perhaps to be explained partly in light of their familiarity through liturgical use in the synagogue and perhaps in the Christian assembly as well; in any event, a survey of Paul's psalm citations shows that he often selects passages that reinforce the Isaianic theme of Gentile inclusion (as in Rom. 15:9–11, quoting Ps. 18:49 and 117:1) or passages that dramatize God's righteous judgment of Israel (as in Rom. 3:4, quoting Ps. 51:4; Rom. 11:9–10, quoting Ps. 69:22–23). There are a few isolated instances in which Paul reads a psalm christologically (Rom. 15:3, 1 Cor. 15:27),[28] but most of the psalm texts are employed in service of the same ecclesiocentric themes that Paul finds in Isaiah and Genesis: in the psalmist's words the Christian community's experience of judgment and grace is figured.

Deuteronomy is the most surprising member of Paul's functional canon within the canon. One might expect this book of conditional blessings and curses to bear witness—as it apparently does in Gal. 3:10, 13—to precisely the sort of performance-based religion that Paul wants to reject. In fact, however, none of Paul's other references to the book is pejorative in character; nowhere else is Deuteronomy disparaged as a retrograde voice of legalism. Instead, as we have seen, the words of Deuteronomy become the voice of The Righteousness from Faith. Furthermore, in addition to Paul's specific citations, we have noted numerous allusions, especially to the Song of Moses in Deuteronomy 32. Why is Deuteronomy such an important text for Paul, and how does he understand the relationship between its threats and promises?

Gerhard von Rad, arguing for theological continuity between Deuteronomy and the New Testament, highlights the Deuteronomist's emphasis on God's gracious initiative in covenant election, apart from Israel's merit.[29] This theme is indeed suggested, as we have noted, by Paul's editorial decision to introduce the quotation of Deut. 30:12 with the formula, "Do not say in your heart," drawn from other passages (Deut. 8:17 and 9:4) that stress the unmerited character of God's action. It will not do, however, to read Deuteronomy as a simple precursor of the doctrine of justification by faith. The problem, from the point of view of Pauline theology, is that God's gracious action creates in Deuteronomy a covenant that is rigorously conditional in character and that pronounces terrifying curses upon Israel for disobedience. How can this text, the source of "the curse of the Law,"[30] serve as a prefiguration of Paul's gospel? Paul gives us an important clue in his startling reading of Deut. 30:11–14 (in Rom. 10:6–10). As Dan O. Via, Jr., has observed, there is a deep structural affinity between the theology of the word in Deuteronomy and in Paul: "God's life-giving action seems to be interpreted in Deuteronomy as his life-giving word."[31] Thus, Paul can read Deut. 30:11–14 to mean that the presence of God's word in the community of God's people empowers the obedience of faith.

But even that affirmation fails to address the enigma of Israel's disobe-

dience. That is where the Song of Moses, read as a prophetic prefiguration of God's dealings with Israel through the gospel, becomes in Paul's
hands a hermeneutical key of equal importance with the prophecies of
Deutero-Isaiah. The song describes in sequence God's election of and
care for Israel (Deut. 32:6–14), Israel's inexplicable rebellion (Deut. 32:15–
18, cf. 32:5), God's judgment upon them (Deut. 32:19–35), and—ultimately and mysteriously—God's final deliverance and vindication of his
own people (Deut. 32:36–43). The point is not just, as Via argues, that
Deuteronomy and Romans are both performances generated by "the
comic genre."[32] The relation between scriptural subtext and Pauline reflection is far more complex and specific. In Deuteronomy 32, Paul finds
not only the prophecy of Israel's lack of faith and ultimate restoration but
also the prefiguration of God's intention to "stir them to jealousy"
through embracing the Gentiles (Deut. 32:21), who are invited to join
with his people in praise (Deut. 32:43). It is hardly coincidental that Paul
quotes both of these verses explicitly (Rom. 10:19, 15:10). Deuteronomy
32 contains Romans *in nuce.*

Thus, Deuteronomy fits the profile of the other texts given the greatest
canonical weight in Paul's scriptural interpretation, because—on Paul's
reading—it renders an account of God's mysterious action through the
word to bring the whole world, the Jew first and also the Greek, to
acknowledge his unconditional lordship:

> See now that I, even I, am he,
> and there is no other god beside me;
> I kill and I make alive;
> I wound and I heal;
> and there is none that can deliver out of my hand.
>   (Deut. 32:39)

Deuteronomy parallels Isaiah's crucial hermeneutical turn: both texts
have already read the history of Yahweh's dealing with Israel typologically,[33] as a prefiguration of a larger eschatological design. That is
why these two texts, above all others, are the privileged predecessors of
Paul's discourse. For both, the exodus has already become a metaphor
that comprehends the ongoing life of the people of God in history; for
both, Israel's return to the promised land has become transmuted into a
sign of eschatological hope. Thus, these texts undergird Paul's account of
the accordance between the word of Scripture and the word of his gospel.
His typological reading strategy extends a typological trajectory begun
already in the texts themselves.

Scripture as Word of Address

Paul's readings characteristically treat Scripture as a living voice that speaks to the people of God. The Bible for Paul is not just a chronicle of revelation in the past; the words of Scripture sound from the page in the present moment and address the community of believers with authority. This hermeneutical stance sometimes yields readings that appear whimsical in their effects, for it causes words spoken to characters in biblical narratives to miss their original addressees and to fly into the faces of bystanders previously uninvolved in the action. If the effect seems comic to an unsympathetic reader, however, that is contrary to Paul's design. He believes himself, along with his churches, to stand in a privileged moment in which the random clutter of past texts and experiences assumes a configuration of eschatological significance, because all has been ordered by God to proclaim the gospel to those who read what Paul writes.

Even the most mundane apodictic pronouncements in Scripture gain unforeseen spiritual gravity when read with the ruling conviction that Scripture must speak to us and must speak of weighty spiritual matters. A telling illustration is Paul's interpretation of Deut. 25:4 in 1 Cor. 9:8–10. In the course of arguing that "those who proclaim the gospel should get their living by the gospel" (1 Cor. 9:14) (a right that Paul is choosing to forego at Corinth), he cites "the Law of Moses"—which, significantly, he juxtaposes to a merely human authority: "Am I speaking these things in a human way (*kata anthrōpon*), or doesn't even the Law say these things? For it is written in the Law of Moses, 'You shall not muzzle a threshing ox.' Does it matter to God about oxen, or does he speak entirely for our sake? For it is written for our sake that 'the plowman ought to plow in hope and the thresher to thresh in hope of sharing.' " The commandment of Deut. 25:4 cannot merely be a helpful tip on the care of livestock, because it is written *di' hēmas* ("on account of us"), and it concerns *us*. Paul buttresses his interpretation by adducing another text with the word *thresher* in it,[34] but the underlying hermeneutical assumption of his reading of both texts is articulated in the emphatic *di' hēmas pantōs legei* (he speaks entirely for our sake).

Of course, Paul's rhetorical flourish plays on the contrast between animals and humans as the objects of God's concern, but we miss the real force of his argument if we suppose unreflectively that his *di' hēmas* is synonymous with a more neutral *di' anthrōpous.* In view of Paul's habit of finding himself and his churches prefigured in Scripture, we should probably understand him to be claiming that the words of the Law of Moses find their true and primary referent in the financial arrangements pertaining to his own ministry. This hunch is supported by the simple observation that the pronoun *hēmas* (us) of verse 10 must have the same antecedent—that is, Paul and Barnabas (cf. vv. 4–6)—as the *hēmeis* (we) of verse 11: "It was written on account of *us*. . . . If *we* sowed spiritual things for you, is it a big deal [*mega*] if *we* harvest fleshly things from you?" To describe Paul's interpretation of Deut. 25:4 as allegorical[35] or as an instance of *gezerah shawah,* though both these descriptions are correct, overlooks the remarkable distinctive emphasis here: Paul reads the text as bearing direct reference to his own circumstances and reads this commandment of the Law of Moses as a word addressed directly to Gentile Christians. (Still more remarkably, he follows a course opposed to what the text—on his own reading—requires.)[36]

Allegorization is not one of Paul's primary hermeneutical strategies, as many scholars have noted.[37] If allegorical reading were an important tool for him, he could have allegorized the scriptural commandments dealing with circumcision and *kashrut,* thus sparing himself a great deal of anguish. It is striking that he does not adopt such a strategy. This observation suggests that the allegorizing reading that Paul gives the "threshing ox" text is a secondary and accidental effect generated here by his more deliberate policy of reading the text as a direct word of address, a policy pursued with some consistency throughout the letters.

In Rom. 4:23–24, for example, he concludes his exposition of the Abraham story by asserting that the text's ascription of righteousness to Abraham applies also to all who place their trust in the One who raised Jesus from the dead: "It was not written on account of him only that 'It was reckoned to him,' but also on account of us to whom it is going to be reckoned." The words *elogisthē autō* in Gen. 15:6 are spoken with reference to Paul and his readers, as well as to Abraham. Again, as we have seen in 1 Cor. 10:11, Paul asserts that the scriptural account of Israel in the wilderness was written explicitly "for our instruction [*pros nouthesian hēmōn*]." In Rom. 15:4, this claim is generalized into a poignant pedagogical maxim: "For whatever things were written beforehand [*proegraphē*] were written for our instruction [*eis tēn hēmeteran didaskalian*], in order that through endurance and through the consolation of the Scriptures we might have hope." Though these texts differ slightly in emphasis, they share the conviction that Scripture is rightly read as a word of address to the eschatological community of God's people. The mode of reading that they prescribe is in fact practiced by Paul in all his dealings with the scriptural text.

Some of the most vivid instances of such reading have been noted in the preceding chapters. We rehearse a few of them here as an invitation to the reader to extend the inventory of examples. In 1 Cor. 5:13, Paul turns Deut. 17:7 into an authoritative word spoken directly to the Corinthians: "Drive out the evil person from among yourselves." In Gal. 4:30, Sarah's demand to Abraham becomes the direct word of *Graphē* to the Galatians: "Cast out the slavewoman and her son, for the son of the slavewoman shall not inherit with the son of the freewoman." And, of course, the example par excellence, which not only illustrates the phenomenon but also provides the hermeneutical warrant for it, is Rom. 10:5–10, in which The Righteousness from Faith speaks directly to the readers: "But what does it say? 'The word is near you, in your mouth and in your heart.'"

Here speaks the master hermeneutical trope that governs all the intertextual play of Paul's letters. The trope is simple but almost infinitely potent: the word of Scripture is read as the word of God to us. The text was written by some human author long ago, written to and for an ancient community of people in Israel, but original writer and readers have become types whose meaning emerges with full clarity only in the church—that is, only in the empirical eschatological community that Paul is engaged in building. Even utterances that appear to be spoken to others in another time find their true addressees in *us*. When God blesses Abraham, he is speaking to us. When Moses charges Israel, he is speaking to us. When Isaiah cries comfort to Jerusalem, he is speaking to us.

Paul did not invent this trope. This metaphorical strategy of reading had already been worked out long before (*proegraphē*) in Israel, preeminently in Deuteronomy: "The Lord our God made a covenant with us in Horeb. Not with our fathers did the Lord make this covenant, but with us, who are all of us here alive this day" (Deut. 5:2–3; cf. Deut. 26:5–9). Paul tightens the tension of the trope, however, stretching the word not only across time, as the Deuteronomist did, but also across ethnic boundaries. Will it break? Paul is confident that it will not. The promised nearness of the word guarantees both its flexibility and its durability.

Of course, to affirm that the word is near, to identify the hermeneutical conviction that the scriptural text is a word addressed to us, does not necessarily allow us to predict what we will hear in Scripture's word. Paul exploits the master trope to generate a stream of novel readings. These readings are contingent acts of imagination, not fixed doctrinal formulations. They take shape only within the intertextual chemistry of his letters: provoked by a challenge, struck by an analogy, Paul draws Scripture and pastoral situation together, making metaphors at the intersections. These metaphors are not haphazard; as we have already

argued, a particular imaginative construal of the overall message of Scripture shapes the way in which the voice of Scripture is heard. Still, the
relation between the word and its reading is genuinely dialectical: the
word is effectual, speaking in ways that cannot be fully controlled or
manipulated by Paul, bringing into being the people that it addresses.

That is why Paul's hermeneutic places special emphasis on the formation of community. The enfleshment of the word in the church makes the
meaning of Scripture knowable. Where Scripture remains only an inscribed text, it becomes *gramma,* indicting the readers with aching consciousness of their distance from what the text promises or alienating
them with speech that seems incomprehensibly remote. But where Scripture speaks as a living word, it creates communities whose lives are
hermeneutical testimonies, embodying the word, making its speech palpable. That is what we meant by speaking of an ecclesiocentric hermeneutic, and that is what Paul meant when he called his Corinthian
readers "a letter from Christ." Scripture, then, continues to speak in
order to call into existence the community in which it can be heard rightly.

Hermeneutics at the Turn of the Ages

The community that Scripture addresses is conceived by Paul as an
eschatological community. That observation has been made repeatedly in
these pages; nevertheless, we must offer some further summary reflections on the hermeneutical implications of Paul's eschatology.

In 1 Cor. 10:11, Paul discloses the eschatological perspective that informs his interpretation of Scripture: "These things happened to them
[i.e., Israel] typologically, but they were written for our instruction, upon
whom the ends of the ages have come." The exact exegesis of the unusual
phrase *ta telē tōn aiōnōn* (the ends of the ages [both nouns plural]) is
disputed. Does it refer, as Johannes Weiss contended, to the end of the
old age and the beginning of the new, so that Christians see their own
time as the hinge where two ages meet?[38] Or does Paul mean that all past
ages have simultaneously met their consummation in his own time? Either way, the formulation claims for Paul's present moment a uniquely
privileged temporal perspective. He sees himself and his readers standing at the climactic time, the *kairos* that imposes upon all past time a new
and shocking valuation. Because God has acted in Jesus Christ to initiate
the turn of the ages, everything past must be read with new eyes.[39]
Scripture, of course, is not exempt from this eschatological reassessment;
Paul insists, as we have seen, that his privileged position in the climactic
chapter of the story of God's dealing with Israel allows him to perceive

patterns—both unities and ironies—that were hidden from previous actors and readers. Consequently, the eschatological perspective becomes the hermeneutical warrant for major shifts and revisions in the reading of Scripture.

Shifts are necessary because God's eschatological action is fraught with surprise: "God chose what is foolish in the world to shame the wise, God chose what is weak in the world to shame to strong" (1 Cor. 1:26–27). "The word of the cross" enacts such a sweeping reversal that it looks like nonsense to the world. To see the unexpected interpretive consequences of this eschatological word of the cross, we need only consider the case of Paul's reading of Deut. 21:23 in Gal. 3:13. Scripture spoke the truth when it said, "Cursed is every one who is hanged upon a tree,"[40] but Paul now construes that truth in an ironic mode: by hanging upon the tree, Jesus became cursed in order that blessing might accrue to others. The eschatological *apokalypsis* of the cross[41] has wrought an inversion in Paul's reading of the text.

God's election of Gentiles into the people of God and concomitant turning of his back to Israel participates in this pattern of reversal. The present reality of communities in which Gentiles join with Israel in praising God for his mercy (Rom. 15:7–13) compels a new reading of Scripture that will account for what has taken place. If the gospel's gathering of such communities is the manifestation of the righteousness of God, then Scripture cannot have meant exactly what Israel had supposed. Yet, when Scripture is refracted through the hermeneutical lens provided by God's action in the crucified Messiah and in forming his eschatological community, it acquires a profound new symbolic coherence.

The exegetical outworking of this reversal is most startling in Gal. 4:21–31, where Hagar becomes a symbol for "the present Jerusalem . . . in slavery with her children," while Isaac becomes a symbol for Gentile believers. Once the pattern of eschatological reversal is recognized, however, its presence as a hermeneutical key throughout the letters can be discerned. It would be possible to describe virtually every citation of Scripture in the letter to the Romans, for example, as a performance of this pattern of ironic reversal. The reversal pattern is deeply rooted in Israel's prophetic tradition, as the citations of Hosea in Rom. 9:25–26 (to take a single instance) show, but Paul's eschatological perspective sharpens the irony by transposing it into a new temporal framework.

That new temporal framework is signaled in Paul's discourse by the most obvious of devices: when he echoes scriptural texts, he frequently transforms the verb tenses. Isaiah's "I shall not be ashamed" becomes "I am not ashamed." Psalm 94's "God will not cast off his people" becomes "God has not cast off his people." The tense changes mark the turn of the ages.

From the perspective of the eschatological community, temporal boundaries start to dissolve, so that Scripture can be said to have "pre-preached the gospel" to Abraham, and so that the word spoken by Moses becomes contemporary with Paul's readers as the word of The Righteousness from Faith. Such temporal warps are not the result of carelessness or naivete in Paul's presentation: they are indicators of what has happened to time at the turn of the ages. All that God has ever done in the past converges toward the eschatological community, and all past words of Scripture find their sense rooted in the present graced time. Consequently, Paul can read Moses' turning to behold the glory of the Lord in Exodus 34 as a parable figuring the experience of the church; the hidden eschatological meaning of the text is disclosed in the eschatological community, for whom the veil is taken away.

Thus, Paul's intertextual readings create a convergence of time upon his communities. This hermeneutical phenomenon reveals far-reaching differences between Paul and other ancient Jewish interpreters. Though the working method of this study has not been comparative, a quick glance over the shoulder at certain Jewish analogues highlights the audacity of Paul's reading strategies.

James Kugel has drawn attention to the "sense of time" that characterizes postbiblical Judaism; on his reading, apocalyptic visionaries, Alexandrian allegorizers, and rabbinic midrashists were haunted in their different ways by a common perception "that the present world was somehow discontinuous with the Bible's, and that the Bible's simple, 'consequential' view of God's workings could not be extended in linear fashion to cover recent history."[42] Their hermeneutical strategies in the face of this situation are diverse, but all of them betray the awareness that the present time can no longer be read as continuous with the "God-dominated events"[43] of the Bible. Philo and the apocalyptic writers strive in various ways "to dress up present reality in biblical trappings."[44] But the response of rabbinic midrash to this temporal gap is of a different kind:

> [M]idrash . . . generally views Scripture as a world unto itself, without direct connection to our own times; as one critic has phrased it, "God acted (in the past), will act (in the eschatological future), but is not acting in between." Messianism, however important it may be, never becomes the bridge between the biblical past and the mid-

rashist's present. Such a bridge, if it exists at all, is the halakhic one: the Bible informs the present as the source of those practices which Jews undertake to adhere to. But there is no bridge between the Bible's *time* and our time: God has acted and will act, but for now his activity is suspended in a majestic state of kingship.[45]

Between this rabbinic time sense and Paul's lies a great gulf. The difference is dramatized by their divergent interpretations of Deut. 30:11–14, as traced in the first chapter of this book. For the rabbis, God's word is a deposit stored up in time past and entrusted to the community's ongoing interpretation; for Paul, God's word is alive and active in the present time, embodied in the community's Spirit-empowered life and proclamation. In both communities the work of interpretation goes forward, but their different temporal sensibilities engender radically different norms of community life, radically different modes of reading.

Paul stands, however presumptuous it may be for him to do so, directly in Israel's prophetic biblical tradition. He does experience present time as a time of God-dominated events; he does see his own ministry as part of the consequential flow of time from Abraham to the present. He does believe that God is speaking through him. Hence, the freedom of his intertextual tropes. The circumspect sense of temporal estrangement from Bible time is completely lacking from his readings of the text. Also lacking, therefore, is the dutiful desire to preserve and repeat the precise words of a holy "once upon a time" when God was present and spoke to his people; God speaks now. This is nowhere more compellingly expressed than in 2 Cor. 5:20–6:2:

> On behalf of Christ, then, we are ambassadors; God is appealing to you through us. We beseech you, for Christ's sake, be reconciled to God. . . . But we also speak to you as your fellow-workers, adding our exhortation that you should not let God's proffered grace go for nothing.[46] For he says, "At the acceptable time I have heard you, and in the day of salvation I have helped you." Behold, now is the well-favored[47] time; behold, now is the day of salvation.[48]

The day of salvation that Isaiah prophesied has dawned. Therefore, for Paul there is no question of dressing up the present in nostalgic biblical trappings; on the contrary, the meaning of the Bible is only brought to light through the revelation of the righteousness of God in the present time. All of this is a direct consequence of Paul's eschatological hermeneutic and a direct cause of the offense posed by his gospel.

The closest analogy within first-century Judaism to Paul's temporal sensibility is to be found in the Qumran texts, especially the *hodayot* and the biblical commentaries (*pesharim*). The Dead Sea covenanters, with their self-interpretation as a privileged eschatological community now granted the true readings of Scripture, present significant parallels to Pauline hermeneutics.[49] The following hymnic passage, for instance, celebrates the community's knowledge of the true interpretation of the Law as an anticipation of eternal blessedness:

> My eyes have gazed on that which is eternal,
> on wisdom concealed from men,
> on knowledge and wise design
> (hidden) from the sons of men;
> on a fountain of righteousness
> and on a storehouse of power,
> on a spring of glory
> (hidden) from the assembly of flesh.
> God has given them to his chosen ones
> as an everlasting possession,
> and has caused them to inherit
> the lot of the Holy Ones.
> He has joined their assembly
> to the Sons of Heaven
> to be a Council of the Community,
> a foundation of the Building of Holiness,
> an eternal Plantation throughout all ages to come.[50]

In the *pesharim*, we learn that the community's revealed knowledge includes a system of esoteric interpretation in which scriptural prophecies are read as coded figurations of the Qumran community and its enemies. A detailed comparative study would disclose at least three fundamental differences between the covenanters and Paul: whereas Paul uses Scripture to justify the inclusion of uncircumcised Gentiles in the people of God and to relativize the Law's ritual requirements, Qumran exegesis operates in service of a rigorously exclusive sectarian Judaism that regards mainstream Jewish practice as ritualistically lax; the scrolls contain no parallel to Paul's conviction that the decisive eschatological event had already occurred; and Qumran biblical commentary is characteristically apologetic, seeking to vindicate the community's practices against outsiders, whereas Paul uses Scripture to nurture and warn the community. Still, despite these differences, the "sense of time" at Qumran is analogous to Paul's in urgency and revisionary boldness. In neither case do we find a consciousness of disjunction from Israel's past or a reluctance to speak of God's activity in the present.

Reading Scripture at the culmination of the ages, Paul discovers himself and his readers at the center of God's redemptive purposes. Through Jesus Christ, so Paul's gospel declares, God has configured a people whose vocation is to proclaim the message of reconciliation by embodying the righteousness of God (cf. 2 Cor. 5:20–21). Insofar as that embodiment occurs, the right interpretation of Scripture will be enacted through the metaphorical correspondence between biblical text and eschatological community.

Conclusion: Strategies of Intertextual Echo

Having surveyed Paul's interpretive practices, can we render a synoptic characterization of the overall relation between Scripture and Paul's reading of it? I have contended that categories such as midrash, typology, and allegory offer insufficient power of discrimination to probe the distinctive properties of Paul's interpretations. In place of these conventional categories, I propose an analytic framework adapted from Thomas M. Greene's *The Light in Troy: Imitation and Discovery in Renaissance Poetry.*

Greene sketches a typology of four "strategies of humanist imitation," seeking to distinguish the ways in which humanist poets of the Renaissance recapitulate classical models and subtexts; their rhetoric of imitation varies widely in its subtlety and in its "implicit perspective on history." Greene proposes that the act of literary imitation necessarily implies some imaginative construal of the past and of the historical distance that separates the writer from it. The writer's perspective on this gap between past and present may be implicit or even unconscious, or it may be thematized, in more historically self-conscious texts, as an explicit structural element of the literary work.[51] Greene's critical examination of the strategies by which poets relate their creations to textual precursors reveals the following spectrum of options:

1. *Sacramental imitation.* (Or "reproductive imitation.") The poem venerates a precursor by imitating it with slavish precision.
2. *Eclectic imitation.* (Or "exploitative imitation.") The poem mingles allusions to various texts and traditions, without binding itself in a determinative fashion to any one subtext.
3. *Heuristic imitation.* The poem "singles out one text as its putative genesis and it defines itself through its rewriting, its 'modernizing,' its *aggiornamento* of that text. . . . The poem becomes a kind of

rite de passage between a specified past and an emergent present."[52] The result of this strategy is that heuristic imitations *"distance themselves* from the subtexts and force us to recognize the poetic distance traversed."[53]

4. *Dialectical Imitation.* The poem engages the precursor in such a way that two symbolic worlds are brought into collision so that each is vulnerable to criticism and interpretation by the other. "And just as heuristic imitation involves a passage from one semiotic universe to another, so dialectical imitation, when it truly engages two eras or two civilizations at a profound level, involves a conflict between two *mundi significantes.*"[54] If the poem succeeds, it presumably achieves a synthesis of the two worlds, but the genius of dialectical imitation is to produce the synthesis within the text of a literary work that *sustains* the tension between worlds rather than resolving it.

The variable that distributes texts along the typological axis is not stylistic or verbal correspondence; it is, rather, the writer's stance toward the past expressed in the symbolic world of the subtext.

While Greene has created this typology to analyze strategies of poetic imitation, I would suggest that his categories can be applied analogically to any text that performs intertextual reflection. If so, Paul's strategy of intertextual echo can be evaluated in these terms. (I leave it to the reader to decide whether my use of Greene is exploitative or heuristic.)

Paul, of course, is not writing imitations of scriptural texts. An imitation presumably must remain within the same genre as its original, at least approximately. The Qumran *hodayot* might be read as imitations, in Greene's sense, of the canonical Psalms, or the Book of Jubilees read as an imitation of Pentateuchal narrative. Ephesians might be an imitation of the authentic Pauline letters. Paul's letters, however, do not belong to the same literary genre as any Old Testament text. Still, his hermeneutical stance toward Scripture as precursor can be profitably scrutinized through analogical application of Greene's categories, using them as descriptions of strategies of intertextual reading.

No one would take Paul's readings of Scripture to be sacramental. His freedom with regard to the wording of his citations, and his transformative reversals of tradition mark his hermeneutical style as belonging to a different mode altogether. Indeed, there are few examples of purely reproductive intertextuality in the Bible. Even when Matthew and Luke incorporate large blocks of Mark's gospel, they place the material into a very different narrative and theological framework, thus creating an intertextual chemistry that is more heuristic than reproductive. Perhaps the Pastoral Epistles approximate the strategy of sacramental intertextuality. For really good illustrations, however, we would have to turn to the source from which Greene draws his terminology: the church's later liturgical traditions.[55]

Eclectic strategies of reading appear here and there in Paul's letters. The "threshing ox" text in 1 Cor. 9:8–10 is a good example, as is the citation of Ps. 19:4 in Rom. 10:18, where Paul transmutes the psalmist's graceful depiction of the heavens' glory into a description of the universal scope of Christian preaching. In cases such as these, there is no indication that Paul has wrestled seriously with the texts from which the citations are drawn. He has simply appropriated their language to lend rhetorical force to his own discourse, with minimal attention to the integrity of the semiotic universe of the precursor. This mode of intertextual reading is traditionally stigmatized as prooftexting, but that pejorative label misconstrues the rhetorical function of such intertextual strategies in Paul. The citation of Ps. 19:4 does not prove that Jews have had the opportunity to hear the gospel; rather, it gives Paul a "vocabulary of a second and higher power"[56] with which to *assert* that they have heard it. Commentators sometimes fret over the apparent logical illegitimacy of such eclectic hermeneutical strategies in Paul, because, as scrupulous but unimaginative readers, they ascribe to Paul's intertextual tropes a literal assertive weight that they cannot and should not bear.

If Paul's readings of Scripture were predominantly of this eclectic sort, his discourse would lose much of its gravity. We might admire the passing cleverness of this or that echo, but the intertextual links would not add up to anything. Scripture would be treated not as a coherent word of witness but as a pool of symbols to be drawn out and used wherever they suit Paul's purposes, "a vast container whose contents can be disarranged endlessly without suffering damage."[57] The Gospel of Matthew is the clearest instance in the New Testament of a text whose hermeneutical strategy in relation to Israel's Scripture is almost unrelievedly exploitative, in Greene's sense. Our investigation of Paul, however, has shown how seldom his intertextual echoes function in this eclectic mode. They characteristically require the reader to engage in serious sustained deliberation about the relation between Scripture's *mundus significans* and the new situation that Paul is addressing.

If Paul's intertextual strategies are not eclectic, then, are they heuristic? Does he labor so hard in the reading of Scripture in order to win freedom from its constraints? The traditional Christian distinction between Old Testament and New Testament, as popularly understood, presupposes and perpetuates this heuristic relation between Israel's Scripture and its Christian reading, placing the Old Testament decisively in *Vergangenheit* and marking our temporal distance from it. Traditional interpretations of Paul's Letter to the Romans and of the letter-spirit juxtaposition in 2 Corinthians 3 have understood Paul to be working out a classic heuristic rewriting of Scripture, forcing Moses and Abraham into a dichotomous Law/gospel scheme, producing a revision of the precursor that makes it a foil for his own theological vision. The result of such a strategy would be to emphasize the distance between subtext and its interpretation, to place the Old Testament in antithetical typological relation to the New Testament, as antithetical as Adam is to Christ. It has been the burden of this study to show that such an assessment of Paul's intertextual reading strategies is subtly but tragically mistaken.

Among the Pauline letters, only Galatians can justly be described as an instance of heuristic intertextual reading; even in Galatians, however, there are, as we have seen, signals that Paul is uneasy with the relentlessly antithetical implications of his own argument (Gal. 3:21, 5:6, 6:15). In light of his subsequent reworking of similar issues in Romans, Galatians looks like a preliminary heuristic probe, staking out a strong position that had to be articulated along the way to discovering a more complex hermeneutical strategy. Our analyses of the argument of Romans and of the metaphorical language of 2 Corinthians 3, as well as of the Israel/Church typology in 1 Corinthians and Galatians, have demonstrated that Paul's fundamental reading strategies are profoundly *dialectical*. The word of Scripture is not played off as a foil for the gospel, not patronized as a primitive stage of religious development, not regarded merely as a shadow of the good things to come. Paul's urgent hermeneutical project, rather, is to bring Scripture and gospel into a mutually interpretive relation, in which the righteousness of God is truly disclosed.

This distinction between the heuristic and dialectical conceptions of Paul's intertextual poetics can be rightly grasped only if the nuances of Greene's typology are honored. Heuristic imitation, in the classical mode that Greene explores, is not a hostile ploy by the poet to subjugate the precursor, nor is dialectical imitation a smoothly harmonious means of integrating two different symbolic worlds. In both strategies there is friction between subtext and surface text. The difference between these modes of imitation lies in the extent to which the subtext is finally allowed by the poet to retain its own voice, to answer back, to challenge the poet's own attempts at integration. The heuristic reading strategy seeks to overcome the estrangement between past and present by positing a diachronic resolution of the intertextual tension; the dialectical strategy, disavowing diachronic resolution, allows the intertextual tension to remain but thereby achieves a fuller contemporaneity with the past, for the precursor goes on speaking in the derivative text. To return to the terms that I have used earlier, heuristic imitation is a form of *supersessionist* hermeneutics: the symbolic world of the earlier text is assimilated without remainder into the *mundus significans* of the later. The Letter to the Hebrews is the paradigmatic illustration in the New Testament of a heuristic construal of the relation between Scripture and gospel. Paul's Letter to the Romans, however, is a paradigmatic case of dialectical intertextuality. Paul's proclamation needs the blessing of Scripture, and Scripture's witness to God's election of Israel stands in judgment of all formulations of the gospel. On the other hand, Scripture's witness gains its eschatological coherence only in light of the gospel, and the gospel stands in judgment of Israel's unbelief. The voices contend in counterpoint.

In two different ways, the intertextual strategies that we have seen in Paul allow this dialectical process to continue without premature closure. First, Paul's allusive manner of using Scripture leaves enough silence for the voice of Scripture to answer back. Rather than filling the intertextual space with explanations, Paul encourages the reader to listen to more of Scripture's message than he himself voices. The word that Scripture speaks where Paul falls silent is a word that still has the power to contend against him. In fact, when Paul reaches the climactic conclusion in Rom. 11:26 that "all Israel will be saved," we suspect that Scripture, at least for the moment, has gained the upper hand. Second, the ecclesiocentric character of Paul's hermeneutic may represent a respectful concession to the actual shape of Scripture's witness. To read Scripture as a book of messianic testimonies that point to the crucified Messiah, Jesus, requires a great deal more ingenuity than to read it as a narration that foreshadows God's purpose to raise up a worldwide community of people who confess his sovereignty and manifest his justice. Because Paul stresses the latter themes, there is much common ground on which the dialectical engagement between Scripture and gospel can occur. This observation suggests that the ecclesiocentric focus of Paul's readings can be explained not merely by the historical contingency of the pastoral problems to which he was speaking but also by the continuing autonomy of Scripture's voice in Paul's dialectical hermeneutical strategy: Scripture refuses to be assimilated to a one-sidedly christocentric reading.

By reading Scripture under the conviction that God's word is near, in the mouths and hearts of the eschatological community, Paul collapses the distance between past and present. Scripture retains tremendous power as an instrument of God's speech, yet at the same time the community's acts of interpretation manifest great freedom. This is not really a paradox: the notion that hermeneutics is a zero-sum game in which the authority of the text must cancel the creativity of the interpreter (or vice versa) poses a rationalistic conundrum that Paul would find unintelligible. For him the nearness of the word at the end of the ages insures that faithful readers, for whom the veil is removed, will be empowered by the Spirit to generate imaginative intertextual readings that illuminate the witness of the Law and the Prophets to the gospel of God's righteousness. The "original" meaning of the scriptural text, then, by no means dictates Paul's interpretation, but it hovers in the background to provide a *cantus firmus* against which a *cantus figuratus* can be sung.

PAUL'S LETTERS AS HERMENEUTICAL MODEL

I exhort you, then: become imitators of me.
1 COR. 4:16

It will have occurred to many thoughtful readers long before now to wonder whether we too should take our turn at improvising a counterpoint to the Word. Should we interpret Scripture with the same freedom that Paul did?

One of my students recently wrote to me, mulling over a similar problem:

I read *Dietrich Bonhoeffer: Meditating on the Word*, edited by David McI. Gracie, about a month ago. I liked the book a lot, but it was unsettling. It raised a recurring issue: how a believer can interpret and appropriate passages of Scripture. There is on pages 97–98 of this book an excellent example: "The decision to leave the safety of America, where he had been invited to lecture, and return to Germany in the summer of 1939, seemed to find confirmation for him in the Losung text for June 26th of that year: "Do your best to come before winter" (2 Tim. 4:21). He wrote about the text: 'That follows me around all day. It is as if we were soldiers home on leave, and going back into action. . . . "Do your best to come before winter"—it is not a misuse of Scripture if I apply that to myself.'" It is as if Bonhoeffer begs the question about his use of Scripture in this instance. I suppose if a text followed me around all day then I would think God were speaking. It may be as simple as that. But I wonder if there is another issue at stake. Perhaps all the concern in seminary classes over *Sitz im Leben* and canonical context has diverted my attention or dulled my willingness

to let the Word live freely, notwithstanding its original context. . . . I
see NT authors use the same sort of freedom Bonhoeffer employs.
How is this done responsibly? Can it be done on behalf of others? Say,
from the pulpit? Maybe you know better than I do what the issue is
and what my questions concern. I think that you know that I am not
wondering whether the Scriptures are addressed to me; I know they
are.[58]

This student's questions probe to the core of the matter: Bonhoeffer's
direct personal appropriation of this verse from 2 Timothy is reminiscent
of Paul's own way of appropriating Scripture, yet it seems to violate
common sense and critical training. How can Paul's instructions to Timothy[59] in an ancient letter become God's direct summons to a German
pastor almost nineteen hundred years later? The dissonance between
Bonhoeffer's faithful reading and the constraints of critical reading forces
us to pause and address the long-deferred normative questions. Does
Paul offer a good model of how to interpret the Bible? How does our study
of Paul's readings of Scripture bear upon our reading of Paul's writings as
Scripture? These questions will strike different readers with different
force.

Some will be content to view Paul's interpretations of Israel's Scripture as one example of the universal phenomenon of intertextuality. He
may be an interesting case study because his readings are so curious and
because he stands near the source of a movement that was destined to
shape Western culture, but no great consequence hangs on the legitimacy
of his interpretations. (Indeed, the critical operation of introducing intertextuality as an analytical category will perhaps appear—to some—to
have foreclosed questions of truth and falsehood.)[60] For readers who
operate within this frame of reference, the fact that Paul's letters
eventually became part of the Christian Bible—a circumstance that belongs to the history of interpretation—places the interpreter under no
special obligation to decide whether to believe what Paul wrote or to
puzzle out what such belief might require.

Other readers, however, belong to communities for which Paul's
readings of Scripture are either gospel or anathema. For such readers the
question of legitimacy cannot be finessed. Unable to participate in the
cheerful postmodern agnosticism about a transcendental signified, they
will continue to suppose that the appropriateness and truth of Paul's
interpretations are not only matters patient of reasoned adjudication but
also matters of great urgency. Since I belong to such a community, I feel
obliged to conclude this study with some reflections about the theological

implications of the analysis put forward in this book. The question that lies before us is this: can we learn how to read Scripture rightly within the community of faith by studying Paul's example?[61]

The question of the appropriateness of Paul's readings of Scripture can be considered more precisely if the issue is broken into three components:

1. Are Paul's specific *interpretations* of Scripture materially normative?
2. Are Paul's interpretive *methods* formally exemplary?
3. What are the appropriate *constraints* on interpretive freedom?

Differing answers to these questions generate diverse ways of relating the Bible to confession and theology.

Percy Gardner, for example, previously cited as an illustration of an experiential-expressive approach to Paul, regards Paul's handling of the Old Testament as riddled materially with errors, which are caused by his use of inadequate methods: "he interprets in the manner of the rabbis of his time, and therefore, it is needless to say, not in accordance with true critical methods."[62] No equivocation here: Gardner would answer an emphatic "no" to questions 1 and 2, and he would apparently presuppose, with regard to question 3, that the appropriate constraints on interpretive freedom are provided by modern historical-critical methods.

A different position is articulated by Richard Longenecker:

> What then can be said to our question, "Can we reproduce the exegesis of the New Testament?" I suggest that we must answer both "No" and "Yes." Where that exegesis is based upon a revelatory stance, where it evidences itself to be merely cultural, or where it shows itself to be circumstantial or *ad hominem* in nature, "No." Where, however, it treats the Old Testament in more literal fashion, following the course of what we speak of today as historico-grammatical exegesis, "Yes." Our commitment as Christians is to the reproduction of the apostolic faith and doctrine, and not necessarily to the specific apostolic exegetical practices.[63]

Longenecker answers my analytic questions quite specifically: yes, Paul's readings are materially normative (we are committed to "the reproduction of the apostolic faith and doctrine"), and no, we cannot follow his methodological example except where it happens to coincide with modern "historico-grammatical exegesis." Longenecker differs from Gardner in ascribing some of Paul's startling interpretations to revelation rather than to sheer error, and he shows far greater historical understanding and sympathy for first-century Jewish exegetical practices, but he appears in the end to share Gardner's views that many of Paul's interpretive practices are "merely cultural" and that modern critical methods (are these methods something other than "merely cultural"?) must serve as the determinative constraints on exegetical freedom for the community of faith in the present time.

These illustrations are chosen not because they are distinctive or of special importance in their own right but because they exemplify widely held positions on the question of the normative value of Paul's hermeneutics. Gardner assumes that Pauline exegesis is odd but incidental; the real substance of his faith lies elsewhere, in his "religious experience." That account of the matter fails, however, to reckon seriously with Paul's own urgent emphasis on Scripture interpretation. Furthermore, in the long run, it is difficult to see how such a condescending approach is compatible with reading Paul's letters as part of the Christian Scriptures. The letters become a window onto the spiritual experiences of early Christians; those experiences, then, become themselves the normative center of gravity, whereas Paul's writings, with their odd hermeneutical procedures, are reduced to the status of secondary rationalizations.[64]

Longenecker, on the other hand, takes Paul's interpretive activity far more seriously; indeed, by reverently attributing many of its idiosyncrasies to revelation, he places Paul on a theological pedestal. We are to believe and "reproduce" his teachings but not to emulate the freedom with which he reads Scripture. This recommendation would bind Christian discourse to what Greene calls reproductive (or *sacramental*) imitation. I would contend, however, that the position recommended by Longenecker is inherently unstable: it commits us to a peculiar intellectual schizophrenia in which we arbitrarily grant privileged status to past interpretations that we deem unjustifiable with regard to normal, sober hermeneutical canons. (Let us not deceive ourselves about this: Paul would flunk our introductory exegesis courses.) Despite the intended piety of the position, it cuts the lifeline between Paul's time and ours. Ironically, Longenecker's attitude toward the New Testament is formally identical to the view of Scripture that Kugel observes among the rabbis (see pp. 170–71 above): Scripture belongs to a holy past in which we no longer can presume to participate. Whatever the virtues of this attitude toward Scripture (humility would head the list), those who hold such views are strange successors to Paul, whose letters are models of hermeneutical freedom. Longenecker has circumscribed this freedom for Paul's followers[65] by granting hermeneutical veto power to a modern critical method of which Paul himself was entirely innocent. From the perspective of faith it is not clear why this should be so.

Besides, (and this is the more fundamental objection to Longenecker's formulation) the "apostolic faith and doctrine" cannot be extricated so cleanly from apostolic exegesis. Our investigation of Paul's letters has shown above all how his message is rooted in intertextual reflection. C. H. Dodd argued cogently that "the substructure of all Christian theology" lay in the early church's patterns of interpreting Old Testament material.[66] Consequently, the "chief regulative ideas" of the apostolic faith were organically fused at the root with the specific exegetical practices that Longenecker would like to declare merely cultural and nonnormative. Scriptural interpretation was not just a peripheral activity of the early church, not just an embellishment of the message; it was, as Longenecker's own work also shows, integrally bound up with the formulation of the Christian proclamation.[67] Scripture interpretation is the theological matrix within which the kerygma took shape; removed from that matrix, it will die. Longenecker would like to pluck and preserve the flower of apostolic doctrine, but severed from its generative hermeneutical roots that flower will surely wither.

There is no possibility of accepting Paul's message while simultaneously rejecting the legitimacy of the scriptural interpretation that sustains it. If Paul's way of reading the testimony of the Law and the Prophets is wrong, then his gospel does constitute a betrayal of Israel and Israel's God, and his hermeneutic can only lead us astray. If, on the other hand, his material claims are in any sense true, then we must go back and learn from him how to read Scripture.

Of course, it is theoretically possible to hold the inverse of Longenecker's position: that Paul's actual interpretations are materially wrong or outdated but that his hermeneutical method is nevertheless a good model. Virtually no Christians have ever advocated such a view, but Marks—whose trenchant essay avoids identifying its hermeneutical proposals with the commitments of any religious community—has sketched the outlines of such a position. "There are some, however, who would prefer to take Paul's *act* [of revisionary interpretation] or attitude as authoritative. They would know the 'dispensation of the Spirit' as a straining toward freedom, knowing that this always involves a struggle against one's own patrimony in the deepest sense. . . . Within the temporal framework that the Bible insists on, they would recognize that the content of the gospel is never fixed."[68] Marks thus presents Paul as a paradigmatic strong misreader whose true disciples will emulate his iconoclastic assault on received tradition, presumably including the canonical Paul himself. This profile of a true Pauline disciple is exemplified, as Marks recognizes, by Marcion. I have already argued that Marks's selective reading misrepresents Paul's attitude toward Scripture; however, that criticism does not in principle invalidate Marks's formal proposal. It is difficult, though, to see how one could combine such a stance with Christian faith.[69] Marks's reading transmutes Paul's gospel about God's gracious act in Jesus Christ into "another gospel" (cf. Gal. 1:6–9) about the hermeneutical *exousia* of the *Überleser*.

Against all of the above options, I would argue that the only theologically appropriate response to our study of Pauline hermeneutics is to answer "yes" to both questions 1 and 2: Paul's readings are materially normative (in a sense to be specified carefully) for Christian theology and his interpretive methods are paradigmatic for Christian hermeneutics.[70] His letters help us to understand both what the Old Testament means and how it should be read. I hasten to add, however, that these affirmations must be understood only in light of the findings of the foregoing pages: Paul's readings of Scripture enact a certain imaginative vision of the relation between Scripture and God's eschatological activity in the present time. To learn from Paul how to read Scripture is to learn to share that vision, so that we can continue to read and speak under the guidance of the Spirit, interpreting Scripture in light of the gospel[71] and the gospel in light of Scripture. In short, to gain Paul's kind of reader competence we must learn from him the art of dialectical imitation, bringing Scripture's witness to God's action in the past to bear as a critical principle on the present, and allowing God's present action among us to illumine our understanding of his action in the past. Paul exhorted his readers to become imitators of him (1 Cor. 4:16, 11:1; Phil. 3:17).[72] Surely to imitate him faithfully we must learn from him the art of reading and proclaiming Scripture.

If we did imitate Paul's interpretive practices, how would our reading of Scripture be shaped by his example? The simplest way to grasp the normative implications would be to recapitulate the discussion of the first part of this chapter, converting its descriptive observations into prescriptions. Without repeating all that has already been said, however, a brief summary can highlight some important facets of my proposal.

If we learned from Paul how to read Scripture, we would learn to read it primarily as a narrative of election and promise, as a witness to the righteousness of God. God's faithfulness ensures that the story of his dealings with Israel extends into the present time and encompasses it. This hermeneutical perspective erodes conventional distinctions between Christianity and Judaism, because God's covenant with Israel is read—in the light of clues from Isaiah 40–55 and Deuteronomy 32—as part of his larger narrative design to raise up a people to declare his praise, called from among the Gentiles as well as from among the Jews: the Gentiles are grafted into Israel. A corollary of this hermeneutical strategy is that the present circumstances—in which many Gentiles believe God's indication of his righteousness (the death and resurrection of Jesus) while most Jews do not believe—must be understood as a temporary complication of the plot. If we have learned anything from Scripture's story about the character of Israel's God, we can trust that he will not permit this anomalous situation of division and unbelief to terminate the story of election.

The story that Paul finds in Scripture is an account of God's dealing with a people. Consequently, *if we learned from Paul how to read Scripture, we would read it ecclesiocentrically,* as a word for and about the community of faith. Scripture discloses its sense only as the text is brought into correlation with living communities where the Holy Spirit is at work. The point is not that Scripture must be made "relevant," as though its meaning could first be discerned through abstractable critical methods and then secondarily applied by analogy to our contemporary situation; rather, the meaning of Scripture will never be understood at all until it is read in communities that embody the obedience of faith. Thus, true interpretation is a retrospective activity of communities whose reading is shaped by the grace of God in their midst. Under the guidance of the Spirit, we discover the operation of God's grace among us to be prefigured in Scripture, and we find the Scripture that we thought we knew transfigured by the grace at work among us.

Because the sense of Scripture is disclosed only in the nexus between text and community, interpretation should never be severed from preaching. *If we learned from Paul how to read Scripture, we would read it in the service of proclamation.* Christian biblical interpretation has its original and proper *Sitz im Leben* in preaching or (as in Paul's letters) in pastoral counsel—that is to say, in acts of reading that construe Scripture as a word of direct address to the community. When Bonhoeffer read in 2 Tim. 4:21, "Do your best to come before winter," and took it as God's word to him, he was operating with hermeneutical assumptions faithful to Paul's example. This may not be good exegesis, but it was never proposed as exegesis of the text; rather, it was a charismatic, prophetic transference of the text's sense. Indeed, Paul's way of using Scripture suggests that homiletical and prophetic readings can sometimes be more faithful than rigorously exegetical ones. Exegesis gives us critical distance from the text; preaching thrusts the text's word directly into our faces. The word is near us, and it demands a response. This strategy of reading is risky, because it strips away critical controls, exposing us to the danger of arbitrary or manipulative interpretations. On the other hand, unless we learn from Paul to read Scripture as a word addressed directly to us, we will never proclaim the word of God with power. Only those who have studied or taught in seminary know how ill-prepared our preachers are to read Scripture in this way. Yet, the classic theologians canonized by our curricula (Augustine, Luther, Calvin, Wesley) did their work of interpretation, imitating Paul's example, preeminently as a form of proclamation. If we fail to follow this example, something is amiss.

The presupposition for Paul's practice of reading Scripture as a word addressed immediately to his community is his urgent conviction that they are the ones "upon whom the ends of the ages have come." *If we learned from Paul how to read Scripture, we would read as participants in the eschatological drama of redemption.* Of all the hermeneutical prescriptions offered us by Paul's example, this one is the hardest to swallow. Can we join with Paul in regarding ourselves as people of the endtime? Or have the passing centuries discredited his eschatological vision? If so, then his hermeneutical strategies can only perpetuate illusion. It is impossible to adopt Paul's interpretive practices without sharing his eschatological perspective. Demythologized atemporal translations of his eschatology will ultimately undermine his hermeneutic.[73] Why? Because intertextuality posits temporal sensibility. Any act of intertextual reflection creates a relation between the reader's time and the past time of the text, and (the dialectical counterthrust seems inevitable) the reader's consciousness of temporality will shape the way in which the text is read.

Through interpreting Scripture, we locate our present time in relation to the story of God's dealing with humankind. Paul believed that his stance at the turn of the ages gave him a warrant for his radically revisionary readings because it gave him a privileged perspective from which to discern the thematic unity of time past and future. If we are unable to share Paul's sense of participating in the community of the endtime, then his reading strategies will appear arbitrary and grandiose; we would do better to adopt hermeneutical practices that more adequately correspond to our own modest sense of temporal location and historical relativity. (This is precisely what has happened in Christian communities where historical criticism is granted a normative constraining hermeneutical role.) If, on the other hand, we can confess with Paul that "now is the day of salvation," that the present is God-dominated time, and that we await the liberation of all creation from its bondage to decay (Rom. 8:21), then his readings of Scripture might begin to make sense, and his strategies of reading might become paradigmatic for us.

At this point, simple reproductive imitation of Paul is impossible. The passage of a hundred generations in which the parousia has not yet occurred is a fact of experience no less hermeneutically formidable for us than the refusal of his Jewish contemporaries to believe the gospel was for Paul. Our historical experience, therefore, demands a hermeneutical response no less imaginative, no less faithful. Our imitation of Paul's eschatology will necessarily take on a dialectical character, as we appropriate his hope for God's redemption and healing of creation while offering revisionary readings of texts which pin that hope to the imminent return of the Lord.[74]

Above all, Paul provides us with a model of hermeneutical freedom. *If we learned from Paul how to read Scripture, we would learn to appreciate the metaphorical relation between the text and our own reading of it.* Thus, we would begin to cherish the poetics of interpretation, allowing rhetoric to lie down peacefully with grammar and logic.[75] In our own proclamation of the word, we would grant a broad space for the play of echo and allusion, for figurative intertextual conjunctions, and even—if our communities were sufficiently rooted in Scripture's symbolic soil—for metalepsis. The troping of the text would be the natural consequence of locating our lives within its story.[76]

Only when we understand Paul's readings of Scripture in this metaphorical mode will we glimpse the intelligibility of the paradox posed by simultaneously affirming both their normative status and their exemplary value. The dilemma is this: if we read Scripture with the same imaginative freedom Paul employed, will we not inevitably contradict his particular construals of it? Will we not, in fact, produce readings of Paul's own letters that cut across the grain? The way out of the dilemma is to recognize the figurative mode of the intertextual connections created in Paul's readings. Anyone who does not recognize that "the rock was Christ" is a metaphor is a dull reader indeed. But biblical scholars have been slow to recognize, for example, the metaphorical character of Paul's equation between the word of the covenant in Deuteronomy 30 and the word of the gospel in Romans 10. To describe this equation as metaphorical is not to deny its truth; rather, it is to insist that it be granted the sort of acknowledgment proper to its own metaphorical mode of assertion. Thus, when I affirm that such an interpretation of Deuteronomy 30 is materially normative for Christian theology, I am proposing that Paul's metaphorical reading is a trustworthy model of an appropriate hermeneutical stance toward Deuteronomy and toward Torah as a whole. Recognizing the metaphorical character of the intertextual relation will prevent us from literalizing or absolutizing Paul's reading. Indeed, Paul's own example would lead us to expect that the community, under the guidance of the Spirit, will remain open to fresh readings of the same text, through which God will continue to speak.

While we will continue to recognize Paul's readings of Scripture as abidingly valid figurations, we will also create new figurations out of the texts that Paul read, and we will do so in part by weaving Paul's own writings into the intertextual web, perhaps discerning correspondences that did not occur to Paul himself. Let us consider a single example of how such a constructive intertextual reading might proceed.

We noted in our discussion of Romans 9 that Paul supports his association of Isaac with *promise*, rather than with *flesh*, by quoting from Gen. 18:10, 14 God's word of promise to Abraham: "According to this time [*kata ton kairon touton*] I will come, and there will be for Sarah a son." At the explicit level of argumentation, this quotation simply advances Paul's argument a small step by proving that Isaac's birth was promised by God. But when we read Rom. 9:6–9 in intertextual counterpoint with the allegory of Gal. 4:21–31, new interpretive possibilities arise. The Galatians passage, as we have seen, identifies Gentile Christian believers as "children of promise according to Isaac" and takes the reference in Gen. 21:10 to "my son Isaac" as a figure for the Christian community (see Gal. 4:30–31).[77] What if this interpretation of Isaac were carried over into Romans 9, which also cites Genesis 21 (Gen. 21:12, in Rom. 9:7)? Then Paul's citations of Gen. 21:12 and 18:10, 14 (Rom. 9:7, 9) would not merely prove the general proposition that God can be selective if he wants to; rather, they would already whisper veiled prophecies of God's specific intention to call Gentiles into the people of God. These texts would ring in the reader's ears with the resonances of eschatological prophecy. "This time" (*ton kairon touton*) for Paul is the moment pregnant with the fulfillment of promise; it is "the now time" (*en tō nyn kairō* [Rom. 3:26]) in which the righteousness of God is being revealed, the time to which all the promises of Scripture are addressed. Given Paul's predilection for reading Scripture in general and the Abraham story in particular as a word of promise addressed to the present time, is it bad reading to construe Gen. 18:10 as such a word? When we read in Rom. 9:9 of God's promising Abraham, "I shall come and there will be for Sarah a son," should we think of the coming of Jesus Christ as God's promise-fulfilling act that gives Sarah a son by calling into being a community of Gentile believers?

Exactly such a reading is worked out carefully and explicitly in Galatians, but if Paul still bears it in mind here in Rom. 9:6–9, he does not say so; the argument in Romans 9 works neatly without reference to the Galatians allegory. If we are "doing exegesis" as a problem-solving ac-

tivity, we had best invoke Ockham's razor and excise this latent allegorical sense from our interpretation of Rom. 9:9. But if we are reading the
text in a way that seeks to grasp its full semantic range, how can we filter
out the intertextual resonances triggered by Paul's quotation? He introduces the text with the sententious formula, "This is the word of promise," and then leaves it dangling at the end of a paragraph unit without
further interpretive comment; consequently, the quotation stirs the air
with lingering echoes.

There is no reason to think that Paul's Roman readers had read Galatians or that they were given any clues that would permit them to hear in
the quotation of Gen. 18:10 the overtones that I have described. In this
case the transumed text (Gal. 4:21–31) is not within the canon shared by
Paul's original readers; instead, it is a text within the New Testament
canon. As a result, later readers can hear in Rom. 9:9 an intertextual trope
that might well have been within the range of Paul's sensibility but that
would almost surely have eluded his original readers. This case illustrates
dramatically the difference between historical exegesis and intertextual
canonical reading. Even if Paul did not intend latent resonances between
Rom. 9:9 and Gal. 4:21–31, these resonances do in fact exist for readers
who now have these texts together within the church's canon; furthermore, the resultant prophetic interpretation of Gen. 18:10 is consistent
with and complementary to the whole argument of Romans 9–11 that
God always intended to create a new elect community (cf. also Romans
4). Thus, to hear in Rom. 9:9 echoes of Gal. 4:21–31, even if that is not
what Paul meant when he was writing to the Romans, is to read Paul with
the same sort of intertextual hermeneutic sensibility that Paul brought to
his reading of Scripture.[78]

Is such a method of reading legitimate? And, in interpreting Paul, is
legitimacy discerned according to the flesh or according to promise? This
example should remind us that "legitimacy" is a metaphorical way of
speaking about the parentage of our interpretations. I would suggest that
the reading I have just proposed of Rom. 9:9 is a legitimate one in the
sense that Paul is its true father (or perhaps its grandfather). It is certainly
not a valid historical exegesis of Rom. 9:9 by normal exegetical standards,
and still less is it a valid exegesis of Gen. 18:10. Nonetheless, in the *poiēsis*
of proclamation, this intertextual reading could be employed effectively
and faithfully. It is exactly the sort of reading that Paul's own example
would encourage.[79]

Do we then overthrow the canon by this hermeneutic? On the contrary, we uphold the canon. Will the imaginative freedom of Paul's example ultimately destroy Scripture's authority if we dare to read the text as

freely as he did? On the contrary, only when our interpreters and preachers read with an imaginative freedom analogous to Paul's will Scripture's voice be heard in the church. We are children of the Word, not prisoners.

Such reading is dangerous. It might seem that the Christian community is flirting with intellectual suicide if it encourages emulation of Paul's free-ranging hermeneutical innovation: our readings might diverge so radically from the community's traditions of interpretation that there would no longer be substantive continuity between the faith that Paul proclaimed and the faith that we promulgate. Consequently, it might appear safer to posit a doctrine of revelation that grants Paul and the other New Testament writers an apostolic license to read innovatively and authoritatively under a special dispensation no longer available to subsequent generations. Paul's readings would then define the contours of a new orthodoxy to which subsequent Christian readers must conform. Though this strategy appears safer, the appearance is deceptive, for two reasons.

First, the ideal of a perspicuous authoritative text that contains an unchangeable meaning is untenable because it denies the necessary contribution of the reader and the reader's community in the act of interpretation. No longer can we think of meaning as something contained by a text; texts have meaning only as they are read and used by communities of readers. Therefore, our normative proposals about the role of Scripture in the community must take account of our own hermeneutical agency.

Second, as I have already argued, the attempt to separate Paul's hermeneutical freedom from ours cuts off the word at its roots. It is ironically unfaithful, in the most fundamental way, to the teaching of the apostle who insisted that "the word is near you, in your mouth and in your heart." Those who would be faithful to Paul's word must take the risks of interpretive freedom. Those who do not take and acknowledge such risks will either stifle the word of God by parroting fixed formulas or turn the notions of inspiration and revelation into a smokescreen for self-deception, because they will in fact continue to generate their own transformative readings of Scripture while pretending not to do so.

It is better by far to imitate Paul's example of dialectical engagement with Scripture: we acknowledge that Scripture forms our identity, even while we read it with imaginative freedom.[80] Indeed, insofar as the Pauline letters function as Scripture—and therefore form our communal identity—they teach us to read with freedom, for we learn in them that we, who once were no people, are now God's people, elected and called to act in freedom with the guidance and empowerment of the Holy Spirit.

This action in freedom necessarily includes responsibility for ongoing interpretation of Scripture to address the needs of the community. By what authority do we undertake the risks of interpretation? "Such is the confidence that we have through Christ toward God. Not that we are competent of ourselves to claim anything as coming from us; our competence is from God, who has made us competent to be ministers of a new covenant, not of the script but of the Spirit" (2 Cor. 3:4–6a). We are authorized to perform imaginative acts of interpretation because as people of the new covenant we find the Law written on our hearts, and we discover in our own corporate life a letter from Christ whose import is open to all, whose message is in the deepest sense congruent with the message of Scripture.

If we claim such bold hermeneutical privilege, however, how do we respond to the dangers of self-deception and radical discontinuity? Will the community's figurative readings of Scripture deviate so drastically from Paul's interpretations that our gospel will become a different gospel? Will our hermeneutical freedom become an opportunity for the flesh? The danger is a serious one. It forces us to return to the third analytic question posed in the beginning of this discussion: what are the constraints on interpretive freedom? If there are no such constraints, Scripture will lose its power to form the identity of the community: it will become a lump of clay to be shaped according to the whim of the reader.

Paul already faced this problem in his own time: his readings of Scripture seemed so scandalously revisionary that he had to defend their continuity with the Torah. In the course of that defense, he acknowledged, either implicitly or explicitly, certain fundamental constraints or criteria by which the validity of his readings could be assessed. In order to carry to completion my proposal that Paul's own hermeneutical practice be taken as paradigmatic for ours, I would suggest that we must acknowledge the same constraints that he acknowledged. (That, I take it, is part of what it means to recognize his writings as Scripture.) But if the normative constraints on our reading are to be the same as Paul's, historical criticism, however useful it may be for other purposes—such as stimulating analogical imagination—should not be burdened with theological responsibility for screening the uses of Scripture in Christian proclamation.[81] If it were entrusted with such a normative task, many of Paul's readings would fail the test. What then were the constraints that he recognized, and what would it mean for us to imitate him in recognizing them?

We have already noted that his hermeneutical constraints are substantive rather than methodological. The task of identifying these constraints is dauntingly complex, but at least two criteria seem to loom large in Paul's mind. The first of these is, as we have seen, the criterion of God's faithfulness to his promises: "let God be true though every man be false." No reading of Scripture can be legitimate if it denies the faithfulness of Israel's God to his covenant promises. That criterion binds Paul's interpretive freedom to a relation of continuity with Israel's story. But a second, equally important constraint must be recognized: Scripture must be read as a witness to the gospel of Jesus Christ. No reading of Scripture can be legitimate if it fails to acknowledge the death and resurrection of Jesus as the climactic manifestation of God's righteousness. That criterion binds Paul's interpretive freedom to a relation of faithfulness to the Christian kerygma. The tension between these two fundamental constraints defines the field within which the work of interpreting Scripture in the church must be performed. Or, to use a different metaphor, these two convictions bond together to create the nucleus around which all interpretation must orbit.

Our examination of Paul's interpretive practices, however, has identified still one more hermeneutical constraint, more exacting than the other two; in the end, it is the most powerful check against arbitrariness and error. Because readers who discern the true message of Scripture behold the glory of God in Jesus Christ, Paul tells us, they are "changed into his likeness." No reading of Scripture can be legitimate, then, if it fails to shape the readers into a community that embodies the love of God as shown forth in Christ. This criterion slashes away all frivolous or self-serving readings, all readings that aggrandize the interpreter, all merely clever readings. True interpretation of Scripture leads us into unqualified giving of our lives in service within the community whose vocation is to reenact the obedience of the Son of God who loved us and gave himself for us. Community in the likeness of Christ is cruciform; therefore right interpretation must be cruciform. "For while we live we are always being given up to death for Jesus' sake so that the life of Jesus may be manifested in our mortal flesh" (2 Cor. 4:11). Any reading of Scripture that requires of us something other or less than this is a false reading.

Wayne Meeks has called for "a hermeneutics of social embodiment," a theological hermeneutics whose goal "is not belief in objectively true propositions taught by the text nor the adoption by individuals of an authentic self-understanding evoked by the text's symbols, but the formation of a community whose forms of life correspond to the symbolic universe rendered or signaled by the text."[82] Paul's hermeneutical practice answers Meeks's formal description paradigmatically: he invested his life in seeking to form communities that would embody the gospel of

Jesus Christ crucified. Such communities are the best constraint on aberrant interpretation and the best hope for nurturing imaginative readers
who will be able to hear the word that is near them. Of course, it is
possible to trust that such communities will be simultaneously imaginative and faithful only if one trusts, as Paul did, in the power of the Spirit to
disclose truth and give life.

To speak of this kind of community formation as "theological hermeneutics" is to speak a quaint metaphorical dialect that Paul would not
have understood. He would have understood, however, that the meaning of Scripture is ultimately written on the tablets of fleshy hearts. That is
why his tireless efforts to read Scripture rightly are always directed towards forming the church into a text that glorifies God. "For whatever
was written before was written for our instruction, in order that through
steadfastness and through the encouragement of the Scriptures we might
have hope. May the God of steadfastness and encouragement grant you
to live in such harmony with one another, in accord with Christ Jesus,
that together you may with one voice glorify the God and Father of our
Lord Jesus Christ."[83]

Notes

PREFACE

1. Robert Alter and Frank Kermode, eds., *The Literary Guide to the Bible* (Cambridge: Harvard University Press, 1987).
2. "The Good Books," *The New Yorker* (January 11, 1988), 94–98, quotation on p. 97.
3. Dietrich-Alex Koch, *Die Schrift als Zeuge des Evangeliums: Untersuchungen zur Verwendung und zum Verständnis der Schrift bei Paulus* (BHT 69; Tübingen: J. C. B. Mohr, Paul Siebeck, 1986).
4. Alfred Rahlfs, ed., *Septuaginta* (Stuttgart: Deutsche Bibelstiftung, 1935).

CHAPTER ONE

1. The Greek phrase is *hē ek pisteōs dikaiosynē*. Paul's hypostatization of "righteousness" is, of course, a momentary poetic device, not a doctrinal proposition.
2. See his own account of this disjuncture in Phil. 3:2–14.
3. *Baba Meṣia* 59b. The translation is from I. Epstein, ed., *The Babylonian Talmud*, vol. 20 (London: Soncino, 1935), 352–53.
4. I refer here, of course, to the character in the talmudic story; I am making no claim about the trustworthiness of the text's attribution of this reading of Deut. 30:12 to a particular historical figure.
5. For a discussion of the way in which interpretation of Scripture is inevitably governed by some such global construal, or imaginative characterization of the "discrimen," see David Kelsey, *The Uses of Scripture in Recent Theology* (Philadelphia: Fortress, 1976), 158–81.
6. An illuminating discussion of this phenomenon within rabbinic tradition is provided by David Weiss Halivni, *Midrash, Mishnah, and Gemara: The Jewish Predilection for Justified Law* (Cambridge: Harvard University Press, 1986).
7. The Hebrew text of Exod. 23:2 is problematical. For a brief discussion of

the difficulties, see Brevard S. Childs, *The Book of Exodus* (Philadelphia: Westminster, 1974), 450, 481.

8. The LXX translators certainly understood the text in this sense: "You shall not be with a multitude for evil. You shall not join with a crowd to incline with a multitude so as to incline [tilt] justice." Likewise, *Mekilta* Kaspa 2 (Lauterbach II, 161–62) understands the text as a directive to judges not to cast the decisive vote for conviction of an accused person: "Suppose eleven are for acquittal and eleven are for conviction and one says: I do not know. Behold, there is a warning to the judge not to swing the vote except for acquittal. For Scripture says: 'Neither shalt thou speak up in a cause to turn aside after a multitude to pervert justice.' " In relation to these other Jewish interpretations, R. Jeremiah's handling of the text looks all the more peculiar.

9. My colleague Steven Fraade suggests to me that the rabbis, with their conviction that nothing in Torah was superfluous, solved the problem of the apparently redundant *lĕhaṭṭōt* by repunctuating the sentence, creating an elliptical clause out of the final three Hebrew words; consequently, the quotation attributed to R. Jeremiah in *Baba Meṣia* 59b corresponds verbatim to the final three words of Exod. 23:2. The fact that this construal of the words makes no sense in context—indeed, contradicts the first part of the same verse—was a matter of minor consequence for rabbinic hermeneutics.

10. James Kugel remarks that "there is often something a bit joking about midrash. . . . The ultimate subject of that joke is the dissonance between the religion of the Rabbis and the Book from which it is supposed to be derived— and . . . more precisely the dissonance between that book's supposedly unitary and harmonious message and its actually fragmentary and inconsistent components" ("Two Introductions to Midrash," in Geoffrey H. Hartman and Sanford Budick, eds., *Midrash and Literature* [New Haven: Yale University Press, 1986], 77– 103, quotation on 80).

11. Wayne A. Meeks, "A Hermeneutics of Social Embodiment," *HTR* 79 (1986): 182.

12. The hermeneutical importance of the "contingency" of Paul's letters, interacting with the "coherence" provided by certain foundational convictions, has been stressed particularly by J. Christiaan Beker, *Paul the Apostle: The Triumph of God in Life and Thought* (Philadelphia: Fortress, 1980). More recently, Beker has summarized his approach to Paul's theology by declaring that "Paul is a hermeneutic theologian rather than a systematic theologian" ("The Faithfulness of God and the Priority of Israel in Paul's Letter to the Romans," *HTR* 79 [1986]:10). This is an excellent formulation; however, Beker's work may not fully do justice to the fact that Paul's hermeneutic theology was worked out not only by interpreting the *gospel* for particular situations but also by interpreting Israel's *Scriptures*. On the contingency of the letters, see also Nils A. Dahl, "The Particularity of the Pauline Epistles as a Problem in the Ancient Church," in *Neotestamentica et Patristica: Freundesgabe Oscar Cullmann* (NovTSup 6; Leiden: Brill, 1965), 261–71.

13. For a brief historical survey with bibliographical data, see E. Earle Ellis, *Paul's Use of the Old Testament* (Edinburgh: Oliver and Boyd, 1957) 2–5.

14. George A. Lindbeck, *The Nature of Doctrine: Religion and Theology in a Postliberal Age* (Philadelphia: Westminster, 1984), 16 et passim.

15. Percy Gardner, *The Religious Experience of Saint Paul* (New York: G. P. Putnam's Sons, 1913), 215. I am indebted to Leander Keck for this reference.

16. Adolf von Harnack, "Das Alte Testament in den Paulinischen Briefen und in den Paulinischen Gemeinden," *Sitzungsberichte der Preussischen Akademie der Wissenschaften*, Philosophisch-historische Klasse (1928):124–41. In defense of Harnack's assertions, it can be observed that Paul does not conduct exegetical arguments in his earliest letter (1 Thessalonians) and that—in contrast to some of his Jewish contemporaries—he does not write biblical commentaries. But the view that Paul appeals to Scripture only as a concession to his adversaries fails to reckon sufficiently with the pervasiveness of scriptural allusion in Paul's discourse, including 1 Thessalonians. For further comment on this point, see Richard B. Hays, "Crucified with Christ: A Synthesis of the Theology of 1 and 2 Thessalonians, Philippians, Philemon, and Galatians," in David J. Lull, ed., *Society of Biblical Literature 1988 Seminar Papers* (Atlanta: Scholars, 1988), 318–35.

17. Rudolf Bultmann, *Theology of the New Testament*, trans. Kendrick Grobel (New York: Scribner's Sons, 1951–55), 1.187–352. However, D. Moody Smith argues in a forthcoming essay ("The Pauline Literature," in D. A. Carson and H. G. M. Williamson, eds., *"It Is Written": Scripture Citing Scripture: Essays in Honor of Barnabas Lindars, SSF* [Cambridge: Cambridge University Press, 1988], 265–91) that Bultmann's interpretation of Pauline anthropology is fundamentally— though only implicitly—grounded in Old Testament conceptions.

18. R. Bultmann, "The Significance of the Old Testament for Christian Faith," pp. 8–35 in Bernhard W. Anderson, ed., *The Old Testament and Christian Faith* (New York: Harper & Row, 1963), 14.

19. Ibid., 17.

20. Ibid.

21. Ibid., 31–32.

22. The work of Leonhard Goppelt illustrates this tendency: "The church's relationship to the historical Christ and to God's revelation in the Old Covenant must not be replaced by a nonhistorical, syncretistic myth. Typology demonstrates not only the nature of the new in comparison with the old but it also shows that the new is founded directly and solely on redemptive history" *(Heilsgeschichte) (Typos: The Typological Interpretation of the Old Testament in the New*, trans. D. H. Madvig [Grand Rapids: Eerdmans, 1982], 151–52). Goppelt's work, originally published in 1939, had considerable impact upon Ellis, and its influence can still be observed in, e.g., David L. Baker, "Typology and the Christian Use of the Old Testament," *SJT* 29 (1976):137–57; and Walter C. Kaiser, Jr., *The Uses of the Old Testament in the New* (Chicago: Moody, 1985).

23. All the writers cited in n. 22 fit this description, with the exception of Kaiser, who defends the "stonewall" position that there is no gap at all between the original sense of the Old Testament texts and Paul's use of them: "types cannot be 'read into' or 'read back' into the OT from the NT in some sort of canonized *eisegesis*" *(Uses of the OT*, 121). More typical is the cautiously apologetic comment of Ellis: "If Paul's presuppositions as to the nature of the OT and of its history are accepted, little fault can be found with his handling of the individual texts" *(Paul's Use of the OT*, 148).

24. Richard N. Longenecker, *Biblical Exegesis in the Apostolic Period* (Grand Rapids: Eerdmans, 1975), 121.

25. In addition to the studies of Goppelt and Ellis, the landmark works are Otto Michel, *Paulus und seine Bibel* (BFCT 2/18; Gütersloh: Bertelsmann, 1929 [reprint, Darmstadt: Wissenschaftliche Buchgesellschaft, 1972]); J. Bonsirven, *Exégèse rabbinique et exégèse paulinienne* (Paris: Beauchesne, 1939); C. H. Dodd, *According to the Scriptures: The Sub-Structure of New Testament Theology* (London: Nisbet, 1952); Barnabas Lindars, *New Testament Apologetic* (London: SCM, 1961). A major new contribution to the discussion is offered by Dietrich-Alex Koch, *Die Schrift als Zeuge des Evangeliums*.

26. I borrow the description from Leander Keck, "Pauline Studies: Retrospect" (Address delivered in the Pauline Epistles Section of the Society of Biblical Literature Annual Meeting, Atlanta, 1986). The situation has not changed materially since Merrill P. Miller's assessment of the situation in 1971: "Recent major studies of the OT in the NT have dealt mostly with questions of the text form of OT citations in the NT and the implications of this for the milieu and *Sitz im Leben* of the writing" ("Targum, Midrash, and the Use of the Old Testament in the New Testament," *JSJ* 2 [1971]:29–82; quotation on p. 64). A. T. Hanson, *Studies in Paul's Technique and Theology* (London: SPCK, 1974) has given serious attention to the theological implications of focusing on Paul as interpreter of Scripture, but— despite numerous important insights—his exegetical proposals are frequently convoluted and unpersuasive. Koch's *Schrift als Zeuge* is an important step in the right direction, but his analysis of Paul's *Verständnis* of Scripture does not match the depth and sophistication of his account of Paul's *Verwendung* of Scripture, i.e., the technical data on text-critical matters and incidence of citation.

27. A classic statement charging Paul with fundamental incomprehension of the role of Law in Judaism is that of Hans-Joachim Schoeps, *Paul: The Theology of the Apostle in Light of Jewish Religious History*, trans. Harold Knight (Philadelphia: Westminster, 1961), 168–218. More recently, Heikki Räisänen (*Paul and the Law*, [WUNT 29; Tübingen: J. C. B. Mohr, Paul Siebeck, 1983])—arguing that "Paul vacillates in his theological attitude to the law" (201)—agrees with Schoeps that "Paul misconstrues Jewish 'soteriology,' ignoring the pattern of gratuity on which it was based as well as the role accorded to man's repentance" (200).

28. For example, Gerd Theissen, *The Social Setting of Pauline Christianity*, ed. and trans. John H. Schütz (Philadelphia: Fortress, 1982); Wayne Meeks, *The First Urban Christians: The Social World of the Apostle Paul* (New Haven: Yale University Press, 1983); Norman R. Petersen, *Rediscovering Paul: Philemon and the Sociology of Paul's Narrative World* (Philadelphia: Fortress, 1985).

29. For example, Hans Dieter Betz, *Galatians* (Hermeneia; Philadelphia: Fortress, 1979). For a recent summary and assessment with extensive bibliography, see Wilhelm Wuellner, "Where Is Rhetorical Criticism Taking Us?" *CBQ* 49 (1987):448–63.

30. For example, E. P. Sanders, *Paul and Palestinian Judaism* (Philadelphia: Fortress, 1977); *Paul, The Law, and the Jewish People* (Philadelphia: Fortress, 1983); Beker, *Paul the Apostle*. Significant exceptions are Koch, *Schrift als Zeuge;* and Hans Hübner, *Gottes Ich und Israel: Zum Schriftgebrauch des Paulus in Römer 9–11* (FRLANT 136; Göttingen: Vandenhoeck & Ruprecht, 1984).

31. The interpretive yield of such studies is, on the whole, surprisingly meager. Some detailed studies of particular passages, however, have produced helpful insights: notably, Wayne A. Meeks, "'And Rose Up to Play': Midrash and

Paraenesis in 1 Cor. 10:1–22," *JSNT* 16 (1982):64–78; William Richard Stegner, "Romans 9.6–29—A Midrash," *JSNT* 22 (1984):37–52; E. Earle Ellis, *Prophecy and Hermeneutic in Early Christianity* (WUNT 18; Tübingen: J. C. B. Mohr, Paul Siebeck, 1978).

32. This capacious use of the term allowed Renee Bloch ("Midrash," *DBSup* 5.163–81) to find midrash already within the Old Testament canon and to argue that the New Testament writers' use of the Old Testament always involved "midrashic actualization." Bloch's important dictionary article is now available in an English translation by Mary H. Callaway in W. S. Green, ed., *Approaches to Ancient Judaism*, vol. 1 of *Brown Judaic Studies* (Missoula, Mont.: Scholars, 1978), 29–50. The same volume also contains a translation by W. S. Green and W. J. Sullivan of Bloch's essay, "Note methodologique pour l'étude de la littérature rabbinique" (51–75), originally published in *RSR* 43 (1955):194–227. For more precisely focused introductory treatments of midrash, see Jacob Neusner, *Midrash in Context: Exegesis in Formative Judaism* (Philadelphia: Fortress, 1983); Gary G. Porton, *Understanding Rabbinic Midrash* (Hoboken, N.J.: KTAV, 1985).

33. James A. Sanders, for instance, champions the creation of a discipline called "comparative midrash," which would place Paul and other NT writers within a continuum that leads from the earliest biblical writings to the rabbinic midrash compilations; see, e.g., *From Sacred Story to Sacred Text* (Philadelphia: Fortress, 1987), 20 et passim.

34. For a clear example, see Hanson, *Paul's Technique*, 209–24.

35. Philip S. Alexander, "Rabbinic Judaism and the New Testament," *ZNW* 74 (1983):244. As Alexander notes, NT critics would never treat the Gospels as uncritically as they treat rabbinic texts. Cf. also Jacob Neusner, "Comparing Religions," *HR* 18 (1978):177–91.

36. As, for example, has been done by Geza Vermes, *Scripture and Tradition in Judaism*, 2d ed. (Leiden: Brill, 1973).

37. See Ellis, *Prophecy and Hermeneutic*, 217–19; Stegner, "Romans 9:6–29."

38. Examples in Ellis, *Prophecy and Hermeneutic*, 214–16.

39. For an illustration of the problem, see Nils A. Dahl, "Contradictions in Scripture," *Studies in Paul* (Minneapolis: Augsburg, 1977), 159–77. For exposition and critique of Dahl's proposal, see Richard B. Hays, *The Faith of Jesus Christ: An Investigation of the Narrative Substructure of Galatians 3:1–4:11* (SBLDS 56; Chico: Scholars, 1983), 218–21.

40. See Alexander, "Rabbinic Judaism," 242–44.

41. I.e., "turnings" of language to figurative ends.

42. Jacob Neusner, "Judaism and the Scripture: The Case of Leviticus Rabbah," *BTB* 14 (1984):96.

43. David Daube, "Rabbinic Methods of Interpretation and Hellenistic Rhetoric," *HUCA* 22 (1949):239–65; "Alexandrian Methods of Interpretation and the Rabbis," in Henry A. Fischel, ed., *Essays in Greco-Roman and Related Talmudic Literature* (New York: KTAV, 1977), 165–82. See also Alexander, "Rabbinic Judaism," 246.

44. As Dahl comments at the conclusion of his effort to show that Paul is using a rabbinic style of argumentation in Galatians 3, "In no other place does Paul deviate more from the views of the rabbis" (*Studies in Paul*, 175), despite the putative formal similarities.

45. See, e.g., Susan A. Handelman, *The Slayers of Moses: The Emergence of Rabbinic Interpretation in Modern Literary Theory* (Albany: State University of New York Press, 1982), and the essays in Hartman and Budick, *Midrash and Literature*. But see also the demurral of William Scott Green, "Romancing the Tome: Rabbinic Hermeneutics and the Theory of Literature," *Semeia* 40 (1987):147–68.

46. Michael Fishbane, *Biblical Interpretation in Ancient Israel* (Oxford: Clarendon, 1985); for Bloch, see n. 32 above.

47. Michael Fishbane, "Inner Biblical Exegesis: Types and Strategies of Interpretation in Ancient Israel," in Hartman and Budick, *Midrash and Literature*, 36.

48. See Johannes Munck, *Paul and the Salvation of Mankind*, trans. F. Clarke (Richmond: John Knox, 1959), 11–35; Krister Stendahl, *Paul Among Jews and Gentiles* (Philadelphia: Fortress, 1976), 7–23.

49. Contemporary biblical critics are often less sensitive to phenomena of literary allusion than were their nineteenth-century predecessors, who were broadly educated in classical literary traditions. It is very instructive to read Benjamin Jowett ("On the Quotations from the Old Testament in the Writings of St. Paul," *The Epistles of St. Paul to the Thessalonians, Galatians, Romans, with Critical Notes and Dissertations*, vol. 1 [London: John Murray, 1859], 401–16) or Franklin Johnson (*The Quotations of the New Testament from the Old: Considered in the Light of General Literature* [Philadelphia: American Baptist Publication Society, 1896]).

50. Julia Kristeva, *Semiotiké* (Paris: Seuil, 1969); *La Révolution du langage poétique* (Paris: Seuil, 1974); Roland Barthes, *S/Z* (Paris: Seuil, 1970); "Theory of the Text," in Robert Young, ed., *Untying the Text: A Post-Structuralist Reader* (Boston: Routledge & Kegan Paul, 1981), 31–47. Cf. also Gérard Genette, *Palimpsestes: La littérature au second degré* (Paris: Seuil, 1982). For a helpful discussion of these and other works on intertextuality, see Jonathan Culler, "Presupposition and Intertextuality," *The Pursuit of Signs: Semiotics, Literature, Deconstruction* (Ithaca: Cornell University Press, 1981), 100–18.

51. Culler, *Pursuit of Signs*, 103.

52. Petersen's *Rediscovering Paul* is an example of a similar approach to Paul. Jacob Neusner, *Canon and Connection: Intertextuality in Judaism* (Lanham, Md.: University Press of America, 1987), blasts Susan Handelman in particular for perpetuating the traditional orthodox Jewish convention of treating Scripture and the rabbinic texts as a system in which we must "read everything in light of everything else," without regard to diachronic historical considerations. My working model of intertextuality seeks to incorporate a serious concern for diachronic issues, without making them the center of attention.

53. Thomas M. Greene, *The Light in Troy: Imitation and Discovery in Renaissance Poetry* (New Haven: Yale University Press, 1982), 51.

54. Ibid., 50.

55. In addition to the works of Theissen, Meeks, and Betz (nn. 28 and 29 above), special note is due to the studies of Abraham J. Malherbe, e.g., "'Gentle as a Nurse': The Cynic Background of I Thess ii," *NovT* 12 (1970):203–17; "Ancient Epistolary Theorists," *Ohio Journal of Religious Studies* 5 (1977):3–77; "Exhortation in First Thessalonians," *NovT* 25 (1983):238–55; *Social Aspects of Early Christianity*, 2d ed. (Philadelphia: Fortress, 1983); *Paul and the Thessalonians: The Philosophic Tradition of Pastoral Care* (Philadelphia: Fortress, 1987); "Hellenistic Moralists and the New Testament," *ANRW*, 2d pt., vol. 26.1 (forthcoming).

56. T. S. Eliot, *Selected Essays* (New York: Harcourt, 1950), 4.

57. The term, borrowed from Claude Lévi-Strauss, is applied to poetic practice generally and to Blake, Dante, and Eliot in particular by Northrop Frye, *The Great Code* (New York: Harcourt Brace Jovanovich, 1982), xxi.

58. Harold Bloom, *The Anxiety of Influence* (New York: Oxford University Press, 1973); *A Map of Misreading* (New York: Oxford University Press, 1975); *Kabbalah and Criticism* (New York: Seabury, 1975); *Poetry and Repression: Revisionism from Blake to Stevens* (New Haven: Yale University Press, 1976); *Agon: Towards a Theory of Revisionism* (New York: Oxford University Press, 1982); *The Breaking of the Vessels* (Chicago: University of Chicago Press, 1982). For one discerning critique of Bloom's critical project, see Frank Lentricchia, *After the New Criticism* (Chicago: University of Chicago Press, 1980), 318–46.

59. Bloom, *Anxiety of Influence*, 94. This citation illustrates a point that must be kept clearly in mind: in Bloom's critical universe, all reading is "misreading."

60. Ibid., 30.

61. See Bloom, *Map of Misreading*, 5.

62. See Bloom, *Poetry and Repression*, passim. The term *parent poem* is deliberately chosen.

63. This is the point of contact between Bloom and deconstructionist criticism.

64. For one helpful review, see Thaïs E. Morgan, "Is There an Intertext in This Text?: Literary and Interdisciplinary Approaches to Intertextuality," *American Journal of Semiotics* 3, no. 4 (1985):1–40. See also Dayton Haskin, "Studies in the Poetry of Vision: Spenser, Milton, and Winstanley," *Thought* 56 (1981):226–39.

65. Bloom, *Anxiety of Influence*, 31.

66. Reuben Brower, *Alexander Pope: The Poetry of Allusion* (Oxford: Clarendon, 1959), viii.

67. Barbara Kiefer Lewalski, *Protestant Poetics and the Seventeenth-Century Religious Lyric* (Princeton: Princeton University Press, 1979); George deForest Lord, *Classical Presences in Seventeenth-Century English Poetry* (New Haven: Yale University Press, 1987); Joseph Anthony Wittreich, *Visionary Poetics: Milton's Tradition and His Legacy* (San Marino, Calif.: Huntington Library, 1979); Francis Blessington, *Paradise Lost and the Classical Epic* (Boston: Routledge & Kegan Paul, 1979). For another example, see E. Talbot Donaldson, *The Swan at the Well: Shakespeare Reading Chaucer* (New Haven: Yale University Press, 1985).

68. "I have not attempted anything like a systematic taxonomy of allusive echoic patterns" (John Hollander, *The Figure of Echo: A Mode of Allusion in Milton and After* [Berkeley: University of California Press, 1981], ix). This methodological modesty contrasts with the more "scientific" taxonomic efforts of Genette, *Palimpsestes*.

69. Hollander, *Figure of Echo*, ix.

70. Ibid., 111.

71. Robert Alter, "The Decline and Fall of Literary Criticism," *Commentary* 77, no. 3 (March 1984):50–56.

72. Ibid., 55.

73. The terminology can be traced back at least to Quintilian. For a treatment of its history, see Hollander, *Figure of Echo*, 133–49.

74. Ibid., 115.

75. The question of anachronism is a fair one. I offer a brief threefold answer.

First, allusions, even of the "poetic" kind that Hollander considers, are not found only in poetry. They are poetic because they create new figurations, not because they appear in a self-consciously artistic text. Meaning-generating allusions of this type are by no means uncommon in potent prose writing. Second, Paul writes in the language of "primary reflectivity," not the language of second-level theological abstraction. (See Hays, *Faith of Jesus Christ*, 20–28.) It is, in Paul Ricoeur's phrase, "a conceptual language which preserves the tensive character of symbolic language" ("Biblical Hermeneutics," *Semeia* 4 [1975]:36) because it is tightly interwoven with the foundational language of faith. This means that Paul's discourse, for all its expository features, retains much of the evocative character—and allusive multivalence—of poetic discourse. Finally, and most importantly, the literary critic's heightened sensitivity to verbal resonances within the poetic canon of English literature is a near analogue (perhaps the closest approximation in the experience of most modern readers) to the phenomenon represented by Paul's tendency to apprehend all experience through the language and symbols of the scriptural text. When we bend the ear, then, to echoes and allusions in Paul, we are not treating him anachronistically; rather, we are proposing that the intertextual echoing that Hollander traces in English poetry is a phenomenological correlate of the intertextual echoing that occurs within the Bible, a correlate which enables us to recover by way of analogy something of the sensibility that Paul had as a thinker who lived "within" Scripture.

76. Fishbane, "Inner Biblical Exegesis," 34.

77. Hollander, *Figure of Echo*, 65.

78. No Philippians passages are listed in the tables of quotations provided by Ellis (*Paul's Use of the OT*, 150–52) and by Koch (*Schrift als Zeuge*, 21–23). Ellis does list eight instances of Old Testament allusions in Philippians (*Paul's Use of the OT*, 154).

79. Could or would the Philippians have discerned the echo? It is impossible to say so with confidence. The question is of historical interest, but it is not decisive for present purposes. See further discussion of this issue below.

80. On the notion of "assertorial weight" in metaphorical discourse, see Philip Wheelwright, *The Burning Fountain: A Study in the Language of Symbolism* (Bloomington: Indiana University Press, 1968), 92–96.

81. I am indebted to Elizabeth Randall for calling my attention to this echo.

82. I cite the RSV here, which translates the Hebrew text; the LXX differs slightly.

83. This air, by the way, creates an intertextual fusion of Job 19:25–26 with 1 Cor. 15:20.

84. The full text of Hollander's poem appears in *Figure of Echo*, v. Italics are Hollander's.

85. Hollander, *Figure of Echo*, 99.

86. Greene, *Light in Troy*, 53.

87. Ibid.

88. The categories are those of Krister Stendahl, "Biblical Theology, Contemporary," *IDB* 1.418–32. Cf. the remarks of Bultmann, *Theology of the NT*, 2.251.

89. The phrase is borrowed—with a certain revisionary freedom—from A. K. M. Adam, "Giving Jonah the Fish-Eye," (S.T.M. Thesis, Yale Divinity School, 1987; forthcoming in *Semeia*).

90. Often overlooked in the discussion of authorial intention is the fact that W. K. Wimsatt, Jr. and Monroe C. Beardsley, in their landmark essay, "The Intentional Fallacy," *The Verbal Icon: Studies in the Meaning of Poetry* (Lexington: University of Kentucky Press, 1954), did not exclude in principle the possibility of gaining information about the author's intention in all texts. Indeed, they asserted that "practical messages"—as distinguished from "poetry"—"are successful if and only if we correctly infer the intention" (5). Their primary point was that "the design or intention of the author is neither available nor desirable *as a standard for judging the success of a work of literary art*" (3, emphasis mine). This is a proposal about aesthetics, not a skeptical stricture on historical knowledge.

91. Thus, my present work is subject to some of the same criticisms that I directed at Norman Petersen's *Rediscovering Paul* (review in *JAAR* 54 [1987]:173–75).

92. Whether the actual original readers of the letters fit this description is a question that must be distinguished carefully from the literary question about the implied reader as an intratextual phenomenon. Some such characterization of Paul's actual readers, however, is not implausible. Cf. Gal. 4:21, where he addresses the Gentile Galatians as "you who want to be under Law."

93. Hollander, *Figure of Echo*, 64.

94. Koch, *Schrift als Zeuge*, 32–48.

95. For further discussion, see chapter 4 below.

96. This test is similar to the method employed by Dodd in his section on "The Bible of the Early Church" (*According to the Scriptures*, 61–110).

97. Frank Kermode, *The Genesis of Secrecy: On the Interpretation of Narrative* (Cambridge: Harvard University Press, 1979), 17.

98. Hollander, *Figure of Echo*, 65–66.

99. Consider, for purposes of comparison, an example proposed by Wimsatt and Beardsley: is Eliot's line, "I have heard the mermaids singing, each to each," an allusion to a line of Donne? They argue that the literary critic should address the question not by writing Eliot a letter but through "the way of poetic analysis and exegesis, which inquires whether it makes any sense if Eliot-Prufrock *is* thinking about Donne" (*Verbal Icon*, 18). From their point of view, if the allusion does make sense in the text, it makes no difference whether Eliot intended it. Another example of the phenomenon of authorially unpremeditated echo is my allusion to Mark 13:14 on p. 27 above; in this case, I hate to spoil the joke by explaining it.

CHAPTER TWO

1. Other unusual features also point to a pre-Pauline source for this affirmation: the emphasis on Jesus' Davidic descent, the adoptionist christology of v. 4, and the odd locution "Spirit of Holiness" rather than "Holy Spirit." None of these elements is characteristic of Paul. For discussion, see the commentaries: C. K. Barrett, *The Epistle to the Romans* (HNTC; New York: Harper & Row, 1957), 18–21; Ernst Käsemann, *Commentary on Romans*, trans. G. W. Bromiley (Grand Rapids: Eerdmans, 1980), 10–14; C. E. B. Cranfield, *A Critical and Exegetical Commentary on The Epistle to the Romans*, 2 vols. (ICC; Edinburgh: T. & T. Clark, 1975, 1979), 1.57–

65; Ulrich Wilckens, *Der Brief an die Römer* 3 vols. (EKK; Zurich-Einsiedeln-Koln: Benziger, 1978, 1980, 1982 and Neukirchen-Vluyn: Neukirchener Verlag, 1978, 1980, 1982), 1.56–61.

2. These figures are taken from Koch, *Schrift als Zeuge*, 21–24. Ellis (*Paul's Use of the OT*, 150–52) gives a similar tabulation, finding 93 citations in the corpus and 53 in Romans; this count includes 6 quotations from Ephesians and the Pastorals, which Ellis treats as authentically Pauline. Though Romans is the longest letter, it constitutes only about a third of the authentic letter corpus.

3. See the essays collected in Karl Paul Donfried, ed., *The Romans Debate* (Minneapolis: Augsburg, 1977). See now also Peter Stuhlmacher, "Der Abfassungszweck des Römerbriefes," *ZNW* 77 (1986):180–93.

4. "The voices of Israel's teachers will struggle to speak anew in traditions and words handed down from the past: Jacob and his exegetical imagination will always be a supplanter seeking the blessing of antiquity" (Fishbane, "Inner Biblical Exegesis," 34).

5. Beker, "Faithfulness of God," 11.

6. As Brevard Childs (*The New Testament as Canon* [Philadelphia: Fortress, 1984], 262) contends, "the canonical shape of Romans" permits it "to transcend the original concrete historical setting."

7. The term is borrowed from Hollander, *Figure of Echo* (e.g., 50, 100).

8. Note Paul's use of *alētheia* with precisely the same covenantal connotations in Rom. 3:7 and especially Rom. 15:8.

9. For a clear exposition of these revisions, see Eldon Jay Epp, "Jewish-Gentile Continuity in Paul: Torah and/or Faith (Romans 9:1–5)," *HTR* 79 (1986):80–90.

10. Cranfield, *Romans*, 1.86–87.

11. Käsemann, *Romans*, 22; similarly, Wilckens, *Römer*, 82. Cf. C. K. Barrett, "I Am Not Ashamed of the Gospel," *AnBib* 42 (1970):19–50.

12. Bultmann, "aischynō, ktl.," *TDNT* 1.190.

13. The LXX of Isaiah reads *ou mē aischynthō*, expressing emphatic negation of a future possibility through *ou mē* with the aorist subjunctive. See BDF ¶365.

14. The literature on Paul's interpretation of Hab. 2:4 is voluminous. The best summary of the issues is D. Moody Smith, "Ho de dikaios ek pisteōs zēsetai," in B. L. Daniels and M. J. Suggs, eds., *Studies in the History and Text of the New Testament in Honor of Kenneth Willis Clark* (SD 29; Salt Lake City: University of Utah Press, 1967), 13–25. For other useful discussions, see T. W. Manson, "The Argument from Prophecy," *JTS* 46 (1945):129–36; Dodd, *According to the Scriptures*, 49–51; James A. Sanders, "Habakkuk in Qumran, Paul, and the Old Testament," *JR* 39 (1959):232–44; Lindars, *New Testament Apologetic*, 229–32; A. Strobel, *Untersuchungen zum Eschatologischen Verzögerungsproblem* (NovTSup 2; Leiden: Brill, 1961), 173–202; Hanson, *Paul's Technique*, 40–45; H. C. C. Cavallin, "The Righteous Shall Live by Faith: A Decisive Argument for the Traditional Interpretation," *ST* 32 (1978):33–43. For further literature and discussion see Hays, *Faith of Jesus Christ*, 150–57.

15. Hab. 1:2, 13 (LXX).

16. Again, this translation follows the LXX rather than the MT. See the discussion in the following paragraphs.

17. For a discussion of the history of interpretation of the passage by Jews and Christians in antiquity, see Strobel, *Verzögerungsproblem*.

18. Ibid., 7–170.

19. A similarly off-center analogical use of Habakkuk is made in Acts 13:41: Luke has Paul quote Habakkuk's warning of military destruction (Hab. 1:5) as a prefiguration of the judgment that may come upon Israel for their failure to believe the deed of God that Paul declares to them.

20. On the correctness of the reading *ek pisteōs mou*, see Dietrich-Alex Koch, "Der Text von Hab 2:4b in der Septuaginta und im Neuen Testament," *ZNW* 76 (1985):68–85.

21. A third reading is also possible if *ho dikaios* is read as a designation of the Messiah. For a summary and assessment of the evidence, see Richard B. Hays, "'The Righteous One' as Eschatological Deliverer: A Case Study in Paul's Apocalyptic Hermeneutics," forthcoming in M. L. Soards and J. Marcus, eds., *Apocalyptic and the New Testament* (Sheffield: JSOT, 1989).

22. The reference in the margin of Nestle-Aland[26] to Isa. 28:22 appears to be a typographical error.

23. In Rom. 8:35, however, the echo bounces back in a different direction, as *thlipsis kai stenochōria* head the list of dire trials that might hypothetically separate us from the love of Christ. Here Paul executes an effective inversion of Isa. 8:22: despite the threat of eschatological "tribulation and distress," the judgment prophesied by Isaiah will not fall upon us because Christ Jesus intercedes on our behalf (Rom. 8:34). (Incidentally, the Nestle-Aland margin once again errs here by referring to Rom. 8:25 rather than 8:35. My sampling of cross references leads me to think that a systematic review might be in order.) But the echo carries additional overtones: Isaiah's oracle of judgment constitutes part of a striking passage in which the prophet depicts himself and his small band of disciples as a faithful remnant in the midst of the unfaithful nation, waiting in hope for God's justice to appear: "Bind up the testimony, seal the teaching among my disciples. I will wait for the Lord who is hiding his face from the house of Jacob, and I will hope in him. Behold, I and the children whom the Lord has given me are signs and portents in Israel from the Lord of hosts, who dwells on Mount Zion" (Isa. 8:16–18). Can it be an accident that Paul—seeing himself as a member of the faithful remnant in Israel (Rom. 11:1–8) and writing a letter whose major purpose is to explain how God, even while "hiding his face from the house of Jacob," can yet be deemed faithful and just—draws on this selection of Isaiah for imagery to describe the judgment on those who fail to respond in faith to God's promise? Unlike the writer of Hebrews (cf. Heb. 2:10–13), Paul neither cites Isa. 8:16–18 nor offers a christological interpretation of it. Instead, the echo of the phrase *thlipsis kai stenochōria* creates a metaleptic link that subliminally suggests Isaiah and his followers as figurations of Paul's own community of Christians, who hope for that which they do not see and wait for it with patience (cf. Rom. 8:18–25), while those who "do not obey the truth" experience the confusion and darkness, the tribulation and distress prophesied by Isaiah as the fate of the disobedient nation.

24. When Paul's allusion to Deuteronomy is taken fully into account, one time-worn issue of Pauline exegesis solves itself: "the curse of the Law" from which Christ redeems us (Gal. 3:13) is not the Law itself regarded as a curse, but

the curse that the Law *pronounces* in Deuteronomy 27 (correctly noted by F. F. Bruce, *Commentary on Galatians* [NIGTC; Grand Rapids: Eerdmans, 1982], 163–64). Pace Betz (*Galatians*, 149), the distinction is an important one.

25. The most thorough discussion of the maxim is offered by Jouette Bassler, *Divine Impartiality: Paul and a Theological Axiom* (SBLDS 59; Chico, Calif.: Scholars, 1982).

26. See the discussion of Rom. 10:5–10 in the final section of this chapter.

27. Here I follow Cranfield's proposal (*Romans*, 156–57) to construe *physei* with the preceding words, *ta mē nomon echonta*. For further discussion, see Paul Achtemeier, "'Some Things in Them Hard to Understand': Reflections on an Approach to Paul," *Int* 38 (1984):254–67.

28. Again, I concur at this point with Cranfield. This reading is a minority view in the history of interpretation, but it yields an excellent sense, especially when Rom. 2:14–15 is read in conjunction with 2 Cor. 3:2–3.

29. This is another clear instance of Paul's dependence on the LXX. The MT reads, "Their rulers wail, says the Lord, and continually all the day my name is despised" (RSV). The phrases "on account of you" and "among the Gentiles" appear only in the LXX.

30. In this case, Paul's citation agrees more closely with the MT than with the LXX. For discussion of the text-critical problems, see Koch (*Schrift als Zeuge*, 66–69), who argues that Paul is dependent on a Hebraizing Greek recension rather than directly on a Hebrew text.

31. See Leander Keck, *Paul and His Letters* (Philadelphia: Fortress, 1979), 117–30.

32. The expression *ta logia tou theou* occurs only here in Paul. While the expression could be synonymous with *ho logos tou theou* (Cranfield, *Romans*, 178–79), the word choice may suggest something of the oracular quality of the revelation given to Israel: they had the words, but lacked the hermeneutical key to interpret the oracles rightly. Cf. 2 Cor. 3:14–16, discussed in chapter 4 below.

33. The phrase *pas anthrōpos pseustēs* (every man false)—juxtaposed in Rom. 3:4a to "let God be true"—is an echo of Ps. 115:2 LXX (Ps. 116:11 MT).

34. E.g., R. Bultmann, "*Dikaiosynē theou*," *JBL* 83 (1964):12–16; H. Conzelmann, "Die Rechtfertigungslehre des Paulus: Theologie oder Anthropologie?" *EvT* 28 (1968):389–404; G. Klein, "Gottes Gerechtigkeit als Thema der neuesten Paulus-Forschung," *Rekonstruktion und Interpretation* (Munich: Chr. Kaiser, 1969) 225–36; Cranfield, *Romans*, 1.92–99, 2.824–26.

35. See David R. Hall, "Romans 3.1–8 Reconsidered," *NTS* 29 (1983):183–97.

36. Fishbane, *Biblical Interpretation*, 404–05. For more detailed discussion of the psalm superscriptions in relation to narrative texts, see Brevard Childs, "Psalm Titles and Midrashic Exegesis," *JJS* 16 (1971):137–50; and E. Slomovic, "Toward an Understanding of the Formation of Historical Titles in the Book of Psalms," *ZAW* 91 (1979):350–80.

37. On this rhetorical trap, see Richard B. Hays, "Relations Natural and Unnatural: A Response to John Boswell's Exegesis of Romans 1," *JRE* 14, no. 1 (1986):194–95.

38. For an analysis of the composition of this catena, which may be a pre-Pauline composition, see L. E. Keck, "The Function of Romans 3:10–18—Observations and Suggestions," in J. Jervell and W. A. Meeks, eds., *God's Christ and His*

People: Studies in Honor of Nils Alstrup Dahl (Oslo: Universitetsforlaget, 1977), 141–57.

39. This is a striking instance where Paul clearly uses *ho nomos* as a synonym for *hē graphē*. None of the texts in the catena come from the Pentateuch; most are from the Psalms, with possible additional echoes of Eccl. 7:20, Isa. 59:7, and Prov. 1:16.

40. For further discussion, see Richard B. Hays, "Psalm 143 and the Logic of Romans 3," *JBL* 99 (1980):107–115.

41. For a long list of commentators who regard 3:21 as the beginning of a new unit, see Hays, ibid., 109 n. 11.

42. The translation here reflects my earlier work on Paul's *pistis Iēsou Christou* formulations; see *Faith of Jesus Christ*, especially 170–74 and the literature cited there. Particularly helpful on this matter is Luke Timothy Johnson, "Romans 3:21–26 and the Faith of Jesus," *CBQ* 44 (1982):77–90. For more recent support of the position, see now Brendan Byrne, *Reckoning with Romans* (Good News Studies 18; Wilmington, Del.: Michael Glazier, 1986), 79–80; Sam K. Williams, "Again Pistis Christou," *CBQ* 49 (1987):431–47.

43. For a summary of the debate, see M. T. Brauch, "Perspectives on 'God's Righteousness' in Recent German Discussion," in E. P. Sanders, *Paul and Palestinian Judaism*, 523–42. A slightly more recent discussion is offered by Marion L. Soards, "The Righteousness of God in the Writings of the Apostle Paul," *BTB* 15 (1985):104–09.

44. A significant exception to this generalization is Nils A. Dahl, "The Doctrine of Justification: Its Social Functions and Implications," *Studies in Paul*, 95–120.

45. For a suggestive discussion of Paul's reading of Torah in a narrative mode, see James A. Sanders, "Torah and Christ," *Int* 29 (1975):372–90; reprinted in *Sacred Story*, 41–60.

46. For a technical explanation and defense of this translation, see Richard B. Hays, "'Have We Found Abraham To Be Our Forefather According to the Flesh?': A Reconsideration of Rom. 4:1," *NovT* 27 (1985):76–98.

47. Cf. Dahl, "The One God of Jews and Gentiles (Romans 3:29–30)," *Studies in Paul*, 178–91.

48. This reading of the text is consistent with the hermeneutical principles elucidated by Lloyd Gaston, "Abraham and the Righteousness of God," *HBT* 2 (1980):39–41, 59.

49. Philo, *De Abr* 88. The translation is that of F. H. Colson, *Philo*, vol. 6 (*LCL*; Cambridge: Harvard University Press, 1935).

50. Cranfield, *Romans*, 1.440.

51. See the discussion of Paul's ecclesiocentric hermeneutics in chapter 3 below.

52. Ps. 43:17–24 LXX.

53. As Dahl (*Studies in Paul*, 142) notes, one of Paul's major purposes in Romans is "to prove that he is neither an antinomian nor an apostate from Judaism."

54. The fundamental studies are Israel Levi, "Le sacrifice d'Isaac et la mort de Jesus," *REJ* 64 (1912):161–84; Hans-Joachim Schoeps, "The Sacrifice of Isaac in Paul's Theology," *JBL* 65 (1946):385–92; Shalom Spiegel, *The Last Trial*, trans. Judah Goldin (New York: Schocken, 1969); Geza Vermes, "Redemption and Gen-

esis xxii—The Binding of Isaac and the Sacrifice of Jesus," *Scripture and Tradition in Judaism*, 2d ed. (Studia Post-Biblica 4; Leiden: Brill, 1973) 193–227; Nils A. Dahl, "The Atonement: An Adequate Reward for the Akedah?" *The Crucified Messiah* (Minneapolis: Augsburg, 1974), 146–60.

55. The phrase is borrowed from Hans Frei, *The Identity of Jesus Christ* (Philadelphia: Fortress, 1975), 74–84, 102–15.

56. Paul's imperfect indicative verb *ēuchomēn* ("I [could] pray") should probably be understood to express a desire to pray for something unattainable or inappropriate. For a careful argument in support of this translation, see Cranfield, *Romans*, 2.454–57.

57. The suggestion is often made that Paul is recalling the story of Moses' offering of himself to atone for the sin of Israel (Exod. 32:30–34). There are, however, no direct verbal echoes of the Exodus text in Rom. 9:3.

58. Note that the bodies (plural) of believers are to be presented as a sacrifice (singular). The image reveals a crucial element of Paul's theology: the obedience of faith is manifest in the corporate life of a community, not just in individual conduct.

59. This last sentence articulates a possibility created for subsequent readers by the intertextual matrix that Paul has woven; Paul himself does not express such an idea explicitly, but see Col. 1:24.

60. See, e.g., the analysis of Robert Badenas, *Christ the End of the Law: Romans 10:4 in Pauline Perspective* (JSNT Sup 10; Sheffield: JSOT Press, 1985), 94–96. For more extensive discussion, see C. K. Barrett, "Romans 9:30–10:21: Fall and Responsibility of Israel," *Essays on Paul* (Philadelphia: Westminster, 1982), 132–53.

61. The RSV translation of Rom. 9:7 renders Paul's argument incoherent by reversing the terms: "not all are children of Abraham because they are his descendants." But Paul's point, as the citation of Gen. 21:12 shows, is precisely the reverse: Abraham has many children (*tekna*), but not all of them belong to his "seed" (*sperma*).

62. See the discussion of the passage in James W. Aageson, "Scripture and Structure in the Development of the Argument in Romans 9–11," *CBQ* 48 (1986):268–73. For the argument that the pattern of exposition here is midrashic in form, see Ellis, *Prophecy and Hermeneutic*, 219; and Stegner, "Romans 9:6–29."

63. For a thorough discussion of Paul's exegesis here, see John Piper, *The Justification of God: An Exegetical and Theological Study of Romans 9:1–23* (Grand Rapids: Baker, 1983).

64. In addition to Jer. 18:3–6, we can hear echoes here of Job 9:12, 10:8–9; Isa. 29:16, 45:9, 64:8; Sir. 33:10–13. (I am indebted to Maggi Despot for bringing some of these references to my attention.) A detailed investigation of these subtexts would demonstrate the complexity of the intertextual matrix from which Paul's metaphor emerges.

65. This insight is brilliantly developed by Karl Barth, *Church Dogmatics* II.2, trans. G. W. Bromiley et al. (Edinburgh: T. & T. Clark, 1957), 223–38.

66. For an account of Paul's manipulation of the text, see Koch, *Schrift als Zeuge*, 166–68.

67. This phrase, taken not from Isaiah but from Hos. 2:1 LXX, serves as an artful transition to the quotation of Isa. 10:22.

68. E.g., RSV, NEB, JB, NIV, TEV.

69. In both cases, the calling that Paul envisions is a calling through the gospel of Jesus Christ. There is no doctrine in Paul of separate but equal covenants for Jews and Christians; the remnant that will be saved is composed of Jewish Christians, like Paul himself.

70. Paul gives no overt sign here of interpreting *sperma* christologically, as he does in Gal. 3:16. Still, readers who know Galatians may wonder whether Rom. 9:29 might bear a latent christological sense. See the last part of chapter 5 below for a discussion of the problems posed by this kind of canonical intertextuality.

71. A faint ironic echo—or inversion—of this text also hovers about Luke 3:19–20.

72. This verb, another standard element of the lament psalm vocabulary, is taken up prominently in early Christian interpretations of Jesus' death and resurrection as a fulfillment of the suffering-vindication pattern in these Psalms. See especially Mark 15:34 ("My God, my God, why have you forsaken [*egkatelipes*] me?"), quoting Ps. 22:1 (Ps. 21:2 LXX); and Acts 2:27 ("You will not abandon [*egkataleipseis*] my life to Hades"), quoting Ps. 16:10 (Ps. 15:10 LXX).

73. Barth (*Church Dogmatics* II.2, 270) calls attention to the fact that in 1 Kings 20:15—following hard upon God's promise (1 Kings 19:18) to leave seven thousand in Israel who have not fallen into idolatry—the number of "all the people of Israel" is given as seven thousand! Barth remarks: "It is these seven thousand men, and not the unfaithful majority, who represent Israel as such. By 'leaving them' God holds fast to Israel as such, and it is decided that He has not rejected His people. When therefore . . . the solitary Elijah is consoled by reference to these seven thousand men, he does not stand alone, but as the holder of his commission he is invisibly surrounded by these seven thousand. . . . Even in his loneliness he stands effectively before God for the whole of Israel, for Israel as such. In just the same way Paul does not stand alone. . . . He can and must, therefore, appeal to his existence as a Jew and as a Gentile missionary as a valid proof that God has not rejected his people." (I am grateful to Sherry Jordan for calling my attention to this passage.)

74. The syntax of Rom. 15:9a is difficult. For inventories of possible construals, see Cranfield, *Romans*, 2.742–44; Wilckens, *Römer*, 3.106. The most natural reading of the sentence would be to take *doxasai* as an aorist optative active rather than as an aorist infinitive, so that the clause would express a prayer wish: "May the Gentiles glorify God for his mercy." The translation given here, however, follows the interpretation given by Barrett, *Romans*, 271–72.

75. Käsemann, *Romans*, 387.

76. Käsemann (ibid., 386) thinks that the speaker must be Paul himself: "the apostle to the Gentiles finds his own task delineated in Scripture." The messianic interpretation, proposed by M. J. Lagrange (*Épitre aux Romains* [Paris: Gabalda, 1950], 347), is accepted by Cranfield (*Romans*, 2.745) and by Wilckens (*Römer*, 3.108).

77. William Sanday and Arthur C. Headlam, *A Critical and Exegetical Commentary on the Epistle to the Romans* (ICC; Edinburgh: T. & T. Clark, 1906), 289. Their opinion is followed by Longenecker, *Biblical Exegesis*, 121–23.

78. M. Jack Suggs, "'The Word Is Near You': Romans 10:6–10 within the Purpose of the Letter," in W. R. Farmer, C. F. D. Moule, and R. R. Niebuhr, eds., *Christian History and Interpretation: Studies Presented to John Knox* (Cambridge:

Cambridge University Press, 1967), 289–312; Koch, *Schrift als Zeuge*, 153–60; J. D. G. Dunn, "'Righteousness from the Law' and 'Righteousness from Faith': Paul's Interpretation of Scripture in Romans 10:1–10," in G. F. Hawthorne and O. Betz, eds., *Tradition and Interpretation in the New Testament: Essays in Honor of E. Earle Ellis for His Sixtieth Birthday* (Grand Rapids: Eerdmans, 1987), 216–28.

79. Barth, *Church Dogmatics* II.2, 245–47; Ellis *Paul's Use of the Old Testament*, 123; Cranfield, *Romans*, 2.522–26; Käsemann, *Romans*, 283–92.

80. The verb *katelaben* can include the idea of intellectual comprehension: cf. its use in John 1:5.

81. Again here Paul's citation of the LXX is loose; see Koch, *Schrift als Zeuge*, 50–51.

82. Barth, *Church Dogmatics* II.2, 259, argues that this quotation speaks eloquently about what God has done for Israel: "To this very people God never . . . grew weary of offering Himself, of condescending to it, and repeatedly proving His loyalty. God is the One who has mercy on this people."

83. The detailed study of Badenas (*Christ the End of the Law*) has made a compelling case for the "teleological" interpretation of *telos* as "goal" or "completion." Both Cranfield (*Romans*, 2.515–20) and Wilckens (*Römer*, 2.222–23) had already reached a similar conclusion. See also the nuanced discussion of Paul Meyer, "Romans 10:4 and the End of the Law," in J. L. Crenshaw and S. Sandmel, eds., *The Divine Helmsman: Studies on God's Control of Human Events, Presented to Lou H. Silberman* (New York: KTAV, 1980), 59–78. The burden of proof lies strongly on any interpreter who reads *telos* as "termination."

84. The conjunction *de* in 10:6 does not necessarily carry adversative force. See the technical discussions in Badenas, *Christ the End of the Law*, 121–25; Cranfield, *Romans*, 2.520–23; Meyer, "Romans 10:4," 68–69; Barth, *Church Dogmatics* II.2, 245.

85. Indeed, Rom. 10:3b ("they did not submit [*hypetagēsan*] to the righteousness of God") is be explicated by cross-reference to Rom. 8:7 ("The mindset of the flesh is inimical towards God, for it does not submit [*hypotassetai*] to the Law of God"). The apparent equivalence in these formulations between "righteousness of God" and "Law of God" is theologically noteworthy.

86. E.g., Käsemann, *Romans*, 284–87; C. H. Dodd, *The Epistle of Paul to the Romans* (New York: Harper and Brothers, 1932), 165–66.

87. The use of Lev. 18:5 in Gal. 3:12 is an entirely different matter. As in so many other particulars, Paul argues very differently in Romans from the way that he had argued earlier in Galatians. Whether it is possible, as Barth thinks (*Church Dogmatics* II.2, p. 245), to reinterpret Gal. 3:12 in light of this reading of Romans 10 is a question too complicated to address here. Likewise, a full exegesis of Rom. 10:5–6 must take into account Phil. 3:9, which juxtaposes "my own righteousness derived from Law" to the righteousness that comes "through the faithfulness of Christ, the righteousness from God based upon faith." Whatever the interpreter decides to do about synthesizing Paul's apparently divergent statements about the Law in the various letters, the harmonizing impulse must not override the internal logic of the argument in Romans 10.

88. For detailed discussion of the exegetical problems, see Badenas, *Christ the End of the Law*, 108–33.

89. The personification of Righteousness is of course a figurative device.

Though this device parallels the emergent Christian convention of reading certain scriptural passages as utterances of Christ, Barth presses the identification between Christ and the *dikaiosynē ek pisteōs* much too hard: "Who is speaking here? Obviously not a 'personified' idea, but the very man of whom Moses has written that he will live as the *kelal* of the Law. . . . He is Himself the righteousness before God" (*Church Dogmatics* II.2, 245). This is a good example of the failure of an earnest and discerning theological reader to reckon with the metaphorical lightness of Paul's assertions.

90. Cf. Koch, *Schrift als Zeuge*, 185–86.

91. This point is noted by Franz J. Leenhardt, *The Epistle to the Romans*, trans. Harold Knight (London: Lutterworth, 1961), 268–69, as well as by Cranfield (*Romans*, 2.523).

92. LXX reads here the plural *dikaiosynas:* (presumably "righteous actions"). To this formulation, compare Rom. 10:3.

93. Cf. Fishbane's comment ("Inner Biblical Exegesis," 31) on Jer. 2:3: "Indeed, the evocation of an earlier textual authority through the diction and topos chosen for this new prophetic oracle so reactivates the older language as to provide a semantic foil for its revision. A simultaneity of voices is heard—the divine voice speaking the priestly rule through Moses, and the divine voice which uses its own words as it speaks through Jeremiah—and they do not cancel each other out."

94. The later Christian reader might recall Luke 24:5: "Why do you seek the Living One among the dead?" or Mark 16:3: "Who will roll away the stone for us from the door of the tomb?"

95. Suggs, "The Word Is Near You," 306–12.

CHAPTER THREE

1. E.g., by Longenecker, *Biblical Exegesis*, 104–5, 205–9; Ellis, *Paul's Use of the OT*, 115–16; Cranfield, *Romans*, 2.867.

2. 4Q Florilegium 1:10–11. For discussion, see George J. Brooke, *Exegesis at Qumran: 4Q Florilegium in Its Jewish Context* (JSOTSup 29; Sheffield: JSOT, 1985), 197–205; Donald Juel, *Messianic Exegesis: Christological Interpretation of the Old Testament in Early Christianity* (Philadelphia: Fortress, 1988), 59–77.

3. Dennis C. Duling, "The Promises to David and Their Entry into Christianity," *NTS* 20 (1973–74):55–77; Dahl, *Studies in Paul*, 128, 130; Max Wilcox, "The Promise of the 'Seed' in the New Testament and the Targumim," *JSNT* 5 (1979):2–20; Juel, *Messianic Exegesis*, 77–88.

4. See chapter 2, n. 1, above.

5. Matt. 1:22; cf. Matt. 2:15, 2:17–18, 2:23, 3:3, 4:15, 8:17, 12:17–21, 13:35; 21:4–5; 27:9–10. On Matthew's use of Scripture, see Krister Stendahl, *The School of St. Matthew* (Philadelphia: Fortress, 1954); Robert Gundry, *The Use of the Old Testament in St. Matthew's Gospel* (Leiden: Brill, 1967). On John's use of Scripture, see Edwin D. Freed, *Old Testament Quotations in the Gospel of John* (NovTSup 11; Leiden: Brill, 1965).

6. Ellis, *Paul's Use of the OT*, 115. Cf. the criticism of Herbert Marks, "Pauline Typology and Revisionary Criticism," *JAAR* 52 (1984):71–92, especially 75–76.

7. We could equally well speak of a *pastoral* hermeneutic. I prefer the term *ecclesiocentric* because it emphasizes that Paul not only interprets Scripture *for* the church but also construes Scripture to be *about* the church.

8. The christological allegory would be even more natural and compelling here if—as many suppose (see chapter 2, n. 54)—the Akedah tradition is a driving force behind the formation of New Testament christology.

9. The textual witnesses here are divided between *hēmeis* (we) and *hymeis* (you). For the present discussion, the difference does not matter. This translation, with the RSV, follows the reading of ℵ,A,C,D² et al. Bruce M. Metzger (*A Textual Commentary on the Greek New Testament* [New York: United Bible Societies, 1971], 597) prefers *hymeis*.

10. The logical link between Gal. 3:16 and 4:21–31 is Gal. 3:29. See the last section of the present chapter.

11. This formulation assumes the consensus view that Romans is to be dated later than Galatians. For recent discussion of Pauline chronology, see Robert Jewett, *A Chronology of Paul's Life* (Philadelphia: Fortress, 1979); Gerd Lüdemann, *Paul, Apostle to the Gentiles: Studies in Chronology*, trans. F. S. Jones (Philadelphia: Fortress, 1984).

12. Hans Lietzmann, *An die Korinther I/II*, 5th ed. (HNT 9; Tübingen: J. C. B. Mohr, Paul Siebeck, 1969), 135. Cf. R. H. Strachan, *The Second Epistle of Paul to the Corinthians* (MNTC; London: Hodder and Stoughton, 1935), 138: "The relevance of the quotation from Exod. xvi. 8 is not quite apparent, and is largely verbal. It does not really illustrate the principle of 'give and take' as Paul has just expounded it."

13. Hanson, *Paul's Technique*, 176.

14. Alfred Plummer, *A Critical and Exegetical Commentary on the Second Epistle of Paul to the Corinthians* (ICC; Edinburgh: T. & T. Clark, 1915), 245. A similar interpretation is given by Furnish, *II Corinthians* (AB 32A; Garden City, N.Y.: Doubleday, 1984), 420. Hans Dieter Betz notes that Exodus, chapter 16, already had been given an ethical interpretation in Jewish haggadic traditions (*2 Corinthians 8 and 9: A Commentary on Two Administrative Letters of the Apostle Paul* [Hermeneia; Philadelphia: Fortress, 1985], 69–70).

15. See the discussion of the manna motif by Fishbane, *Biblical Interpretation*, 326–29.

16. The key passage in Philo is *Her.* 191. On John's use of the tradition, see Peder Borgen, *Bread from Heaven: An Exegetical Study of the Concept of Manna in the Gospel of John and the Writings of Philo* (NovTSup 10; Leiden: Brill, 1965).

17. The dating of the various parts of Paul's Corinthian correspondence presents a notorious difficulty, because it requires complex judgments about the literary integrity and composition of the edited texts that now appear in the New Testament canon. For a recent judicious discussion see Furnish, *II Corinthians*, 29–55. I follow Furnish in assuming that 2 Cor. 8 belongs to a letter (2 Cor. 1–9) written approximately one year later than our canonical 1 Corinthians.

18. Various attempts to find a history-of-religions explanation for Paul's formulation here (e.g., Joachim Jeremias, "Der Ursprung der Johannestaufe," *ZNW* 28 [1929]:312–20) have been completely unconvincing. Cf. Koch, *Schrift als Zeuge*, 212 n. 54.

19. Hollander, *Figure of Echo*, 115.

20. Cf. chapter 1, n. 80, above.

21. This observation, of course, stands in direct contradiction to Harnack's suggestion ("Alte Testament," 129–30, 134–35) that Paul had given his mission congregations only a minimal acquaintance with Scripture in his original teaching and that he took up detailed scriptural argumentation only when forced by "Judaizers" to confront contested issues.

22. Meeks, "Rose Up to Play."

23. Ibid., 68–71.

24. One significant contribution of Meeks's essay is that his analysis allows him to give an account of the unity of 1 Corinthians 10. The relation of vv. 14–22 to the foregoing scriptural references is often overlooked by commentators. Koch, for example, ignores these verses altogether (*Schrift als Zeuge*, 211–16).

25. Metzger, *Textual Commentary*, 560–61.

26. Of course, there is also an echo here of Gen. 1:26. The effect is complex and ironic: God created human beings for "dominion" over these creatures, but fallen human idolaters now bow before the likenesses of animals.

27. Cf. chapter 2, n. 37, above.

28. Käsemann, *Romans*, 44–47.

29. Deuteronomy 32 is, as we have already seen, a crucial subtext for Paul (cf. Rom. 10:19, 11:11, 14).

30. Note also the possible echo of a phrase from Deut. 32:4 (*theos pistos*) in 1 Cor. 10:13: *pistos de ho theos* ("But God is faithful").

31. The importance of this fact is noted by Meeks ("Rose Up to Play," 72) as well as by Andrew J. Bandstra, "Interpretation in 1 Cor 10:1–11," *CTJ* 6 (1971):5–21 (see especially 9–14).

32. A modern writer—though perhaps not a postmodern one?—would put this information in a footnote.

33. See Eric Auerbach, "Figura," *Scenes from the Drama of European Literature*, vol. 9, *Theory and History of Literature* (Minneapolis: University of Minnesota Press, 1984), 11–76. Cf. Koch, *Schrift als Zeuge*, 216–20.

34. Likewise C. K. Barrett, *The First Epistle to the Corinthians* (HNTC; New York: Harper & Row, 1968), 223; Hans Conzelmann, *1 Corinthians*, trans. James W. Leitch (Hermeneia; Philadelphia: Fortress, 1975), 167. Gordon D. Fee, *The First Epistle to the Corinthians* (NICNT; Grand Rapids: Eerdmans, 1987), 452–53.

35. Marks, "Pauline Typology," 77.

36. For an extensive survey of "kinship relations in Paul's symbolic universe," see Petersen, *Rediscovering Paul*, 200–40.

37. This hypothesis is accepted, e.g., by Meeks ("Rose Up to Play") and by Koch (*Schrift als Zeuge*, 214–16), who thinks it possible to distinguish layers of redaction within the text (cf. 216 n. 69).

38. Some of the Corinthians may have held such a view; if so, Paul is vigorously opposing them. See, e.g., 1 Cor. 4:8, 8:1–3, 10:12.

39. The change from the LXX's future indicative *exareis* to Paul's aorist imperative *exarate* is of negligible semantic significance. Paul has simply altered the peculiar LXX idiom into more normal Greek, which serves to make his point clearer to his Corinthian readers.

40. Rightly noted by Ulrich Luz, *Das Geschichtsverständnis des Paulus* (BEvT 49; Munich: Kaiser, 1968), 122.

41. Auerbach, "Figura," 50.

42. Goppelt, *Typos*, 199, 202; Kaiser, *Uses of the OT*, 107-08.

43. Auerbach, "Figura," 51. Here Auerbach is a precursor of Bloom.

44. This sentence is informed by insights of Northrop Frye (*Anatomy of Criticism* [Princeton: Princeton University Press, 1957], 77-79; and *The Stubborn Structure: Essays on Criticism and Society* [Ithaca: Cornell University Press], 164) and of Paul Ricoeur ("The Narrative Function," *Semeia* 13 [1978]:177-202, especially pp. 182-85). For further discussion, see Hays, *Faith of Jesus Christ*, 20-28, 223-24.

45. A carefully nuanced treatment of typology is provided by Fishbane, *Biblical Interpretation*, 350-79, 408-40. Though Fishbane is dealing with the Hebrew Bible, many of his categories and distinctions are useful in dealing with New Testament typology as well. In addition to the literature on typology already cited, see G. W. H. Lampe and K. J. Woolcombe, *Essays on Typology* (SBT; Naperville, Ill.: Allenson, 1957); Jean Danielou, *From Shadows to Reality: Studies in the Biblical Typology of the Fathers*, trans. W. Hibberd (London: Burns & Oates, 1960); James Barr, *Old and New in Interpretation: A Study of the Two Testaments* (London: SCM, 1966), 103-48; James Samuel Preus, *From Shadow to Promise: Old Testament Interpretation from Augustine to the Young Luther* (Cambridge: Harvard University Press, Belknap Press, 1969); Earl Miner, ed., *Literary Uses of Typology: from the Late Middle Ages to the Present* (Princeton: Princeton University Press, 1977); George P. Landow, *Victorian Types, Victorian Shadows: Biblical Typology in Victorian Literature, Art, and Thought* (Boston: Routledge & Kegan Paul, 1980); Northrop Frye, *The Great Code*, 78-138.

46. This example is cited by Fishbane, *Biblical Interpretation*, 358.

47. Conzelmann, *1 Corinthians*, 166.

48. Marks, "Pauline Typology," 79.

49. The text is cited from Louis L. Martz, ed., *The Anchor Anthology of Seventeenth Century Verse*, vol. 1 (Garden City, N.Y.: Doubleday, 1969), 185-86.

50. For differing elegant discussions of the Herbert poem, see Rosemond Tuve, *A Reading of George Herbert* (Chicago: University of Chicago, 1952; reprint 1982), 112-17; Stanley Fish, "Catechizing the Reader: Herbert's Socratean Rhetoric," in Thomas O. Sloan and Raymond B. Waddington, eds., *The Rhetoric of Renaissance Poetry* (Berkeley: University of California Press, 1974), 180-85; Richard Strier, *Love Known: Theology and Experience in George Herbert's Poetry* (Chicago: University of Chicago Press, 1983), 155-59.

51. On this point, Tuve and Strier differ sharply: while Tuve contends that "there is another dimension to the subject of this poem, beyond the mere conveyance of a particular individual's emotion at a given time, that thin subject with which modern readers have come to be content" (*Reading of Herbert*, 117), Strier insists that the poem provides "a historical and religious *validation* of Herbert's concern with his own experience. 'Each Christian' is now as much a focus of God's works as previously the whole community of Jews was" (*Love Known*, 156).

52. On the structure of Galatians, see Hans Dieter Betz, "The Literary Composition and Function of Paul's Letter to the Galatians," *NTS* 21 (1974-75):353-79.

53. This is the flip side of the argument in Romans; in both cases, Paul is arguing for the inclusion of Gentiles among God's people. In Galatians, he defends his position against demands that Gentiles be circumcised and keep the

Law; in Romans, he defends his position against the charge that it negates the Law.

54. On the importance of Gentile inclusion as a key theme in Galatians, see George Howard, *Paul: Crisis in Galatia: A Study in Early Christian Theology* (SNTSMS 35; Cambridge: Cambridge University, 1979); T. L. Donaldson, "The 'Curse of the Law' and the Inclusion of the Gentiles: Gal 3:13–14," *NTS* 32 (1986):94–112.

55. The logic of this somewhat puzzling claim is elucidated in Gal. 3:16 and 3:29. See further discussion below.

56. E.g., F. F. Bruce, *The Epistle to the Galatians: A Commentary on the Greek Text* (NIGTC; Grand Rapids: Eerdmans, 1982), 155–56.

57. Abraham was not reading a text, of course. It is not easy to visualize what Paul has in mind: one thinks of the dramatic device whereby the narrator in a stage play speaks to one of the characters. Gal. 3:8 is a Pauline analogy to a rhetorical strategy that Hollander (*Figure of Echo*, 102) notes as a frequent phenomenon in "major poetry": "in the structure of the poem's rhetoric, the anterior voice is made to seem the echo of the present one."

58. The verb does appear also in Philo, *Op.* 34 and *Mut.* 158. Cf. Betz, *Galatians*, 143 n. 43.

59. Betz, *Galatians*, 139.

60. In view of Paul's other uses of the prefix *pro* with verbs of writing and proclaiming, we may reasonably wonder whether the temporal force of *pro* obtains here also. If so, the question could be read as a veiled reference to the *scriptural* prefiguration of Christ's crucifixion, which Paul presumably explained to the Galatians (cf. 1 Cor. 15:1–3) in the course of his preaching and teaching among them: "O foolish Galatians, who has bewitched you, before whose eyes Jesus Christ was [shown to be] pre-written as crucified?" (For a development of this interpretation, see P. G. Bretscher, "Light from Galatians 3:1 on Pauline Theology," *CTM* 34 [1963]:77–97.) If this interpretation were correct, it would offer another indication that Paul's letters may presuppose a christological use of Scripture; however, the evidence is ambiguous at best. The more obvious meaning of the text is the one championed by commentators and reflected in the usual translations; the possible reference to a Christ scripturally prewritten as crucified remains a subliminal undertone.

61. Hays, *Faith of Jesus Christ*, 143–49; David Lull, *The Spirit in Galatia: Paul's Interpretation of "Pneuma" as Divine Power* (SBLDS 49; Chico, Calif.: Scholars, 1980).

62. The point stands even if, as Betz persuasively proposes (*Galatians*, 140), *kathōs* is shorthand for *kathōs gegraptai*.

63. For a persuasive and sympathetic reconstruction of the views of the Galatian "teachers," see J. Louis Martyn, "A Law-Observant Mission to Gentiles: The Background of Galatians," *SJT* 38 (1985):307–24 (originally published in *Michigan Quarterly Review* 22 [1983]:221–36).

64. Cf. Hays, *Faith of Jesus Christ* 200–2; Hays, "Righteous One."

65. My formulation of course echoes E. P. Sanders.

66. See the discussion of typology above.

67. I have offered an analysis of the narrative logic of the passage in *Faith of Jesus Christ*, 110–15. See now also Donaldson, "Curse of the Law."

68. "Although Paul has, by the standards of Jewish expectations, dissipated the promise's objective content, he nevertheless remains committed to the view that by his promises to the fathers God obligated himself to Israel" (Dahl, *Studies in Paul*, 136).

69. Philo, *Mig.* 53, 70–71. The whole discussion (1–126) affords an instructive contrast to Paul's reading of the story. Philo's Abraham is a philosopher who leaves behind crude sense-perception in order to gain a vision of immortal wisdom and to progress in virtue.

70. We will never know why it did not occur to Paul to justify his revisionary interpretation of the promise by appealing to a text like Joel 2:28–29, which speaks of the outpouring of the Spirit "on all flesh" (cf. the use made of this passage in Acts 2:16–21). That the text must have been familiar to Paul we know from his citation of Joel 2:32 in Rom. 10:13.

71. Barrett, "The Allegory of Abraham, Sarah, and Hagar in the Argument of Galatians," *Essays on Paul*, 154–70.

72. The translation is that of R. H. Charles, *The Apocrypha and Pseudepigrapha of the Old Testament in English*, 2 vols. (Oxford: Clarendon Press, 1913), 2.38 (emended slightly).

73. I will not object if whimsical readers prefer to take the word *agape* in this sentence as a Greek word rather than an English one: he leaves them *agapē* as the sum of the Law (cf. Gal. 5:14, quoting Lev. 19:18).

74. In order to appreciate the rhetorical effect of this maneuver, the modern American reader might imagine the analogy of a Fourth of July oration that claims to find communism prefigured in the Declaration of Independence.

75. Paul frequently tailors the text of his citations to suit the purposes of his argument; pace Ellis, his interpretive incursions are more sweeping than the textual modifications characteristic of Qumran *pesher* exegesis. See Koch, *Schrift als Zeuge*, 102–98.

76. The fact that Gen. 25:1–6 represents Abraham as having more than two sons is irrelevant to Paul's present purposes.

77. Bruce (*Galatians*, 218), expresses himself incautiously by speaking of "the *historical fact* that Isaac was the ancestor of the Jews, whereas Ishmael's descendants were Gentiles" (emphasis mine).

78. "We find that our Father Abraham observed the whole Torah before it was given, for it is said, because that Abraham obeyed my voice and kept my charge, my commandments, my statutes, and my laws" (*Qiddushin* 82a, citing Gen. 26:5). (The translation is from Epstein, ed., *Babylonian Talmud*, vol. 18 [London: Soncino, 1936], 424.) For discussion of this notion in rabbinic thought, see E. E. Urbach, *The Sages*, trans. Israel Abrahams (Jerusalem: Magnes, 1975), 318–19.

79. For a discussion of possible historical antecedents of such an interpretive strategy within Judaism, see Betz's excursus on Abraham (*Galatians*, 139–40, with further literature cited there).

80. Of course, unequivocal negation of the Sinai covenant creates major theological problems that are left unresolved in Galatians. Paul handles the whole issue more artfully in 2 Corinthians 3 and in Romans.

81. At the risk of trying the reader's patience, I note once more how radically this strategy differs from a supersessionist interpretation of Scripture.

82. One favorite speculation of the commentators is that Paul is punning on an Arabic word *ḥadjar*, which means "rock." If so, one wonders whether the pun was lost on the Galatians (cf. Betz, *Galatians*, 244–45; Bruce, *Galatians*, 219–20). For a careful recent discussion of the passage, which prudently leaves the meaning of Gal. 4:25a unresolved, see Charles H. Cosgrove, "The Law Has Given Sarah No Children, (Gal. 4:21–30)," *NovT* 29 (1987):219–35.

83. On Paul's use of the *paidagōgos* metaphor, see David J. Lull, "The Law Was Our Pedagogue," *JBL* 105 (1986):481–98; Norman H. Young, "*Paidagōgos:* the Social Setting of a Pauline Metaphor," *NovT* 29 (1987):150–76.

84. The verb *exagorazō*, translated here as "liberate," literally refers to buying a slave out of slavery; "redeem," the standard English translation, was originally apt, but it has become so thoroughly absorbed into theological discourse that its metaphorical force is easily lost.

85. E.g., Goppelt, *Typos*, 139–40. More carefully formulated is Bruce's judgment: "[Paul] is not thinking of allegory in the Philonic sense . . . ; he has in mind that form of allegory which is commonly called typology" (*Galatians*, 217).

86. "[God] bids the wise man hearken to the words of Sarah, who charges him expressly to cast forth the bondwoman and her son (Gen. xxi.10). It is well to listen to the voice of virtue [Sarah], above all when she sets before us such a doctrine as this, because the most perfect types of being and the secondary acquirements are worlds apart, and wisdom has no kinship with the sophist's culture. For the latter has for the fruits of all its labor only those persuasions which tend to establish the false opinion, which destroys the soul; but wisdom studies truth and thus obtains that great source of profit to the mind, knowledge of right reason" (*Cher.* 9; cf. *Sob.* 7–9).

87. One way of putting the distinction would be as follows: *typology* is a particular species of the genus *allegorical interpretation*, a species distinguished by its propensity for representing the latent sense of a text as *temporally posterior* to its manifest sense. In typology, the allegorical sense latent in the text's figures is discovered not by a reading that ascends from the material to the spiritual but by a reading that grasps the preliminary in relation to the ultimate.

88. Nor, pace Barrett ("Allegory," 165), do we hear "the command of God to his (angelic) agents."

89. Lest this action seem too uncharitable for this interpretation to be correct, compare the anathema solemnly pronounced on the "troublemakers" in the letter's irate opening sentences (Gal. 1:6–9).

90. The rabbinic references are collected by Meeks, "Rose Up to Play," 69–70. Philo (*Sob.* 8) explains that Ishmael was banished "because he, the bastard, claimed to play on equal terms with the true-born."

91. For a discussion of the Isaiah passage and its history of interpretation see Mary Callaway, *Sing, O Barren One: A Study in Comparative Midrash* (SBLDS 91; Atlanta: Scholars, 1986) 59–90. On 107–13, Callaway discusses Paul's use of the tradition.

92. One question inevitably raised by this analysis is the role of Isa. 52:13–53:12 in Paul's vision. If the citation in Gal. 4:27 evokes echoes of Isaiah 51–54, is the Suffering Servant figure—who "opened not his mouth"—to be seen standing silently behind the text?

CHAPTER FOUR

1. Ernst Käsemann, "The Spirit and the Letter," *Perspectives on Paul*, trans. Margaret Kohl (Philadelphia: Fortress, 1971), 138–66, quotation on 155, with reference to 2 Corinthians 3.

2. Stephen Westerholm, "Letter and Spirit: The Foundation of Pauline Ethics," *NTS* 30 (1984):229–48, quotation on 241.

3. Paul's earthy term *skybala* (Phil. 3:8) is euphemistically rendered by English translations as "refuse" (RSV), "rubbish" (JB, NIV), "garbage" (NEB, TEV). The KJV, with Elizabethan frankness, translates more literally: "dung."

4. For attempts to reconstruct the history of the Pharisaic movement in the pre-70 C.E. period, see Jacob Neusner, *The Rabbinic Traditions about the Pharisees before 70*, 3 vols. (Leiden: Brill, 1971); *From Politics to Piety: The Emergence of Pharisaic Judaism* (New York: KTAV, 1979); Ellis Rivkin, "Pharisees," *IDBSup* 657–63; *A Hidden Revolution: The Pharisees' Search for the Kingdom Within* (Nashville: Abingdon, 1978).

5. It is conventional to treat the pericope as beginning in 2 Cor. 2:14 (despite the linking conjunction *de*) rather than in 3:1. Certainly, major themes of 3:1–4:6 (sufficiency for ministry, commissioning by God) are sounded already in 2:14–17. For the purposes of this book, however, I have chosen to begin with 3:1 because it introduces a new cluster of metaphors related to writing and reading. The difficult metaphors of 2:14–16a belong to an entirely different circle of images. See Stephen B. Heiny, "2 Corinthians 2:14–4:6: The Motive for Metaphor," in Kent Harold Richards, ed., *SBL 1987 Seminar Papers* (Atlanta: Scholars, 1987) 1–22; Scott J. Hafemann, *Suffering and the Spirit: An Exegetical Study of II Cor 2:14–3:3 within the Context of the Corinthian Correspondence* (WUNT 2d ser., vol. 19; Tübingen: J. C. B. Mohr, Paul Siebeck, 1986).

6. Käsemann, *Perspectives*, 138, 159.

7. Koch, *Schrift als Zeuge*, 340. Similarly, Morna D. Hooker, "Beyond the Things That Are Written? St. Paul's Use of Scripture," *NTS* 27 (1980–81):295–309; Marks, "Pauline Typology," 84–85.

8. Alfred Plummer, *A Critical and Exegetical Commentary on the Second Epistle of St. Paul to the Corinthians* (ICC; Edinburgh: T. & T. Clark, 1915), 87. Cf. Furnish, *II Corinthians*, 199–200; Westerholm, "Letter and Spirit," 240–41; Luz, *Geschichtsverständnis*, 123–35.

9. For a brief account of the history of this interpretive tradition, see Robert M. Grant, *The Letter and the Spirit* (London: SPCK, 1957).

10. Ibid., 51.

11. For a good account of scriptural echoes in the passage, see Earl Richard, "Polemics, Old Testament, and Theology: A Study of II Cor., III, 1–IV, 6," *RB* 88 (1981):340–67.

12. For the purposes of this book, it is not necessary to take up the vexed problem of the literary integrity of 2 Corinthians; cf. Furnish, *II Corinthians*, 30–48. Everyone would agree that 2:14–4:6, at least, is a unitary composition.

13. See William R. Baird, "Letters of Recommendation: A Study of II Cor 3:1–3," *JBL* 80 (1961):166–72.

14. The quoted phrases reflect the influence of Furnish's excellent translation (*II Corinthians*, 173, 202).

15. The connection between the passage and the letter's occasion would be considerably diminished by Hans Windisch's hypothesis that 2 Cor. 3:7–18 is a previously composed midrash whose polemic is aimed not against Paul's Jewish-Christian adversaries but against Judaism per se. This theory is still accepted, with qualifications, by Koch (*Schrift als Zeuge*, 332). Note, however, the counterargument of Furnish, *II Corinthians*, 229–30, 242–45. The present chapter will seek to confirm the integral relation of vv. 7–18 to the surrounding argument.

16. Dieter Georgi, *The Opponents of Paul in Second Corinthians* (Philadelphia: Fortress, 1986), 264–71. Georgi's analysis builds on the work of Windisch and of Siegfried Schulz, "Die Decke des Moses. Untersuchungen zu einer vorpaulinischen Überlieferung in II Cor 3:7–18," *ZNW* 49 (1958):1–30.

17. A similar position is taken by N. T. Wright, "Reflected Glory: 2 Corinthians 3:18," in L. D. Hurst and N. T. Wright, eds., *The Glory of Christ in the New Testament: Studies in Christology: in Memory of George Bradford Caird* (Oxford: Clarendon, 1987), 139–50: "We do not need elaborate hypotheses, either of the theology of Paul's opponents or of the textual prehistory of our passage, to make sense of the argument" (141 n. 6).

18. There is, of course, a text-critical problem here. Though RSV reads "your [*hymōn*] hearts," the manuscript evidence strongly favors the reading "our [*hēmōn*] hearts." See Hafemann, *Suffering and the Spirit*, 186–88.

19. Rudolf Bultmann (*The Second Letter to the Corinthians*, trans. Roy A. Harrisville [Minneapolis: Augsburg, 1985], 73) offers several parallels from Greek literature (Thucydides, Isocrates, Plato), but 2 Cor. 3:3 resembles none of these as closely as it resembles Jer. 31:33.

20. Richard, ("Polemics," 344–49) stresses the foundational character of the Jeremiah passage for Paul's exposition.

21. For another instance where "spirit of God" and "finger of god" appear as different transformations of the same tradition, see Matt 12:28, Luke 11:20: "If by the spirit/finger of God I cast out demons, then the kingdom of God has come upon you."

22. In Jeremiah's prophecy, the problem with the old covenant lies in the disobedience of the people, not in some inherent deficiency of the Mosaic Law. See Hans Walter Wolff, "What Is New in the New Covenant?" *Confrontations with Prophets* (Philadelphia: Fortress, 1983), 49–62; cf. Robert P. Carroll, *Jeremiah: A Commentary* (Philadelphia: Westminster, 1986), 610–14.

23. Thus, the present passage is yet another illustration of Paul's ecclesiocentric hermeneutic.

24. This formulation suggests, of course, that Stanley Fish's notion of texts as "self-consuming artifacts" may have roots in Israelite prophecy as well as in the Platonic-Augustinian tradition that he traces. Cf. Stanley Fish, *Self-Consuming Artifacts: The Experience of Seventeenth-Century Literature* (Berkeley: University of California Press, 1972), 5–43.

25. Greene, *Light in Troy*, 25, 26. I reproduce here just one of his illustrations, from William Blake:

> The Human Dress is forged *Iron*,
> The Human Form is a fiery *Forge*,
> The Human Face, a Furnace seal'd,
> The Human Heart its hungry Gorge.

26. Another possibility would be to translate the noun *gramma* as "writ" and the participle *eggegrammenē* as "written."

27. Adolf Schlatter unfortunately makes this mistake, translating *gramma* as "Die Schrift," thereby creating needless interpretive problems for himself (*Die Korintherbriefe* [Stuttgart: Calwer, 1950], 246–48).

28. On the distinction between *gramma* and *graphē*, see G. Schrenk, "*Graphō, graphē, gramma, ktl.*," TDNT 1.742–73, especially 749–69.

29. A classic discussion that weaves 2 Cor. 3:6 together with Romans is that of Augustine, "The Spirit and the Letter," conveniently available to English readers in *Augustine: Later Works*, trans. John Burnaby, *Library of Christian Classics* (Philadelphia: Westminster, 1955), 182–250. Cf. Furnish, *II Corinthians*, 200–1, 228–29.

30. "Claudius of Turin sums up the patristic tradition as it had reached the scholars of Charlemagne's day. The Word is incarnate in Scripture, which like man has a body and soul. The body is the words of the sacred text, the 'letter', and the literal meaning; the soul is the spiritual sense. To explain the literal sense is to expound *litteraliter vel carnaliter; littera* is almost interchangeable with *corpus*." (Beryl Smalley, *The Study of the Bible in the Middle Ages* [Notre Dame: University of Notre Dame Press, 1964], 1.)

31. Westerholm, "Letter and Spirit," 241.

32. The *RSV's* translation of *diakonia* in 2 Cor. 3:7–9 as "dispensation" is unjustifiable and regrettable.

33. Noted by Richard, "Polemics," 352–53; cf. Jacob Mann, *The Bible as Read and Preached in the Old Synagogue*, with a prolegomenon by Ben Zion Wacholder (New York: KTAV, 1971), 1.530–33.

34. Following Hans Windisch, *Der zweite Korintherbrief*, 9th ed. (MeyerK; Göttingen: Vandenhoeck & Ruprecht, 1924), 112–31.

35. James Kugel characterizes midrash as focused precisely on the "surface irregularities" of the text ("Two Introductions to Midrash," 92–93). The best case for reading 2 Cor. 3:7–18 as a midrash on Exodus 34 has been made by J. D. G. Dunn, "2 Corinthians III.17—'The Lord is the Spirit'," *JTS* 21 (1970):309–20.

36. "Paul's interpretation of II Corinthians 3 is a classic example of genuine theological dialectic. He brings to the text the perspective of faith which had learned to hope in Christ (v. 12), but he brings from the text a witness which conversely forms his understanding of God and shapes the Christian life through his Spirit" (Childs, *Exodus*, 624).

37. See the discussion of this passage in chapter 3 above.

38. On the translation of this word, see below. Cf. the translation of Wright ("Reflected Glory," 141): "the Israelites could not look steadily at the face of Moses, because of its glory—which glory was to pass away."

39. Especially if the opponents were already appealing to the Exodus story to support their own self-presentation, Paul would be putting himself in an extraordinarily weak position if he based his argument on his own fictional embellishment of the text.

40. Childs, *Exodus*, 621.

41. Indeed, Wayne Meeks notes several passages in later rabbinic midrash where the glory of Moses' face is explicitly described as unfading ("Moses as God and King," in Jacob Neusner, ed., *Religions in Antiquity: Essays in Memory of Erwin*

Ramsdell Goodenough [NumenSup 14; Leiden: Brill, 1968], 354–71, especially 363–64). Of course, such claims might be a counterreaction to Paul.

42. This point is emphasized by A. T. Hanson, "The Midrash in II Corinthians 3: A Reconsideration," *JSNT* 9 (1980):14.

43. Furnish (*II Corinthians,* 203) argues that the present participle *katargoumenēn* "expresses action contemporary with that of the main verb . . . *egenēthē.*" This is not necessarily so, however, because the participle here is being used attributively rather than predicatively. Consequently, it is impossible to determine on syntactical grounds whether the action that it describes should be understood as contemporary with the main verb or with Paul's own time of writing. The decision must be made on the basis of the sense of the surrounding context, especially v. 10.

44. Consequently, Marks' discussion of 1 Cor. 3:7–11 as an instance of willfully revisionary reading ("Pauline Typology," 84) stands in need of revision.

45. Ralph P. Martin, *2 Corinthians,* Word Biblical Commentary 40 (Waco, Tex.: Word, 1986), 57.

46. This is the view taken by Windisch, Plummer, Strachan, Barrett, Bultmann, Furnish, J.-F. Collange (*Énigmes de la deuxième Épître de Paul aux Corinthiens* [Cambridge: Cambridge University Press, 1972], 96), and Ernest Best (*Second Corinthians* [Interpretation; Atlanta: John Knox, 1987], 32).

47. Among modern interpreters, Martin, Hanson, Matthias Rissi (*Studien zum zweiten Korintherbrief* [ATANT 56; Zurich: Zwingli, 1969], 32–33), Jean Hering (*The Second Epistle of Paul to the Corinthians,* trans. A. W. Heathcote and P. J. Allcock [London: Epworth, 1967], 25), and Badenas (*Christ the End of the Law,* 75–76) advocate the teleological or consummative interpretation of *telos* in this passage. Cf. also n. 49, below.

48. Badenas, *Christ the End of the Law,* 38–80.

49. The clearest statement occurs in Theodoret's commentary on the passage: "[Moses] put a veil on his face, teaching that they were unable to see the *telos* of the Law. 'For the *telos* of the Law is Christ for righteousness to all who believe' [Rom. 10:4]. For he said this 'in order that the sons of Israel might not gaze upon the *telos* of that which is transitory.' He said the law is 'transitory,' i.e., it is ceasing. But the *telos* of that which is transitory is the one proclaimed under the Law, i.e. Christ." (My translation; the Greek text can be found in PG 82.396.) Theodoret's exegetical device of explicating 2 Cor. 3:13 by cross reference to Rom. 10:4 serves to show that he understands *telos* in both passages to mean "goal" or "consummation." (Cf. Badenas' discussion [*Christ the End of the Law,* 7–14] of patristic readings of Rom. 10:4.) Chrysostom's Homily VII on 2 Corinthians does not comment explicitly on *telos;* he argues clearly that the Law is no longer in effect, but he also contends that the Jews are culpable for failing to recognize Christ in the Law: "Why are you disturbed if Jews do not believe in Christ, since they don't believe the Law, either? For that is the reason why they were ignorant also of grace, since they saw neither the old covenant nor the glory that was in it; for the glory of the Law is to turn to Christ." (My translation; Greek text in PG 61.445.) Tertullian uses the passage to argue against Marcion that the God of Moses is not a different God from the God of Jesus Christ, because "Moses spoke of Christ" and "the whole Mosaic system was a figure of Christ" ("Against Marcion," V.xi [ANF 3.453]).

50. Windisch, *Korintherbrief*, 112. Bultmann, (*Second Letter to the Corinthians*, 84) replies, on the contrary, that "3:12–18 most intimately coheres with the train of thought."

51. E.g., Bultmann, *Second Letter to the Corinthians*, 87–88; Furnish, *II Corinthians*, 207.

52. Plummer, *Second Epistle*, 97.

53. Philip Edgcumbe Hughes, *Paul's Second Epistle to the Corinthians* (NICNT; Grand Rapids: Eerdmans, 1962), 110 n. 6.

54. Kugel, "Two Introductions to Midrash," 100.

55. Lord, *Classical Presences*, 40.

56. Culler, *Pursuit of Signs*, 115.

57. Ibid., 116.

58. This is, of course, the feature of the text's rhetoric that gives rise to hypothetical reconstructions of opponents who model their self-presentation on the figure of Moses.

59. Lord, *Classical Presences*, 40–41.

60. Another powerful dissimile is found in Heb. 12:18–20: "For you have not come to what may be touched, a blazing fire, and darkness, and gloom, and a tempest, and the sound of a trumpet, and a voice whose words made the hearers entreat that no further messages be spoken to them. For they could not endure the order that was given, 'If even a beast touches the mountain, it shall be stoned.'"

61. This formulation reflects Exod. 33:11: "Thus the LORD used to speak to Moses face to face, as a man speaks to his friend." (Cf. also Num. 12:7–8.) To be sure, the Pentateuch also preserves side by side with such daring claims another set of traditions that seek to place a more reverent distance between Moses and Yahweh: for instance, Exodus immediately qualifies the audacious formulation of 33:11 with an equivocal little episode in which the LORD forbids Moses to see his face ("for man shall not see me and live") but permits him to see his "back" after he has passed by (Exod. 33:18–23). As 2 Cor. 3:18 shows, however, Paul emphasizes the unmediated character of the encounter and ignores the cautionary note.

62. Again, other Pentateuchal texts suggest something quite different: "The LORD spoke with you face to face at the mountain, out of the midst of the fire" (Deut. 5:4). The very next verse, however, reaffirms Moses' mediatorial role: "I stood between the LORD and you at that time, to declare to you the word of the LORD; for you were afraid because of the fire, and you did not go up into the mountain" (Deut. 5:5). Because 2 Cor. 3:12–18 centers on a reading of Exod. 34:29–35, Paul's comments stress the difference—symbolized by the veil—between Moses, who went into God's presence, and the other Israelites, who did not.

63. This point is grasped and explained clearly by Dunn, "The Lord is the Spirit."

64. This is generally overlooked by commentators, who consequently find themselves puzzled about how to construe *kathaper*. For a summary of proposals, see Furnish, *II Corinthians*, 216.

65. Because the wider context (especially 4:7–12) demands this interpretation, I cannot fully agree with Wright's interesting proposal ("Reflected Glory," 147): "Paul is not saying that one is changed into the same image as Christ. He is asserting that Christians are changed into the same image as each other. That is

why he can be so bold: he and his audience have this in common, that each of them is being changed into the same image, and so is able to behold the glory of the Lord reflected in the other." Wright is probably correct in what he affirms but not in what he denies: if Christians can behold the glory of *the Lord* reflected in each other, then the image into which they are being changed must be the image of Christ.

66. The inbred impulse of biblical critics to seek reduction of ambiguity renders them particularly helpless in the face of a text that so stubbornly resists reduction.

67. This interpretation is rightly argued by John Koenig, "The Knowing of Glory and Its Consequences (2 Cor. 3–5)." Unpublished paper presented in the Pauline Epistles section, annual meeting of the Society of Biblical Literature, Atlanta, 1986. (My thanks to Prof. Koenig for allowing me to consult his manuscript.) Hanson ("Midrash in II Corinthians 3," 15–19) argues that "the right explanation for Moses' veiling his face is, according to Paul, that he wished to hide the glory of the preexistent Christ whom he had seen in the tabernacle." There is something to be said for this proposal, as long as it is not pressed in the oddly literalistic direction that Hanson's essay urges. Hanson's treatment of Paul's fanciful figurative exposition offers a textbook example of a historical critic's inability to tolerate ambiguity or to cope with metaphor: "The narrative in Exodus 34.29f. is not a mere cipher to Paul. He believes it really did happen, but the pattern of events has to some extent been reproduced in the circumstances of the early church. . . . Admittedly Paul's use of the figure of the veil becomes confused when he applies it to his own day: the veil has to stand for *both* Moses' determination that Israel should not see the glory of the preexistent Christ *and* the failure of Jews in Paul's day to acknowledge Jesus Christ. The result is a tendency toward allegory. But this is not Paul's intention, which is firmly based on his concept of salvation history" (p. 23). Here Hanson's predetermined convictions about Paul's univocal intention to ground his thought in history (and therefore to write typology, which is good, rather than allegory, which is bad) smother his own reading of the text.

68. The history-of-religions background to Paul's image of transformation has been the subject of many investigations. For useful summaries of the discussion with judicious conclusions, see Bultmann, *Second Letter to the Corinthians,* 90–96; Joseph A. Fitzmyer, "Glory Reflected on the Face of Christ (2 Cor. 3:7–4:6) and a Palestinian Jewish Motif," *TS* 42 (1981) 630–44.

69. These fragile equations are of course subject to Greene's cautionary word about the complexity of the figurative copula (see n. 25, above), but we blunder ahead.

70. Cf. Rom. 8:29–30, where all this is said explicitly.

71. For an analysis of these shifts in wording, see Koch, *Schrift als Zeuge,* 126–27, 151–52.

72. Ibid., 186–90.

73. Ibid., 338–39.

74. Again, this formulation agrees with Koenig, "The Knowing of Glory."

75. The text of Hopkins' untitled poem is cited from W. H. Gardner, ed., *Poems of Gerard Manley Hopkins,* 3d ed. (New York-London: Oxford, 1948; revised 1961), 95.

76. This presence is so vividly real to Paul that he characteristically treats the Spirit as a datum of experience that can be used as a decisive warrant for theological inferences, as in Gal. 3:2–5. See David J. Lull, *The Spirit in Galatia*, 54–57, 103–04.

77. One possible misunderstanding should be identified here, in order to preclude it: Paul's dichotomy between *gramma* and *pneuma* is in no way anti-Jewish. Paul is no more anti-Jewish than is Jeremiah: both speak from within the covenant community of Israel and both proclaim God's judgment and mercy on that community. Furthermore, both dare to promise a new state of affairs in which the efficacy of grace overcomes human disobedience. As I have repeatedly argued in this book, Paul is developing a new reading of Scripture within Israel's traditions of inner-Biblical exegesis. The more one knows about the actual practice of Jewish (rabbinic) hermeneutics, the more ridiculous it becomes to characterize Jewish interpretation as bound slavishly to the letter. History shows, however, the danger of a Christian misreading of the *gramma/pneuma* polarity as a distinction between Judaism and Christianity.

78. As proposed by Hanson, "Midrash in II Corinthians 3."

79. Kelsey, *Uses of Scripture*, 158–81.

80. For subsequent Christian readers, an intracanonical echo of the Johannine prologue also sounds here, though Paul, of course, could not have anticipated that; nor is there reason to think that the author of the Fourth Gospel was echoing 2 Cor. 4:6. Because both Paul and John echo Genesis 1, their echoes harmonize.

81. This echo is suggested by Collange, *Énigmes*, 138–39.

CHAPTER FIVE

1. The rabbis knew well Scripture's capacity to throw off such sparks: "'Is not my word like fire, declares the Lord, and like a hammer that shatters rock' (Jer. 23:29). As a hammer[stroke] scatters many slivers/sparks so a single Scriptural passage yields many senses" (Sanhedrin 34a, trans. Moshe Greenberg; unpublished article for faculty seminar, Yale University, New Haven, 1986).

2. Even those Christians who have continued to hold the Old Testament Law in high regard theologically (the Calvinist tradition, for example) have hardly upheld the Law in its direct literal sense, i.e., in a sense that the first-century Pharisees or their rabbinic descendants would have regarded as valid.

3. Marks, "Pauline Typology," 80.

4. Ibid., 72.

5. Heikki Räisänen has mounted a vigorous argument that Paul's statements about the Law are hopelessly contradictory, the product of "secondary rationalization" that seeks to cope with the cognitive dissonance created by Paul's defection from his own religious tradition (*Paul and the Law* [WUNT 29; Tübingen: J. C. B. Mohr, 1983]).

6. Here I find myself substantially in agreement with the suggestions of James A. Sanders, "Torah and Christ," *Int* 29 (1975):372–90; reprinted in *From Sacred Story to Sacred Text*, 41–60.

7. Dodd (*According to the Scriptures*) repeatedly drew attention to this phenomenon.

8. Marks, "Pauline Typology," 72.

9. My echo of Handelman is of course ironic, for her "slayers"—unlike Paul—have successfully escaped the charge of anti-Judaism, despite their revisionary hermeneutics.

10. Marks, "Pauline Typology," 87–88, citing Bultmann, *The Presence of Eternity*, (New York: Harper & Row, 1957), 43.

11. Marks, ibid., 88.

12. Someone might argue that Paul's concern for Israel is purely eschatological and theological in character: i.e., that Bultmann is right after all because Paul's interest in Israel no longer pertains to worldly historical matters. But this sort of dualistic reading of Pauline eschatology became possible only in a much later historical period—in the aftermath of Augustine's fateful dichotomy between the *civitas Dei* and the *civitas terrena*—when the church began to redefine its hope in other-worldly terms and thus to lose its grasp of Paul's literal apocalyptic hope for the return of the Lord, the resurrection of the dead, and the redemption of all creation. Romans 9–11, however, shows unmistakably that Paul continues to wrestle with Israel's historical destiny.

13. Bloom, *Anxiety of Influence*, 11. Barry Seltser has proposed to me, in private correspondence, that Marks' analysis might still illuminate Pauline hermeneutics if one transposed it from the *agōn* of individual poetic consciousness to the *agōn* of communal self-definition: Paul is worried not so much about asserting his own personal autonomy against tradition as about asserting the nascent Christian community's hermeneutical autonomy from the conventions and institutions of Jewish scriptural interpretation.

14. "The torah, as the dominant literary influence on Paul's thinking, had to be challenged if Paul was to realize the autonomy he desired; for it was at least partly the experience of its mediating power that had awakened his own yearning for an unmediated covenant. Of course, such a situation was finally an impossible one, as Paul well understood. No matter how boldly he proclaimed his 'new creation,' its presence had always to remain a lie since it could never relieve him from the burden of indebtedness to its own scriptural sources" (Marks, "Pauline Typology," 87).

15. Individualistic interpretations of Paul's "new creation" language are promoted by most English translations of 2 Cor. 5:17a: "Therefore, if anyone is in Christ, he is a new creation" (RSV). The words "he is" are not present in Paul's elliptical Greek sentence: *hōste ei tis en Christō, kainē ktisis*. In view of the fact that Paul characteristically uses *ktisis* and its cognates in a cosmological frame of reference (see, e.g., Rom. 8:19–23) and in view of the scriptural subtexts from which Paul derives this language, it would be far better to complete the ellipsis in a way that would demonstrate that Paul is speaking here not of individual spiritual renewal but of the reconciliation of the *world* to God (cf. 2 Cor. 5:19): "Therefore, if anyone is in Christ—there is a new creation!"

16. For an important discussion of apocalyptic theological motifs in Galatians—a letter lacking explicit elaboration of a future eschatological scenario—see J. Louis Martyn, "Apocalyptic Antinomies in Paul's Letter to the Galatians," *NTS* 31 (1985):410–24.

17. Krister Stendahl's essay, "The Apostle Paul and the Introspective Conscience of the West" (*HTR* 56 [1963]:199–215; reprinted in *Paul among Jews and*

Gentiles [Philadelphia: Fortress, 1976], 78–96), despite certain oversimplifications, describes the problem so compellingly that it should be required reading for anyone starting out to seek an understanding of Paul.

18. Barr, *Old and New in Interpretation*, 143.

19. Longenecker, *Biblical Exegesis*, 114–32.

20. The point is rightly noted by Rowan Greer in James L. Kugel and Rowan A. Greer, *Early Biblical Interpretation*, (Philadelphia: Westminster, 1986), 127. It is questionable, however, whether one should agree with Greer's assertion that the alternative to an explicit concern with methods is simply prooftexting.

21. Cf. Dahl, *Studies in Paul*, 175.

22. See my discussion of midrash in chapter 1 above, with references cited there.

23. Kugel comments that the midrashic writings are "compilations of comments that are usually focused on isolated, individual verses. . . . Our midrashic compilations are in this sense potentially deceiving, since they seem to treat the whole text bit by bit; but, with the exception of certain patterns, these "bits" are rather atomistic, and, as any student of rabbinic literature knows, interchangeable, modifiable, combinable—in short, not part of an overall exegesis at all" ("Two Introductions to Midrash," 94–95).

24. When modern biblical scholars speak of method, they usually mean a systematic procedure that may be applied to a text to determine its meaning, in such a way that different readers using the same method will arrive at similar interpretations. In that sense, typology can hardly be described as a method, because it deals in purely imaginative acts of correlation.

25. E.g., Goppelt, *Typos*, 17–18; Baker, "Typology and the Christian Use," 152.

26. Here again, the influence of Erich Auerbach has clouded the issues. In "Odysseus' Scar," the opening chapter of his influential *Mimesis: The Representation of Reality in Western Literature*, trans. Willard R. Trask (Princeton: Princeton University Press, 1953), he contends that biblical narrative, in contrast to Greek epic, "involves an absolute claim to historical truth. . . . [T]he Biblical narrator, the Elohist, had to believe in the objective truth of the story of Abraham's sacrifice—the existence of the sacred ordinances of life rested upon the truth of this and similar stories" (14). It is of course true that the communal identity of Israel rested upon the stories told by the biblical narrators. But are the claims made by these narratives historical in anything like our modern sense of the word? Here it seems to me that Auerbach falls into the fallacy diagnosed by Hans Frei in *The Eclipse of Biblical Narrative* (New Haven: Yale University Press, 1974): the inability to distinguish between narrative that makes referential historical claims and narrative whose meaning does not depend upon ostensive reference.

27. These figures are derived from Koch, *Schrift als Zeuge*, 33.

28. Another such case, rarely recognized, may be 2 Cor. 4:13; see A. T. Hanson, *Paul's Understanding of Jesus* (Hull: University of Hull, 1963), 10–13; *Paul's Technique*, 17–18; Hays, *Faith of Jesus Christ*, 189 n. 125.

29. Gerhard von Rad, *Old Testament Theology*, trans. D. M. G. Stalker (2 vols.; New York: Harper & Row, 1962), 1.229–31.

30. I reiterate here my assertion that the genitive in Paul's formulation *katara*

nomou must be subjective rather than epexegetical. Cf. chapter 2, n. 24, above.

31. Dan O. Via, Jr., *Kerygma and Comedy in the New Testament* (Philadelphia: Fortress, 1975), 62–63.

32. Ibid., 64. Via's theological reading of Romans, concentrating on existential encounter with God's word, deemphasizes Paul's concern with the particular national fate of Israel.

33. Fishbane (*Biblical Interpretation*, 374) describes Deutero-Isaiah as a "vast typological net."

34. The source of this quotation about the plowman and the thresher is notoriously obscure. Sir. 6:19 is often proposed, but it lacks precisely the key word *aloōn* that links the quotation to Deut. 25:4. Koch (*Schrift als Zeuge*, 41–42) suggests that it is a saying taken over by Paul from the oral tradition of the hellenistic synagogue or of the pre-Pauline hellenistic church, where it was erroneously regarded as a scriptural quotation.

35. Koch, *Schrift als Zeuge*, 202–04.

36. What this extraordinary fact demonstrates is that Paul allows the *imitatio Christi* paradigm (renunciation of privilege for the sake of others) to override all particular ethical rules and prescriptions, even when the rule is a direct command of Scripture.

37. E.g., Michel, *Paulus und seine Bibel*, 110; Ellis, *Paul's Use of the OT*, 51–54; Longenecker, *Biblical Exegesis*, 126–29; Koch, *Schrift als Zeuge*, 202–16, 230–32.

38. Johannes Weiss, *Der Erste Korintherbrief* (MeyerK; Göttingen: Vandenhoeck & Ruprecht, 1910), 254.

39. Cf. J. Louis Martyn, "Epistemology at the Turn of the Ages: 2 Corinthians 5:16," *Christian History and Interpretation* [see chapter 2, n. 78], 269–87.

40. The form in which Paul gives the citation blends Deut. 21:23 with Deut. 27:26.

41. The phrase reflects the insights of Martyn ("Apocalyptic Antinomies," 420–21), who contends that "the focus of Paul's apocalyptic lies not on Christ's parousia, but rather on his death. . . . Thus the subject of his letter to the Galatians is precisely an apocalypse, the apocalypse of Jesus Christ, and specifically the apocalypse of his cross."

42. Kugel, "Two Introductions to Midrash," 88.

43. Ibid., 89.

44. Ibid., 87.

45. Ibid., 90. The "one critic" to whom Kugel refers is Daniel Patte, *Early Jewish Hermeneutic in Palestine* (SBLDS 22; Missoula: Scholars, 1975), 72.

46. This translation of 2 Cor. 6:1 is adopted from Oliver O'Donovan, *Resurrection and Moral Order: An Outline for Evangelical Ethics* (Grand Rapids: Eerdmans, 1986), 172.

47. Rather than repeating the *dektos* of the Isaiah quotation, Paul writes *euprosdektos*, thus subtly heightening the assertion of God's superabundant gracious favor: the *kairos* is not just *dektos*, as Isaiah had prophesied, but *euprosdektos*.

48. This citation of Isa. 49:8 is another remarkable instance of Pauline metalepsis. In its original context, the fragment that Paul quotes here is part of one of Deutero-Isaiah's "Servant Songs." The prophet/servant/Israel is called to proclaim the LORD's salvation to the whole world:

> It is too light a thing that you should be my servant
> to raise up the tribes of Jacob
> and to restore the preserved of Israel;
> I will give you as a light to the nations,
> that my salvation may reach to the end of the earth.
> (Isa. 49:6, RSV)

If this whole depiction of the servant's charge (Isa. 49:1–13) is read in counterpoint with Paul's account of "the ministry of reconciliation" in 2 Cor. 5:18–6:2, as Paul's citation of Isa. 49:8 encourages us to do, both texts take on a new resonance. Even Paul's admonition that the Corinthians not accept the grace of God "in vain (*eis kenon*)" echoes the Servant's lament in Isa. 49:4: "I have labored in vain (*kenōs*), and I have given my strength for vanity and for nothing."

49. For basic studies on the massively-researched topic of Qumran exegesis, see F. F. Bruce, *Biblical Exegesis in the Qumran Texts* (Grand Rapids: Eerdmans, 1959); Joseph A. Fitzmyer, "The Use of Explicit Old Testament Quotations in Qumran Literature and in the New Testament," *NTS* 7 (1961): 297–333; "4Q Testimonia and the New Testament," *TS* 18 (1957) 513–37 (both of these Fitzmyer essays are reprinted in his *Essays on the Semitic Background of the New Testament* [SBLSBS 5; Missoula: Scholars, 1974]; J. Murphy-O'Connor, ed., *Paul and Qumran: Studies in New Testament Exegesis* (Chicago: Priory, 1968); Maurya P. Horgan, *Pesharim: Qumran Interpretations of Biblical Books* (CBQMS 8; Washington: Catholic Biblical Association of America, 1979); Brooke, *Exegesis at Qumran* (chapter 3, n. 2, above).

50. 1QS 11:5–9, as translated by Geza Vermes, *The Dead Sea Scrolls in English*, 2d ed. (Harmondsworth: Penguin, 1975), 92–93.

51. Greene, *Light in Troy*, 16–19, 37–53.

52. Ibid., 41.

53. Ibid., 40, emphasis Greene's. (Can a New Testament scholar read these sentences without thinking of Bultmann's *Theology of the New Testament* as a work of heuristic reinterpretation?)

54. Greene, *Light in Troy*, 46.

55. From the point of view of Christian theology, Greene's choice of the term *sacramental* is not an entirely happy one. Presumably he has in mind the notion that the repetition of a canonically fixed ritual will somehow guarantee the presence of grace. While sacramental liturgies are usually not verbally innovative in their representation of tradition, a more sympathetic interpretation of sacraments might stress the idea that the community's action in worship symbolically bonds past, present, and future in such a way that fresh embodiments of the word occur. *Anamnēsis* should not be confused with mere repetition.

56. Greene, *Light in Troy*, 39.

57. Ibid.

58. Letter from Geoffrey Gwynne, (12 July 1987). The citation, as the letter indicates, is from Dietrich Bonhoeffer, *Meditating on the Word*, ed. and trans. David McI. Gracie (Cambridge, Mass.: Cowley, 1986), 97–98.

59. The question of pseudepigraphy is not crucial for the issue that I am raising here. If anything, the judgment that 2 Timothy is *not* an authentic Pauline letter would make the hermeneutical problem easier rather than harder in this

instance, because "Timothy" would then be already a symbolic figure, a textual cipher for subsequent generations of Christian readers or leaders; thus, Bonhoeffer's reading would be an appropriate response to what Childs likes to call the "canonical shaping" of the tradition (see his *New Testament as Canon*, 373–95). For a recent summary of the issues, arguing for Pauline authorship, see Luke Timothy Johnson, *The Writings of the New Testament* (Philadelphia: Fortress, 1986), 381–407. For the mainstream scholarly view that the Pastorals are pseudepigraphical, see Werner G. Kümmel, *Introduction to the New Testament*, rev. ed., trans. Howard C. Kee (Nashville: Abingdon, 1975), 366–87. The most recent general discussion of the phenomenon of pseudepigraphy with reference to the New Testament is David G. Meade, *Pseudonymity and Canon: An Investigation into the Relationship of Authorship and Authority in Jewish and Earliest Christian Tradition* (WUNT 39; Tübingen: J. C. B. Mohr, Paul Siebeck, 1986).

60. As will be apparent to readers of this book, I do not share this assessment of the matter. Nonetheless, the theological issue—as it has been posed to me by Brevard Childs, Timothy Jackson, and other colleagues—remains a crucial one: if biblical texts are read in light of "secular" literary-critical theories of intertextuality, will Paul's readings be deemed only one chance moment in an endless flux of texts generated out of other texts? Consequently, will the *truth*-claims of the gospel be radically compromised by the methods I have employed? The question cannot be answered satisfactorily without a fully worked-out response to various postmodern challenges to the notions of a "transcendental signified" and of the referential power of language. Though I do not presume to give a full answer to such problems in this book, I have two provisional responses to offer. (1) The problem posed by the loss of transcendent reference is neither created by the introduction of intertextual echo as a critical category nor avoided by reverting to historical-critical methodologies. The literary-critical operation of tracing Paul's readings of scriptural texts is in principle neutral with regard to metatheories about the relation between language and truth. To speak of Paul's practices of intertextual figuration through using literary analytical tools threatens the revelatory authority of Scripture neither more nor less than using methods of historical inquiry to investigate the life of Jesus threatens the Chalcedonian confession. In both cases, the investigation proceeds "from below," trusting that the critical findings will be taken up into a wider framework of theological understanding. Nothing in this book should be construed to mean that Paul's theology is *only* the product of intertextual reflection. (2) Christian theology has a stake in affirming the reality of a "transcendental signified," a God who creates the world through the word and thus invests language with the power to refer truly. Because the community of faith understands Scripture as the word of God, it is believed to be alive and active; its capacity to reveal new senses from old texts is a sign of its divine power as well as of the relativity of human interpretation. If we are engaged in modeling our hermeneutical perspective after Paul's we will hardly find ourselves lapsing into skepticism about the power of the text to disclose extratextual truth.

61. I make no attempt to explain *why* Paul's writings ought to be granted some normative role, because I am conducting a discussion within a historic community that long ago made an irrevocable decision to acknowledge these texts as Scripture. The consequences of such a decision for normative reflection are described

by David Kelsey (*Uses of Scripture*, 208): "Scripture's authority specifically for theology . . . is a function of its authority for the common life of the church. . . . Hence the 'authority of scripture' has the status of a *postulate* assumed in the doing of theology in the context of the practice of the common life of a Christian community in which 'church' is understood in a certain way. In short, the doctrine of 'scripture and its authority' is a postulate of practical theology."

62. Gardner, *Religious Experience*, 215.

63. Longenecker, *Biblical Exegesis*, 219.

64. An analogous hermeneutical program is advocated, with much more sophistication than Gardner, by Elisabeth Schüssler Fiorenza, *In Memory of Her: A Feminist Theological Reconstruction of Christian Origins* (New York: Crossroad, 1983).

65. I reiterate that Longenecker represents a view commonly held among biblical scholars, not an idiosyncratic position.

66. Dodd, *According to the Scriptures*, 127.

67. The work of Lindars (*New Testament Apologetic*) and Juel (*Messianic Exegesis*) has provided further support for Dodd's basic insights.

68. Marks, "Pauline Typology," 88.

69. Some Christian advocates of "process hermeneutics" have recently taken up lines of reflection that resemble Marks's proposal, without, however, showing his Bloomian animus toward tradition. See, for an excellent illustration, David J. Lull and William A. Beardslee, *Biblical Preaching on the Death of Jesus* (Nashville: Abingdon, 1989). Still, the burden of proof is on such interpreters to show how their hermeneutical strategy, if radically conceived, can retain recognizable continuity with the faith that Paul confessed. The position is unstable (a fact that might not disturb its proponents) for reasons diametrically opposite those I mentioned with reference to Longenecker: if Paul's normative value lies not in the particular convictions that he espoused but in the *process* whereby he transformed inherited traditions, then his witness is only an instantiation of a more universal process knowable apart from his writings. Although Paul might continue to serve as a good illustration, the privileged status of his proclamation would be dissolved in the river of hermeneutical flux.

70. When I speak of Paul's interpretations as paradigmatic, I do not intend the affirmation to be understood in a narrowly prescriptive sense. For one thing, the presence of other voices in the canon, other New Testament writers who interpret Scripture in ways very different from Paul, suggests that Paul's way can hardly be the only way. Furthermore, the paradigm must function analogically, not as a cookie-cutter: we are in a different historical situation from Paul, not least because we have the New Testament, whereas he did not (see n. 71, below). My point is simply that our hermeneutical efforts should be informed (not exhaustively determined) by his example.

71. By "gospel," I of course mean Paul's kerygma, not the canonical Gospels, which were written later than Paul's letters; indeed, to follow Paul's example closely, we have to learn how *not* to read the Old Testament in light of the canonical Gospels.

72. See further on the "imitation" motif in Galatians, W. P. De Boer, *The Imitation of Paul* (Kampen: J. H. Kok, 1962), 188–96; Beverly R. Gaventa, "Galatians 1 and 2: Autobiography as Paradigm," *NovT* 28 (1986):309–26; Richard B.

Hays, "Christology and Ethics in Galatians: The Law of Christ," *CBQ* 49 (1987):268–90.

73. Beker (*Paul the Apostle*), inspired by Käsemann, has championed this view. His subsequent book, *Paul's Apocalyptic Gospel: The Coming Triumph of God* (Philadelphia: Fortress, 1982), seeks to confront certain hermeneutical issues that are not addressed in his earlier descriptive account of Paul's thought.

74. Sally Barker Purvis ("Problems and Possibilities in Paul's Ethics of Community," [Ph.D. diss., Yale University, 1987], 202–50) proposes a "relational eschatology" in place of the temporal apocalyptic eschatology that Beker regards as foundational for Paul's thought. Purvis' proposal is an important attempt to grapple with the hermeneutical difficulties posed by a literal apocalyptic eschatology while preserving the critical and normative functions performed by such an eschatology in Pauline theology. For the reasons sketched here, however, I am not persuaded that her proposal will work: Paul's perception of his community's identity was inextricably bound together with his perception of its temporal location.

75. This formulation of the task is influenced by David H. Fisher, "The Phenomenology of Displacement: Tradition, Anti-Tradition, and Liberal Theology," *RelSRev* 13 (1987):314–17.

76. That is perhaps in part what George Lindbeck means by his proposal for a "postliberal theology" whose hallmark is "intratextuality": "a postliberal intratextuality provides warrants for imaginatively and conceptually incorporating postbiblical worlds into the world of the Bible in much the same fashion as did the tradition" (*The Nature of Doctrine,* 123).

77. See the discussion of this passage in chapter 3, above.

78. This way of reading Paul presupposes, of course, that Paul's letters can be treated as Scripture in much the same way that the Old Testament can be treated as Scripture—that the same sort of divinatory hermeneutics that he employed can find apt subject matter in his own writings.

79. To take another example of the same kind, we could read Paul's citation of Isa. 1:9 in Rom. 9:29 ("If the Lord of hosts had not left us a seed (*sperma*), we would have fared like Sodom and been made like Gomorrah") with the echo of Gal. 3:16 (which tells us that the seed is Christ) in our heads. Or, to take a broader and far more challenging case, someone might propose that the historical experience of the Holocaust necessitates a revisionary intertextual reading of Paul that will reclaim the continuity of Paul's proclamation with Israel's Scripture and thus reaffirm God's undying love for Israel. This whole book is in a modest way an illustration of such a reading.

80. Kelsey's analysis converges with the conclusions to which our study of Paul has led: "[I]t is utterly unrealistic to expect either a doctrine about scripture or second-order discussions of scripture and theology . . . to identify *the* way in which scripture can 'control' theology so as to keep it Christianly apt. . . . It surely cannot be supposed that to call scripture 'authority' means that properly employed it could 'guarantee' the correctness of our proposals, if only we could figure out how to employ it properly. . . . Surely, Christianly speaking, it would be improper even to hope for that. For the full *discrimen* by which theological proposals are finally to be assessed includes the active presence of God. No

'theological position' would presume to tell us how to use scripture so as to guarantee that God will be present to illumine and correct us. Theological proposals are concerned with what God is now using scripture to do, and no degree of sophistication in theological methodology can hope to anticipate that!" (*Uses of Scripture*, 215–16).

81. This point must be carefully distinguished from the legitimate role that historical criticism can play in testing readers' intuitions about the presence of specific allusions in a text. (See my remarks on this matter in chapter 1 above.)

82. Meeks, "A Hermeneutics of Social Embodiment," 184–85.

83. Rom. 15:4–6.

Index of Biblical References

Index of Subjects and Authors

Abandonment by God, ix, 59, 68–70. *See also* Israel, fate of; Theodicy

Abraham: circumcision, 2, 56; father of Jews and Gentiles, 54–56, 96; faith of, 56; God's promise to, 57, 65, 105–7, 187; sacrifice of Isaac, 61–62; allegory in Galatians, 86, 111–18; receives God's word, 166–67

Akedah tradition, 62, 210n8

Alexander, Philip, 11

Allegory: of Abraham's two sons, 86, 111–18; use in Pauline interpretation, 166

Allusion: and echo, 18–21, 29, 200n75; example of use, 118–21

Alter, Robert, 19–20

Anamnēsis, 226n55

Apocalyptic: Jewish, tradition, 43; in Pauline hermeneutics, 100, 223n12

Apokalypsis, 36, 169

Arnold, Matthew, 19–20

Auerbach, Eric, 98, 224n26

Augustine, 136, 159, 185

Author, implied, 26–29

Authority of Scripture, 165, 228n61, 229n80

Baba Meṣia 59b, 2

Baptism, 96, 101–2, 121

Barr, James, 160

Barrett, C. K., 111–12

Barth, Karl, 207n73, 208n82, 208–9n89

Barthes, Roland, 15

Bathsheba, 48–50

Baudelaire, Charles, 141

Beardsley, Monroe C., 201nn90, 99

Beker, J. Christiaan, 35, 194n12

Blake, William, 217n25

Blasphemy, 45

Blessing: proclaimed by Moses, 43–44; received by Gentiles through Abraham, 56, 107–9; and grace of God, 144; procured by Jesus, 169

Blessington, Francis, 18

Bloch, Renée, 14, 197n32

Bloom, Harold, 16–17, 158

Bonhoeffer, Dietrich, 178–79, 184, 227n59

Brower, Reuben, 17–18

Bultmann, Rudolf, 7–8, 38, 158–59, 226n53

Bunyan, John, 103

Calvin, John, 185

Canon, Jewish and Christian, 14, 188

Canon, literary, 15

Canon, Paul's, within a canon, 162–63

Childs, Brevard, 133, 141, 202n6, 218n36, 227n59

Christ: 84–85, 101, 168; rock in the wilderness, 2, 97–98; crucifixion and resurrection of, 36, 100, 149; manifests God's glory and righteousness, 36, 52–53, 146, 153, 157; and Gentiles, 72–73, telos of the Law, 75, 79, 137, 219n39; redemption from curse, 109–10, 169, 203n24; seed of Abraham, 85, 121; transforms community of faith, 143–44, 190

Christocentric hermeneutics, 61–63, 84–86, 98–99, 177, 213n60

Christology, Pauline, 120–21

Chrysostom, 219n39